OUR HERITAGE
AND OTHER ADDRESSES

OUR HERITAGE
AND OTHER ADDRESSES

BY

<small>COLONEL THE HON.</small>
HERBERT A. BRUCE
R.A.M.C., M.D., L.R.C.P., F.R.C.S. (Eng.), LL.D.
<small>LIEUTENANT-GOVERNOR OF ONTARIO</small>

Essay Index Reprint Series

Originally published by:

THE MACMILLAN COMPANY OF CANADA LIMITED

BOOKS FOR LIBRARIES PRESS
FREEPORT, NEW YORK

First Published 1934
Reprinted 1968

LIBRARY OF CONGRESS CATALOG CARD NUMBER:

68-54334

MANUFACTURED
BY
HALLMARK LITHOGRAPHERS, INC.
IN THE U.S.A.

To
My Wife

FOREWORD

On many occasions and at various functions a Lieutenant-Governor is expected to speak.   Speech-making is a privilege —a duty inseparable from his office.

These addresses are reproduced here at the request of many friends.   It has been found convenient to print them in chronological order, but they need not be read consecutively. The variety of the subjects discussed leads me to hope that in these addresses there will be found something for everybody.

HERBERT A. BRUCE.

Government House,
Toronto,
November, 1934.

CONTENTS

OUR HERITAGE
AND OTHER ADDRESSES

NEW YEAR'S EVE—1932

A Message Delivered at the New Year's
Eve Service in the City Hall of Toronto,
December 31, 1932

Your Worship, Ladies and Gentlemen:

This is not only the first opportunity afforded me of
addressing the people of Ontario since my accession to the
office of Lieutenant-Governor, but also one of my first
experiences in the use of this marvellous invention, the radio.
With all my heart I welcome the opportunity to wish everyone within hearing of my voice a happier, more useful and
more peaceful year than they have ever had.

The mettle of our people has been subject to the severest
test which has been experienced within the memory of the
oldest of us; the slow attrition which has been worse than
any panic has left its effect upon our morale; but it has left
our Province, as it has our Dominion, with solidarity
unimpaired, prestige undiminished, and the courage of our
people undaunted. We have fulfilled all our obligations as
a nation, our economic structure has been strengthened rather
than weakened by adversity, and the absence of any dislocation in our great financial and commercial institutions
has been the amazement of many other countries.

But perhaps the most significant phase of a distressing
situation, from which I pray God we are emerging, is the
newly-born feeling of sympathy for those less fortunate than
ourselves. It has taken time to beget this sense of responsibility for the weaker sections of our community. We had
become so accustomed to good times, to booming stock
markets and to universal employment at high wages that
the sudden tearing to shreds of the world's economic fabric
was a rude jolt. We were so well satisfied with our material

1

achievements that we could not believe a prolonged era of ill-fortune was at hand. Now we have learned to accustom ourselves to other and more simple modes of life, and what is vastly of more importance, we have learned to help one another and to bear one another's burdens. Whenever we emerge from these years of trial we will, I hope, be a simpler and happier people with our natures attuned to the suffering of others.

An event of great significance within the Empire ushers in the New Year. We are afforded the spectacle of Canada going side by side and hand in hand with the Mother Country to the relief and succour of a sister Dominion. That our country has met her internal and external obligations without question is, in these times, an achievement. That we should be able to help Newfoundland in her hour of stress is an inspiration.

BLUE-STOCKINGS AND THE EDUCATION OF WOMEN

*Some Thoughts Suggested by the Opening
of the New Wing of the Bishop Strachan
School, Toronto, January 18, 1933*

Mr. Chairman, Ladies and Gentlemen:

I wish to congratulate you, Sir, and the Members of the Council and Corporation on the completion today of the architects' original design for this beautiful School for Girls. I wish also to congratulate the architects, Messrs. Sproatt and Rolph, upon giving you buildings of such great beauty in which to house all your activities. I am not unmindful of the fact that the architectural beauty of your chapel was largely responsible for their having been awarded the Gold Medal by the American Institute of Architecture.

The citizens of this Province and of this City are indeed fortunate in having a School of this character in their midst. This School enjoys a unique position in the history of the Province in that your Charter of Incorporation was given you by the First Parliament of Ontario in 1868 at its First Session. I need not remind you of your great asset in Bishop Strachan's distinguished name, for to his exertions were due the establishment of King's College, now the U. of T., and later on Trinity College. You have also been most fortunate in the character of the men who have from the beginning worked toward the development of a school which has acquired a foremost position amongst the women's colleges on this Continent.

I should like especially to refer to the great services of Mr. Beverley Jones, the first Bursar, who is unfortunately not able to be with us today. I am glad to see Mr. Sydney Jones, who has faithfully and loyally carried on this office since 1896. I have only time to refer to a few of your many friends—Mr. William Ince, Rev. John Langtry, Mr. James Henderson.

The old building on College Street, where you carried on so successfully for so many years, is well remembered by many of us.

You have been very fortunate in your Lady Principals, whose influence and work, after all, are more important in developing character and establishing a school's reputation than buildings, no matter how beautiful, or even Councils and Corporations, no matter how necessary. The name and fame of Miss Dupont, your Principal in 1869, and the few following years, is still fresh in our memory. Then came Miss Rose Greer, who filled this position for twenty-three years and to whose memory her pupils dedicated the Sanctuary. She was succeeded by Miss Acres, who continued as Principal for ten years and was responsible for the formation of the B.S.S.A.

Then came Miss Harriet Walsh, M.A., of Dublin, under whose principalship, from 1911 to 1930, your School made great progress. Mr. Jones tells me she rendered valuable assistance in drafting the needs and requirements of the new buildings on College Heights; as also she did later, in transferring the School to its new home without loss of valuable tradition or loyalty of pupils. Her picture, which hangs in this Hall, is an evidence of the appreciation felt for her services by the Council, and will remain to cast a benign influence on the future work of the School.

Everyone appreciates the difficult task the Council had in attempting to fill Miss Walsh's place and I understand it was only after prolonged search that they were fortunate enough to prevail upon Miss E. M. Lowe, B.A., a graduate in Arts of the University of Toronto, to resign her position as Principal of Sheriff Hall, Dalhousie University, Halifax, and come here. I wish her many years of continued success in her new post, and am sure that the traditions of this College will be quite safe in her hands.

When we see the splendid facilities for an education which

girls have here, it causes us to reflect upon the fact that only a little more than two centuries ago not only were schools not provided for the education of women, but their education was not thought necessary. Daniel Dafoe in 1697 said "I have often thought of it as one of the most barbarous customs of the world that we deny the advantage of education to women."

If by education we mean book-learning, the answer is that many, nay, most women, received no education at all. Poor women could neither read nor write nor cast up accounts. Dafoe says "One would wonder, indeed, how it should happen that women are conversible at all. Their youth is spent to teach them to sew and make baubles. They are taught to read, indeed, and perhaps to write their names, and that is the height of woman's education." He proposes to build a woman's college specially designed in shape and approach so that young men (who might presumably divert the ladies from their studies, as did actually happen in that other academy for women pictured in Tennyson's *Princess*) should find it difficult to enter. "In this house the persons who enter should be taught in particular Music and Dancing, French and Italian. They should be taught all the graces of speech and all the necessary air of conversation. They should be taught to read books, and especially history, so as to make them understand the world and enable them to know and judge of things when they hear of them."

One of the earliest women of letters, Lady Mary Wortley Montagu, speaking particularly of her eldest grandchild, said, "Learning, if she has a real taste for it, will not only make her contented but happy in it. No entertainment is so cheap as reading, nor any pleasure so lasting." After giving various other pieces of advice she finishes up by saying "At the same time I recommend books, I neither exclude (needle) work nor drawing. I think it is as scandalous for a woman not to know how to use a needle as for a man not to know how to use a sword."

The boarding-schools for young ladies began to be advertised in the newspapers and journals of the early eighteenth century, although many of them were a kind of polite prison whither the anxious parent sent his daughters out of harm's way, and to be safe from the presumption of ineligible lovers. Often the hoped-for safety was quite illusory and the parent was faced with the unpleasant business of a run-away marriage. In this respect the times have not entirely changed. Indeed, not a few parents preferred to educate their girls at home solely because of the risks, real and imaginary, which were part and parcel of a boarding-school up-bringing.

I think it may be said that Thackeray's creation in *Vanity Fair* of that famous academy for young ladies kept by Miss Pinkerton ended that type of boarding-school. From this time on, education for women took on a new aspect, with the advent of the "blue-stocking". The original "blue-stocking", however, was a man, Benjamin Stilling-fleet—botanist, athlete and conversationalist. His dress was remarkably grave and in particular it was observed that he wore blue stockings. The title at first served both men and women and stood for both wit and wisdom, or rather for a happy union of both qualities. Although Lady Mary had advised that women should strive to be clever, she was careful to advise them to hide their learning lest it might frighten away the men.

The "blue-stockings" were fond of society and believed that good talk was as necessary to any dinner-party as good food. So this era really was the precursor of higher educa-tion for women.

I have indicated somewhat crudely the efforts made in earlier times towards the education of women. What a satisfaction it must be to the members of this Council and Corporation to have been instrumental in providing such advantages for the education of young women, to enable them to take their places on an equality with men in our Universities. What a great heritage you have in the traditions of this School, and what a brilliant future lies before you.

THE ROMANCE OF SURGERY

The Story of Surgeons and Surgery, as told to the Canadian Club of Toronto, February 13, 1933

Mr. President and Gentlemen:

I am emerging very timidly and rather nervously from my professional shell to talk to you as a working surgeon and as a fellow-member. There is so much I owe to the Canadian Club, so many happy and instructive hours I have spent with you that I could not resist the importunities of you, Mr. Chairman, and your committee, to discuss some aspects of the history of my profession, which I have ventured to call "The Romance of Surgery".

I speak to you as a surgeon, and, I earnestly hope, without administering the customary anaesthetic. I trust that this surgery will be of the painless kind and that you will not have occasion regretfully to remember the operation.

I will endeavour to point my lancet with general interest rather than with technicalities. If you leave this meeting feeling that I have not given you sufficient knowledge to enable you to adopt my profession, you will, I know, excuse me—both on the grounds of consideration for your feelings and of natural disinclination to prejudice my own interests by stimulating competition.

A cynic has said that the appendix is an organ no longer of any use to man but of considerable value to surgeons. Be that as it may, many thousands of men and women are living useful lives today because of the surgeon's skill in removing this troublesome relic of a second stomach, and they are but a small part of the great army of people who are now alive because of the progress made in treating malformations and diseases by surgical operations.

It was said only the other day that doctors have aggravated our economic problems by prolonging our lives when society is unable to provide all of us with the promise of a livelihood in our declining years. Such a charge seems to have some foundation in fact. In the past ninety years the life expectancy of a man of twenty has increased from forty-one years to fifty years, for which the surgical profession may modestly claim some credit. How this profession has progressed in knowledge and skill to such a reprehensible efficiency it is now my hope to review briefly for you today.

A barber could speak with as much authority as a surgeon of the early history of surgery in England because there, for many years, "barbery" and surgery were joint professions. In the early ages medicine was practised by the ecclesiastics, but these medical ecclesiastics were forbidden to shed blood. However, much as the ecclesiastical powers frowned upon it, bleeding was then deemed necessary for the curing of most ailments and so it was natural that people turned for assistance to their barbers whom they knew to be dexterous with sharp instruments and well supplied with basins and towels.

When barbers were thus allowed to practise one kind of surgery they ventured further and in the course of time were practising surgery independently of the ecclesiastics. The barber-surgeon still survives in some parts of Europe, notably in Russia where fully qualified surgeons are too few to serve a large and widespread population. But although in England surgery and "barbery" may formerly have been united, it would be wrong to suppose that English surgeons are the successors of barbers. Even during their temporary conjunction with the barbers in a common guild the surgeons held themselves apart as a distinct body.

These surgeons later formed a separate guild with a licence from the City of London authorities and from the Bishop of London or the Dean of St. Paul's. They made an agreement with the barbers the chief provision of which was to give the surgeons control over the practice of surgery. There was thereafter no fusion of the two callings. The company had two distinct sections and two names—Barbers and

Surgeons. In the one section were the barbers, a few of whom practised some simple parts of surgery; in the other section were the surgeons. The surgeons were denied the privilege of shaving people, for which restriction I have always been devoutly thankful, and the barber-surgeons were not allowed to do more than draw teeth. If any of them became surgeons it was only after they had acquired the necessary education.

As the surgeons became more skilled and influential, and surgery became a science as well as an art, even the appearance of a union became more intolerable, and although the barbers were an influential body of citizens in various lines of business, and had always, as they said, "with the greatest deference, submitted to the surgeons in all matters peculiar to them", yet the surgeons insisted on separation. They gave up all claim to any share in the property or other treasures of the joint company and obtained for themselves a separate charter which was the progenitor of the present Royal College of Surgeons.

The earliest known pictures of surgical operations are engraved on the stones over a tomb in Egypt, dating from 2500 B.C. They show the operation of circumcision and operations on the legs and arms, which, with castration, comprised all the surgical operations of the Egyptians. All surgery was then wound surgery. It was performed only upon the surface or the extremities of the body. Forty-three centuries after these records were inscribed surgery was still wound surgery.

Like the Egyptians, the Babylonians had little knowledge of anatomy, although there were surgeons among them. Certain conditions written into their law certainly would have discouraged reckless surgery. For, if as a result of an operation a patient lost his life, the surgeon's hand was cut off as a retaliation. Bad surgery probably explains why surgeons were continually in jeopardy of their lives. In 580 A.D., the king of Burgundy had two surgeons executed upon the tomb of his queen because she died of the plague after they had opened her plague sores. In 1337 a surgeon was thrown into the river Oder because he failed to cure John of Bohemia of blindness, and in 1464 the king of Hungary proclaimed that he would reward the surgeon who cured him of the wound of an arrow, but would put him to death if he failed. Pope John XII burned an unsuccessful surgeon.

A knowledge of human anatomy, so essential to surgery, was not attained by the Greek physicians because Greek philosophy was hostile to any interference with the bodies of the dead. The great Greek physician, Galen, who lived in the second century after Christ, derived his knowledge of anatomy from the pig, the ape, the dog and the ox. He assumed that the structures he found in these animals were identical with the structures of the human body. The hold that Galen's work obtained upon the clerics and physicians of the Middle Ages is indicated by the fact that when Vesalius, in the sixteenth century, showed that Galen's description of the hip bones was wrong, the excuse offered by Galen's followers for his error was that man had changed his shape by wearing tight trousers!

Surgery was so crude and barbarous in the sixth century that Gregory of Tours advised the people to emulate the saints and to endure their pain with patience rather than submit to operation. Even in the eleventh century the armies had no surgeons. In the fifteenth, sixteenth and seventeenth centuries warfare offered the best training available for surgeons, but most surgeons did not care for military life, and in the English army, as late as the seventeenth century, it was necessary to impress them into service. The pay of the English army surgeon was good; a first-class surgeon in the fifteenth century received $200 a year and 12 cents a day for expenses. The high pay of the army surgeon drew many quacks into the service.

It was only after the belief in material resurrection passed away that bodies of criminals became available for dissection. Grave-robbing finally developed into a profession. To avoid the incentive to crime, laws were enacted in the nineteenth century to provide medical schools with unclaimed bodies. It was only in 1831, barely a century ago, that Massachusetts enacted a law making available for dissection bodies that required to be buried at public expense. Subsequently, similar laws have been passed in other countries. The notorious trial in Edinburgh of Burke and Hare, who killed sixteen men and women and disposed of the bodies to a medical school, brought about a realization that the provision of human bodies for dissection was necessary if surgical science was to progress.

But although an exact knowledge of anatomy made the development of surgery possible, no great advancement was made until the discovery of anaesthesia. Before its use the fully conscious victim of the operation was tied with ropes to prevent his escape from the surgeon's knife.

It has been said that necessity is the mother of invention. This is particularly true in regard to the invention of the use of anaesthetics. In 1846, less than a hundred years ago, a dentist named Morton, who had perfected a plate to hold false teeth, found that he could not apply it until all the old roots of teeth had been removed from the jaws of his patients. Such an operation was practicable only when insensibility prevailed in the patient and so, out of necessity, ether came into use. It may be of interest to remind you that this discovery of anaesthesia was made at a time, if not within the memory, at any rate during the lifetime of some of our people.

Morton learned of the anaesthetic properties of ether from Dr. Jackson of Harvard, where ether was sometimes inhaled by medical students at so-called "ether frolics", indulged in for the mild intoxication or "ether jag" which the vapour produced. It was observed that students under the influence of ether appeared to be insensible to pain caused by falling over furniture, which falls were a somewhat logical consequence of their indulgence. Morton saw the possibilities presented by ether and experimented at home; first by appro-

priating the family dog as a subject, and finally by anaesthe-
tizing himself. He first used ether for the extraction of teeth
and subsequently at the Massachusetts General Hospital for a
surgical operation, where it proved entirely satisfactory.

Soon after the successful use of ether, Morton and Jackson
attempted to patent it and to control its use by issuing permits
to physicians, for an annual licence fee.

What a contrast to the action of Dr. Banting,[1] discoverer
of insulin, who immediately handed over his discovery for
the benefit of humanity. When he gave his discovery to
the world, Dr. Banting acted in accordance with the ethics
which govern the conduct of the investigator in medicine
and surgery. For in these professions there is no sectional
or creed consciousness; there are no embargoes or tariffs to
hamper the exchange of knowledge and experience. There
is a world state. The man who discovers new information
or who develops a new technique regards himself as the
agent of the profession at large and his immediate concern
is to place his new knowledge or skill at the disposal of all
his fellow practitioners so that the benefit to humanity will
be most rapidly extended. Since we are discussing the
progress of surgery I should like to say, before I pass on from
Dr. Banting, that in my opinion it was his surgical skill
which was chiefly responsible for the success of his experiments. During these experiments it was necessary to depan-
creatise dogs and repeatedly to puncture their veins to determine the blood sugar content.

In 1847, one year after Morton's discovery of the efficacy
of ether as an anaesthetic, Dr. James Simpson[2], who was

[1] Now Sir Frederick Banting.

[2] Letter, April 11, 1934, from Mr. H. A. Rowland, Superintendent,
Riverdale Isolation Hospital, Toronto, gives the following information:
The student who first administered the chloroform to Dr. Simpson
in 1846 afterwards settled in Canada. His name was Gilbert Tweedie.
According to records he left Edinburgh University before graduating,
came to Canada in 1849 or 1850, graduating from Victoria College of
Medicine in 1860. He practised his profession in Victoria and Kent
Counties until about 1890 when he came to Toronto. He was appointed
first Superintendent of Riverdale Isolation Hospital in 1891. Resigned
owing to ill health in 1905.

anxiously looking for some method of relieving the pain of childbirth, successfully used chloroform for the purpose. He and his use of chloroform in childbirth were denounced by the clergy, who argued that the pain of childbirth was the ordained law of mankind and that to prevent it was a sacrilege. The ecclesiastical attacks laid stress on the biblical injunction to the first woman—"In sorrow shalt thou bring forth children".

Two years after Simpson published his paper on the use of chloroform at childbirth he was able to report that it had been administered to 40,000 patients in Edinburgh, both for childbirth and for surgical operations.

In 1853 Queen Victoria took chloroform for the delivery of her seventh child, Prince Leopold, and this had an enormous influence in popularising anaesthesia at childbirth, not only in Great Britain but in the United States. Simpson was ultimately knighted in recognition of the discovery.

It is recorded by Haggard that when this honour was conferred upon Simpson, Sir Walter Scott wrote and suggested as a coat of arms fitting to commemorate his work on the use of chloroform at childbirth "A wee naked bairn" with underneath the motto "Does your mother know you're out?"

Anaesthesia has made a most important contribution to the progress of surgical science, but the last essential to the development of modern surgery was supplied in 1866 when Joseph Lister discovered a means of preventing infection. Millions of lives have been saved in the little more than half a century that has passed since Lister introduced antisepsis. Prior to Lister's discovery pus, which is a product of infection, was considered a sign of healing and was called "laudable pus". Now the surgeon operates with the certain knowledge that there will be no infection and no pus. Before Lister introduced antisepsis death resulted as readily from the small wound of a minor operation as from the large wound of an amputation. At that time amputations were frequent because nearly all compound fractures ended in amputation and 45 per cent. of the patients who were operated upon died. In other words, in 1866, a compound fracture was almost as dangerous as the bubonic plague!

In hospitals today all wounds which are not infected before the time of operation heal by first intention.

Surgery made considerable progress owing to the demands upon the profession during the war. We were able almost entirely to eliminate tetanus by the use of antitetanic serum so generously supplied by our own Connaught Laboratories.

A new and unexpected development of modern warfare brought added fame to a distinguished Toronto bacteriologist, Colonel George Nasmith. I shall never forget, one day in 1915, seeing a number of our men who had been overcome by a gas attack, stretched out at a casualty clearing station, fighting for breath, enduring an agony so excruciating and terrifying that it chilled even one who for years had been accustomed to see practically all forms of physical and mental suffering. That sight was enough to make a pacifist of any man. It was Colonel Nasmith who first determined the composition of the German gas and suggested the way to combat it. He was in command of No. 5 Canadian Mobile Laboratory, and one day while at the Ypres salient, observed a dense cloud of yellowish-green smoke floating across the British lines. He immediately surmised that it was chlorine gas. Subsequently he verified its nature, wrote directly to General Headquarters and suggested that pads soaked in hyposulphite of soda be used as filters in gas masks. He also suggested that careful search be made on the field to discover the enemy's apparatus for protecting his own men from the gas, and it is interesting to note that when the first German gas masks were captured it was found that they contained pads saturated in this solution.

Then we had the wonderful work done by Gillies and his associates in the later period of the war. Men whose faces had been horribly shattered have had chins, mouths and noses restored. This surgical reconstruction has been so delicately and skilfully carried out that not only useful but exceedingly presentable results have been obtained.

In the advanced casualty clearing stations in France I could not help being impressed with the contrast between the humane and scientific care which the wounded then received and the barbarous and callous neglect which was the lot of the fallen soldier in past conflicts. Our wounded had opiates to relieve their pain and anaesthetics for operations, and at all times the faithful, devoted services of trained women nurses, for there were women nurses right in the front lines.

In the war blood transfusion saved many lives. It was Dr. Bruce Robertson of the Hospital for Sick Children, who, knowing that severely burned infants died as a result of poisoning in their blood, conceived the idea that the best way to combat this was to remove all their blood—exsanguination transfusion is the term we use—and to replace it by a transfusion of normal, healthy blood. When Dr. Robertson went to France he continued to take a leading part in advancing the technique of blood transfusion.

I might explain that it is not necessary to transfuse blood directly from the donor to the recipient, but blood taken from a donor can have a solution of citrate added to it to prevent its clotting and then be kept in cold storage until required. The blood from one man will not necessarily mix with that of another. Blood is divided into four groups, and when collected from donors is typed and labelled according to the group to which it belongs, 1, 2, 3 or 4.

Taking advantage of this fact, the surgeons in France collected quantities of blood from healthy soldiers, grouped it and kept it in cold storage in casualty clearing stations awaiting the time when it would be needed for transfusions. I have seen a dozen or more bottles, each containing two quarts of blood, in an ice box, where it was safely kept for a week or more. When a wounded man was brought in bearing evidence of having lost a quantity of blood he was typed in a few minutes and his group ascertained, and then some of this storage blood was injected into his veins. The effect was most striking; his lips became red, a warm glow came over him and his life was frequently saved.

When nourishment cannot be taken through the mouth some other method of sustaining life must be found. To attain this purpose, Rudolph Matas, a distinguished surgeon of New Orleans, about ten years ago proposed the continuous intraveneous administration of fluids. By giving patients a solution of sugar and salt we are able to maintain life solely by this means for a week or more. This method is in general use here, with an improved technique developed by Dr. R. I. Harris of Toronto.

Many operations are now performed upon the brain. Perhaps the most interesting of these to the lay mind is an operation for the relief of a terribly painful form of neuralgia known as tic doloreux. To give access to the brain a portion of the skull about one and one-half inches in diameter is removed. Through this aperture a spatula is introduced and with it the brain is lifted up so that the surgeon may find the gasserian ganglion, a tiny thing about the size of a small wheat kernel which is located about one and one-half inches from where the opening is made. This ganglion is then separated from the brain, when immediate and permanent relief results. Thirty years ago this was considered a very formidable operation, whereas the technique has been so far improved that now it can be performed with almost as great safety as the removal of an appendix.

As late as 1896 Sir James Paget stated that surgery of the heart had probably reached the limit set by nature and that no new method and no new discovery could overcome the natural difficulties that attend a wound of the heart.

Within recent years, however, surgery of the heart has made considerable progress, and we may still hope that the diseases which affect that organ and which have been responsible for the loss of numbers of our prominent citizens within the last few years, will ultimately yield to surgery. Dr. Cutler of Cleveland has successfully performed operations on the valves of the heart where these had become so thickened as to obstruct the flow of blood. With very delicate instruments he removed parts of these valves of the heart, thus enlarging the opening and restoring normal function. He has operated on patients as young as 11 years and as old as 60, with results that, considering the gravity of the condition and the difficulty attending the operation, are extremely gratifying.

Many operations have also been done for wounds of the heart. The heart is easily exposed by the removal of portions of two or three ribs. A suture may then be passed through the apex of the heart and used to draw the organ into any position desirable to facilitate the repair of wounds.

Only last week a Boston surgeon, speaking in Montreal, reported good results from operations to relieve the pain of angina pectoris. This can be done in two ways, either by an operation to sever the nerves that carry painful sensations from the heart to the brain, or by injecting these nerves with alcohol. The latest reports on the alcohol injection operation indicate that in more than one-half of the cases the patients were entirely relieved of pain and one-quarter were greatly improved. Although this operation does not cure the disease, it makes it more bearable by removing the terrifying symptoms. This new work is still in its infancy and we may confidently expect further progress.

I fear, Mr. Chairman, that the patients are becoming exhausted so I shall not discuss the many various excursions which we make into the abdominal cavity to remove diseased organs, such as the stomach, the spleen, kidney, gall-bladder and appendix. Nature has been generous in creating our physical structure, and these organs may be partially or entirely removed without impairing either health or activity. I should like to impress upon you the fact that the abdomen may now be opened with perfect impunity and entirely without risk. The danger, where such exists in these operations, is due to the disease which the surgeon seeks to relieve.

I have neither the experience in public speaking, nor have I had sufficient time to name the numerous members of my profession in this country who more often than not, without public acclaim or recognition, have, through their own research and skill, made notable contributions to our store of knowledge. This address of mine would not be complete if I failed to express my conviction that in the younger generation of physicians and surgeons in this Province we have ample assurance of brilliant achievement and that our people will in years to come be better served in both medicine and surgery than any age has ever been. A hundred years from now a surgeon looking back on our methods will probably consider many of them clumsy and unscientific. I hope so. For that would be certain evidence of the continued progress which is the objective of all the devoted men and women in whose hands the honour and the advancement of the profession rest.

THE LANGUAGE OF WALES

On the Presentation of the Lieutenant-Governor's Cup to the Duke of York School Choir, Winners of the St. David's Society Singing Festival, March 2, 1933

Mr. Chairman, Ladies and Gentlemen:

I am glad to know that, although this is a cup given in connection with the Welsh Eisteddfod, it has not been necessary for the competitors to learn the Welsh language. I congratulate this School upon its splendid achievement and I am reminded of the growth of the strong national sentiment in modern Wales—the evolution of a new Welsh Renaissance. This revived spirit of nationalism is not due, I am told, to political dissent in Wales, and the question of the vernacular itself is not of necessity bound up in this new movement. But Wales, like Canada, is essentially a bi-lingual country. Every educated Cymro there speaks and reads English with ease, and people in the large towns and districts, such as Cardiff, speak English only. So that, although the landowners and gentry ceased as a body to speak the native tongue generations ago, they are now showing a strong disposition to speak once more the ancient language and read the literature of their country.

I have not forgotten, of course, the young Wales party which has arisen and which seeks to exclude all English ideas and influence. They are opposed, as you would expect, by yet another party—a party which is abnormally suspicious of and hostile to this Welsh renaissance. In the main, however, the bulk of the Welsh nation is content to assert its views in a reasonable manner, that is to say, without recourse to violence.

The National Eisteddfod itself, holding meetings in North and South Wales, indicates the extent of this true spirit of nationalism amongst all classes and sects of Welsh society today. Welsh—the Celtic language spoken by the ancient Britons—is the domestic tongue of the majority of the inhabitants of the principality. It was Edward I who destroyed the independence of Wales; and Wales was united with England during the reign of Henry VIII. Following that the administration of all law and justice was in the English tongue, and I'm afraid that the ancient language of the people was thereby threatened with complete extinction. From such a fate it was happily delivered by the various translations of the Scriptures undertaken at the command of Queen Elizabeth.

As long ago as 1630 only about one per cent. of the people of Wales, other than a few, perhaps, among the clergy, could read their native language. Then, during the earlier part of the seventeenth century about 8,000 Bibles were distributed. That was at a time when there was scarcely any Welsh work of importance in circulation. To make the revival of the Welsh language complete the circulating Welsh charity schools in the eighteenth century resulted in about one-third of the total population being taught to read and write Welsh. The ancient language was coming back in all its power and beauty.

Then early in the nineteenth century came the Eisteddfodau —the ancient bardic contests of music, poetry and learning. More and more people learned to speak and write the Welsh language. It became a popular medium of education and it is computed that in 1893 Welsh was understood or spoken by sixty per cent. of the inhabitants in the twelve Welsh counties.

The Welsh are a nation of singers. Whether it be in their own ancient tongue or in that of their neighbour, their songs and their singing are beautiful.

THE PROPAGATION OF THE UNFIT

*Delivered before the Academy of Medicine
at a Dinner at the Royal York Hotel,
Toronto, Monday, March 27, 1933*

Mr. President and Fellows:

I have listened with great interest to the comparatively recent history of medicine in Toronto, so graphically portrayed by Dr. Anderson. Much as I am honoured, I do not feel deserving of the encomiums he has heaped upon me, and I can only hope that as he is one of my most intimate and valued friends, he will not be called upon to do too severe a penance for his generous words.

The very kind and complimentary remarks made about me by Sir William Mulock and Dr. Cody remind me of a line from Oscar Wilde's play, *A Woman of No Importance*, in which one of the characters said, "After a good dinner one can forgive anyone, even one's own relations." So I feel in a very generous and forgiving mood to these kind friends who have said so many nice things, even though they are undeserved.

You have made me a very happy man tonight. The honour you have done me will be treasured more than I, who have neither the lucidity of our loved Chief Justice nor the eloquence of our revered President of the University of Toronto, can tell you. I am not a technician with words, and my emotion at this moment hinders rather than helps me. So you must be contented not with words to picture my feelings, but with my word that they are feelings of profound gratitude. I have been particularly blessed in the friends that I have made. If success consists in getting what one wants and being satisfied with it, then success has been mine since I have so many good friends.

It has been stated that it is a unique thing for a doctor

to be chosen Governor of this Province. Such appointments must have been more common in early times, for there is an old Hebrew proverb—"Do not dwell in a city whose Governor is a physician."

However, as Dr. Anderson has suggested, I am very pleased to have my appointment considered as a compliment to the medical profession, and shall endeavour so to discharge my duties as to bring added credit to the profession to which I owe so much. I consider that the training a medical man receives is the very best preparation for any career—an education I should like my son to have, in spite of the fact that his present determination is to be a *veterinary* surgeon.

Although the honour to which Dr. Anderson has referred did not materialize, yet I did receive the highest and most priceless decoration that could come to any man, in that my service overseas gave me the opportunity of meeting and bringing back with me my wife. No material decoration of gold or silver or precious stones could have equalled the advantage which I have enjoyed of the loving companionship, help and encouragement of a devoted wife.

Dr. Anderson has also referred to Colonel Price's statement that I am an Irishman. This, he claims, explains why, when I was Inspector of the Canadian Army Medical Corps there were "wigs on the green", but they were not Irish wigs only, and if at times it seemed advisable to lay down the scalpel and wield a shillalah, I hope I had enough Irish in me to make the performance worthy of Donnybrook traditions.

However fraught with danger such overseas activities may have been, there is a suggestion of security here, for to become President of this Academy generally assures longevity. Of the twenty-eight Presidents since its inception twenty-one are living. Although the first President, Dr. J. F. W. Ross, a distinguished surgeon, died at the age of fifty-five as the result of an automobile accident, the second President, Dr. Alexander McPhedran, one of our great teachers in Medicine, is still with us and active at the age of eighty-six. Dr. N. A. Powell, who has taken such a lively interest in the Academy, is eighty-three, and Dr. John Ferguson, who has done so much for the up-building of its Library, is but a few years his junior. If time permitted I would pay tribute to the many able men who have adorned our profession in this city and Province. The only one of my teachers in Surgery living is Mr. I. H. Cameron, whose culture and high principles were an inspiration to us all.

We have gone a long way in surgery since my student days, but even so, one must admire the quality of the surgery done at that time.

During my year as resident in the Toronto General Hospital I recollect seeing only one operation for appendicitis. I have a vivid memory of having assisted in my final year at an operation on a patient in her home. The operation was excision of the elbow joint for tuberculosis, and commenced about 9.30 a.m. with prayer. At 12.30 the surgeon thought we had better adjourn for lunch, and the anaesthetic was continued while in the adjoining room we partook of a leisurely meal preceded by grace. When lunch was finished, one of the assistants relieved the anaesthetist to enable him to have lunch, and the operation was finally concluded about three o'clock. The habit of this surgeon of using his mouth as a receptacle for the scalpel, is good evidence that at this time—just forty years ago—the antiseptic principles of Lister were not thoroughly understood. Most of you will appreciate, I think, the necessity for the prayer! I should tell you that the patient made a good recovery.

The tremendous strides that surgery has made in recent times is due not only to the adoption of the Listerian principles of antisepsis, but also to the discovery of anaesthetics, which it is interesting to recall is within the lifetime, if not the memory of several present here this evening.

We have made great progress in the realms of preventive and curative medicine and surgery. Tomorrow, both because of the character and ability of the young men who are succeeding us, and because these young men will have at their disposal new knowledge and new tools which were not available to many of us when we began to practice, we shall go even further.

But there is an influence that may stultify future efforts of our profession and which even now is working against all progress. It is the problem of racial degeneration, manifest in mental and physical defects, symptomatic of a disease which is slowly and surely eating its way into the heart of the nation. It is a disease whose victims multiply with alarming rapidity, and its spread can be counteracted only by State action. Today we are spectators of a phenomenon that has brought prouder races than ours to ruin.

It is a well-known fact that fertility is in inverse ratio to social status. Consequently, the more efficient sections of the community tend to die out and the less efficient increase in numbers at a terrifying rate. In poor, miserable Finsbury the birth rate is forty-one per thousand; in cultured Westminster it is nine per thousand; so that between these two London districts the future rests with Finsbury. But it is a future to which we look with considerable apprehension.

It is well known that defectives breed and multiply two to six times as fast as normal people. Thieves and other petty offenders, whose stupidity is unquestionable, spring from amongst the most fertile stocks in the community.

What a threat and what a challenge lies in this fact! Already conditions are bad, certainly to an extent beyond public knowledge and perhaps even beyond public belief. In England, in 1926, there were 240,000 who were mentally defective. These were only patients in institutions, whereas thousands more are living in their own homes. Conditions necessarily are worse today because the continued high birth rate of the lowest classes, combined with the low and steadily falling birth rate among the better classes, has caused further deterioration.

In the elementary schools of England and Wales there are a million children so physically and mentally retarded, defective or diseased, as to be unable to derive reasonable benefit from the education provided by the State. During the last stages of the war forty per cent. of the recruits for the British army were rejected as unfit, and only one out of every twenty examined for the police force was of the physical and mental standard desired.

On January 1st, 1932, we had 32,059 patients in Canadian mental hospitals, and their maintenance cost nearly $11,000,000.

In 1931 the United States spent approximately $208,000,000 to maintain 451,245 patients in the mental hospitals.

Warfare accelerated the rate of decadence. In the last year of the war seven out of every nine recruits examined were either definitely infirm or incapable of undergoing exertion, and, in view of their age, could almost be described as physical wrecks. All through the war, the capable and fit, the pick of our manhood, went to drain their blood on the fields of France. The unfit were left at home to breed a generation that, by the immutable laws of heredity, must also be unfit.

The medical profession is engaged in unending warfare against physical ills. It has great achievements to its credit. It is doing all that it can do to improve the race, to extend the span of life and to promote social welfare. But it cannot, itself, go to the root of this great problem of decadence which is properly a problem for the State and which becomes more and more difficult as the years pass.

Today, if we are to make the future secure for our civilization, we must look to State reforms consisting of measures to prevent propagation by the sub-normal and to induce the normal elements of our society to have large families. In this morning's papers there is an Associated Press Dispatch from Rome which tells us that Premier Mussolini's appeal for a seventeen million increase in Italy's population in the next ten years is meeting with such an enthusiastic response that Italian city governments are offering special inducements to promote marriage. It is to be hoped that there are some restrictions whereby these inducements will encourage only the normal and the fit. Otherwise I fear they will later be a cause for regret.

To the medical man, as to all right thinking men, life is a sacred thing. Our profession is devoted to the preservation of life; and religion and moral sense revolt at the suggestion that we can take life into our own hands. But surely there can be no religious or moral scruples against preventing propagation by the unfit. There can be no religious or moral principles which will sanction a reversion to savagery, and that is the road any nation will go if there are no restrictions to prevent the sub-normal and the unfit from over-running the land.

I have dealt briefly tonight with this question of racial degeneration because it is one of supreme importance if our civilization is to be preserved. Public opinion must be awakened to the seriousness of this problem so that the State, which alone can solve it, will take the necessary action. The medical profession may well be expected to lend its leadership in directing public knowledge to the gravity of the situation.

In concluding I must refer again to the honour you have done me. To whatever extent I have deserved it I attribute my adherence to certain rules of conduct which I established early in my professional life. The first of these is to do each day's work to the best of my ability, and having done so, not to waste energy in fruitless worry. Another is to indulge regularly in congenial, healthful exercise, so that physically and mentally I may always be fit. Riding is my hobby, and I feel that every man should have a hobby, but let it be a useful servant to him and under no circumstances assume the character of a master, to the detriment of his regular calling. Another and most important principle is to practise the Golden Rule. And lastly, to cultivate a calm equanimity which alone will permit one to talk with crowds and keep his virtue; to walk with kings nor lose the common touch; and when one meets with triumph or disaster, to treat those two imposters just the same.

From my heart I say "Thank you", both for your tribute tonight and for the distinction I enjoy of being one of you.

FLOWERS

Remarks made at the Opening of the Spring Flower Show, Sponsored by St. Dunstan's Chapter, I.O.D.E. in Toronto, March 28, 1933

Mr. Chairman, Madam Regent, Ladies and Gentlemen:

This fragrant and lovely scene commends more highly than words the enterprise of St. Dunstan's Chapter of the Imperial Order of the Daughters of the Empire and of the Canadian Florists' and Gardeners' Association. I am sure we derive great satisfaction from being able to enjoy the beauty of these spring flowers and at the same time lend deserved support to St. Dunstan's Chapter, which in the past ten years has worked so hard and so successfully in humanitarian interests.

So much is known of this Chapter's generous help to the blind that I need scarcely refer to it, and surely it must seem to us who are admiring these flowers tonight that no effort is too great to help the men and women who are deprived of this privilege by the loss of sight. Most of us are aware that the Chapter administers the fund so generously established by the late Lady Flavelle whereby a four-year University Scholarship is provided for a son of a war widow. We are familiar also with the Mina Barrett Scholarship, created by the Chapter, for a blind girl at the Toronto Conservatory of Music, and we have heard much of the Chapter's contributions to direct relief, to neighbourhood work and to other deserving causes.

I regard this floral display as a tribute not only to the Canadian Florists' and Gardeners' Association but also to the people of Ontario whose love of beauty gives to the work of the Association the wide-spread support which is necessary to warrant such educational efforts. Love of beauty is inherent in all normal human beings. It expresses itself in different ways in different individuals. Nearly always, however, it is also expressed by a fondness for flowers. Among the daintiest and most wonderful works of nature, flowers naturally have an irresistible appeal. They have inspired our greatest painters and finest poets, and we must feel grateful to all who make their fresh loveliness available to us.

Many of the flowers we see tonight are the outcome of long years of work devoted to improving existing varieties and to producing new varieties. A few years ago blooms as beautiful as many of these did not exist. They were originated by careful selection and by skilful crossing of types. This work of hybridizing is perhaps the most interesting of the tasks undertaken by professional florists and growers, and it is gratifying to know that Ontario is well to the fore in such a delicate and difficult art. Professor Crow and Mr. Groff of Simcoe, Mr. Palmer of Vineland and Miss Preston of Ottawa are but a few of the number who should be mentioned for their distinguished work in this connection.

I derive considerable satisfaction from knowing that the retail florists and wholesale growers who are responsible for this show and who enable us to enjoy this early display of spring blooms are meeting with a good response from the public. At least, I assume this is so because I am told that there are in Toronto now 150 florists' shops as compared with only one in 1880, and I understand that to-day hundreds of men in this city are employed growing flowers under glass whereas fifty years ago we had no such industry. I think it is obvious that the flower-loving public owes a debt of gratitude to the commercial and professional growers for producing flowers out of season so that even in the winter months their rich colour, their graceful form and lovely fragrance may gladden our hearts.

Now tonight we are to enjoy not only the beauty of this floral display but also the beauty and interest of a fashion show. I do not propose any longer to keep that added enjoyment from you nor from myself, so with much pleasure and hearty congratulations to all who have contributed to the success of this event, I declare the Spring Flower Show officially open.

THE FARMER AND THE CITY MAN

*A Comparison made at a Complimentary
Banquet Given by the Citizens of North
York, March 31, 1933*

Mr. Chairman, Ladies and Gentlemen:

There is both a disadvantage and an advantage in living close to a great city. The disadvantage is that rural peacefulness is invaded by city dwellers who seek occasional escape from the heat and turmoil of the city and who, all too frequently, leave the wreckage of their picnics behind them and tear to shreds the quiet serenity of country life.

On the other hand the pilgrimage of city men who never, during their busy lives in the city, have lost their love of the country and their desire to live close to Mother Earth again, has certain advantages. Men who come to the country to stay, to spend, shall we say, their declining years, are quite definitely an asset. They conduct what are called model farms—farms which are chiefly valuable because of the blunders made by their well-intentioned owners. These owners are all inspired by a belief which they are at no pains to keep secret, that the knowledge of farming which they acquired in their early days as boys in the country PLUS the business ability which gained them prominence in the city—these together form the sum total of all that is necessary to entitle them to rank as outstanding, experienced, scientific and most efficient farmers. The mistakes they make are many and cry aloud for correction, and their disillusionment is swift and painful but salutary. And yet, for such is human pride, it may be that years will pass before they realize their vast ignorance. I insist, however, that they should be called model farmers if only because most of them are models of what a real practical farmer shouldn't do. And the compensating laws of nature operate here too.   For the very mistakes of a city man who comes to live in the country are a benefit to the community in proportion as they are very costly to himself. They usually are!

In rather more serious vein let me add that it is only too obvious that none of us—city man or farmer—can enjoy prosperity or even reasonable comfort until, through a higher price for his products, the farmer is permitted to resume his place as the chief buyer of all commodities.

May the farmer as the chief consumer of manufactured articles—consuming no less than 80 per cent. of them—may he soon be restored to a position to buy more and more so that the coming of better times for all people may be thereby accelerated.

FREEMASONS AND FREEMASONRY

At a Meeting of Ionic Lodge,
April 5, 1933

Worshipful Sir and Brethren:

It seems fitting that I, as the King's representative, should be a Mason, for in England the craft has allied itself with social order, with the great institutions of the country and, above all, with monarchy, the crowning institution of all. King Edward VII was a Grand Master of English Freemasons and later the Duke of Connaught, our former beloved Governor-General, held a similar post. Our Prince of Wales is Senior Grand Warden of the United Grand Lodge of English Freemasons.

The lustre of many great names has reflected honour on the craft in the past: Napoleon, Lafayette, Voltaire, Franklin, Garibaldi and Washington.

This Lodge numbers amongst its members men who have played a large part in the affairs of this country, and no one has filled so many high offices with more ability and credit than the distinguished jurist, who has so kindly introduced me— my old and revered friend the Chief Justice of Ontario, Sir William Mulock. There are other names—Sir John Aird, Sir Allan Aylesworth, Justice Masten, Justice Riddell, Judge Morson, E. R. Peacock.

The total membership has doubled since 1910; in 1926 it was computed that there were 4,000,000 Masons in the United States and the British Empire.

Masonry gives evidence of a prosperity unparalleled in the annals of any other human institution. It exists where Christianity has not gone; and its claims will be respected even where the superior claims of religion would fail.

At the reorganization of the Craft and the establishment of the present Grand Lodge of England in 1717, we laid aside our operative character, and with it all pretensions to extra-ordinary skill in architectural science. We then became a purely moral and benevolent association, whose great aim is the development and cultivation of the moral sentiment, the social principle, kindly affections, a higher reverence for God, and a warmer love for man. England then became the great central point of Masonry for the whole world. Since the War there have been attempts made to form an International Masonic Association, but these have been abortive owing to Masons in the United States and England refusing to affiliate with foreign bodies who remove the Bible from the Lodge and do not require faith in a Supreme Being as a requisite to membership.

Freemasonry possesses many titles to respect. First, it is of great antiquity; secondly, it is known and practised in every country, in every clime, and in every race of civilized men; and lastly and above all, it has associated itself with human sympathies and charitable institutions. Formerly, through the dim periods of the Middle Ages it carved its records upon the public buildings of Europe. Now it is content to devote itself to works of sympathy and charity and in them it finds its highest praise and reward.

THE RESPONSIBILITIES OF THE TEACHING PROFESSION

Welcoming the Delegates of the Ontario Educational Association in Convocation Hall, April 18, 1933

Mr. President, Ladies and Gentlemen:

The fact that the object of your Association is "to improve the efficiency of the profession of teaching", and to stimulate an intelligent co-operation by all classes in the cause of education is an indication that you are fully alive to the great responsibility that rests upon you. I congratulate you upon being members of the teaching profession, for, next to my own, I consider it the most interesting and beneficent of all professions. What an inspiration to meet daily a classroom filled with children or youth bubbling over with enthusiasm and thirsting for knowledge! What a wonderful opportunity to give direction and to help in the development of character!!

The presence here this evening of so many ladies causes me to reflect that only a little over two centuries ago it was not thought necessary to give women any education at all.

Daniel Dafoe, one of the early advocates of education for women, once said that he thought it one of the most barbarous customs in the world that women were denied the advantages of learning.

Education in the early eighteenth century was a luxury for the few. Lady Mary Montagu, whose letters are so famous, advised women to strive to be clever, but she was careful also to advise them "to hide their learning lest it might frighten away the men." Lady Mary was a "blue-stocking" but not the first of the tribe. It may not be known to you that the wearer of the original blue stockings was a man—Benjamin Stillingfleet, who was famous as a verse-maker and conver-

33

sationalist.   His dress was remarkably grave, and in particular it was observed that he wore blue stockings.   Such was the excellence of his conversation that his absence was felt as so great a loss that it used to be said "We can do nothing without the blue stockings."   The title at first served both men and women, and stood for both wit and wisdom, or rather a happy union of both qualities.   They were famed not only for learning, but for those arts and graces of conversation which could display learning readily, appropriately and with charm. Later, the title became restricted to women.

In the early centuries of the Roman Republic the entire responsibility for the education of his son rested upon the father.   I am glad that we are living in a better age where this responsibility is now assumed by the State.

We have gone a long way since those days and thanks to the Minister of Education and his predecessors and to the able men attached to the Department there has been created a system of education in this Province second to none—with equal opportunities for men and women.

Looking at the individual to be educated, we may say with Plato that the aim of education is to develop in the body and in the soul all the beauty and perfection of which they are capable.   So I say that those who devote themselves to this profession and do their duty with diligence and success are entitled to the very high respect and thanks of the whole community.

STERILIZATION OF THE FEEBLE-MINDED

Before the Canadian Club, Hamilton, at
their Fortieth Annual Dinner, April 28,
1933

Mr. President, Ladies and Gentlemen:

As one who long has enjoyed membership in a Canadian Club, who has spent many happy and profitable hours at its meetings, I realize what Colonel Charles R. McCullough has done for the advancement of Canadian thought and for the development of Canadian opinion by founding the first Canadian Club in 1892.

It is a privilege to break bread with Colonel McCullough tonight, to salute him in gratitude and admiration and to express the hope that his honoured years may long rest as lightly as now upon his capable shoulders. But I wish particularly to thank Colonel McCullough for having founded the Canadian Club in the year 1892. I am delighted that that year should be so greatly honoured, for it was a year of almost infinite importance—and need I say of trepidation—for me. It was the year of my graduation in medicine from the University of Toronto.

Forty years is a considerable period of individual activity in any profession, but it is little in the lifetime of a great organization such as the Canadian Club. However, the Canadian Club and I have this in common; we are both Canadians and we both insist upon looking forward and not backward.

I wonder if Colonel McCullough and his associates of those early years, men like James Ferres, John T. Hall, George D. Fearman, Henry Carpenter (now his Honour Judge Carpenter), Senator Lynch-Staunton and W. Sanford Evans (who was the first Canadian Club President), I wonder if these men had any conception of the enormous potentialities for education and enlightenment possessed by the Club which was founded here in Hamilton. It has spread throughout Canada and has enrolled in its membership thousands of the best brains of the country. Its lifetime is not to be measured by decades. It is still young, it is still virile, and so long as there are men who are devoted to the advancement of knowledge and thought it will be characterized by virility and by the spirit of youth. Because of the good it is doing and its position in the affections of the people I think it may already be regarded as a permanent institution.

I congratulate you, Mr. President, and officers of this Club, and of all the Canadian Clubs, upon the contribution which is being made to the intellectual life and progress of our country, by giving to your members an opportunity to meet and hear our own leaders in all branches of human activity and to listen to the words of distinguished visitors from other lands.

As long ago as 1907, Lord Grey, who was then our Governor-General, stated that "The tendency of the addresses delivered to Canadian Clubs will be to uplift the people out of the valley in which they dwell onto the mountain tops whence their gaze will extend over a wider horizon—to enrich our life by keeping before us high ideals and the well-being of the state."

At this very time, as in 1907, the best minds in the world are seeking solution for a grave economic problem which is causing widespread distress. Economic problems seem to be recurrent and at intervals menace the well-being of the state. But there are other problems of at least equal importance that continuously threaten our welfare and I, who am not an economist, have chosen to speak to you this evening about one of the most terrifying of these problems. It is race degeneration.

That we may all at once realize the importance of the subject, let me begin by quoting from an article entitled "Insanity, the Modern Menace" by Henry Martin Robinson: "If the present rate of increase in mental cases continues for the next three-quarters of a century, half the population of the

United States will be in insane asylums and the other half will labour solely to support them." Life and thought here in Canada are much the same as in the United States and if that dire prediction is a sound one, as it seems to be, we cannot expect a happier outcome in our own country unless action is taken to defeat the disintegrating forces which are now at work unhindered.

Our profession brings us into close, and I might say, intimate contact with mental defectives, mental diseases of all kinds, and the moral perversions which form such dark blots on the pages of every nation's history. We see the horror, the sorrow which neither word nor act can banish, the physical and mental torment, the grim tragedies which engulf whole families in despair and often ruin. For it is to be remembered that the unfortunate individuals of whom I speak are not alone. They have families and friends on whom falls the weight of their suffering.

Since speaking upon this subject a few weeks ago I have received countless letters urging me to engage in a campaign for its control, and many sad cases have been brought to my attention. I shall give you but one. A normal, educated man married a wife of normal intelligence. A son was born, but he made no attempt to speak until he was four. He is now 27 and physically perfect. But he has the intelligence of a boy of four. You can doubtless imagine the quite indescribable mental anguish of his parents. All these years they have been attempting to instruct and bring up this imbecile boy. They love him—their only child. The father, when he brought the boy to see me recently, told me with tears streaming from his eyes that he and his wife had gone through unendurable purgatory for more than twenty years, and that they had reached the very limits of human endurance. They sent the boy to an institution. However, the poor imbecile fretted; the mother, motherlike, worried. She neither slept nor ate until her imbecile boy was restored to her. The father's aunt was insane. The germ of the evil of which I am speaking was there. The father heartrendingly deplored the inescapable fact that the law had not required him to be sterilized, and thus have prevented all this misery.

All the medical science in the world stands helpless before the mental bankruptcy and moral degeneracy of one idiot. And if that poor unfortunate idiot be allowed to propagate, what then, becomes of our race?

We, in the medical profession, can deal effectively with most forms of disease; can cure the greater number of the ills to which flesh is heir. But, notwithstanding this, we are devoting a great deal of time and research to the prevention of these diseases, so many of which are curable. How much more important it is then for all of us, scientists and laymen, to co-operate in an earnest effort to prevent what by no human means can ever be cured!

In order to illustrate the hereditary nature of mental defects and diseases—the inviolable law of nature that like begets like —I shall mention two well-known historic records of the workings of the law of heredity.

First let us look at the bright side of the picture. For it is only by contrast—only by seeing what can be against the dark background of what is that we shall recognize the imperative necessity of putting an end to this malignant growth which threatens the very life of the race. Let us see for a moment how a legacy of good blood or good germ cells may enrich a nation.

Elizabeth Tuthill, a women of splendid qualities, lived nearly two hundred years ago at Hartford, Connecticut. She married Richard E. Edwards, a great lawyer. They had one son and four daughters. That union has left its mark upon American blood. And when anything marks a nation's blood, it marks for weal or woe its ideals, its institutions and its history.

Later in life this same Richard Edwards married an ordinary, commonplace woman. She had ordinary, commonplace children. The splendid heredity of Richard Edwards was swamped by the mating. But the union of two streams of fine blood of similar character begets greater. The son of the first marriage was Timothy Edwards, one of the founders of Yale University. He was the father of Jonathan Edwards, who also married a wonderful woman, Sarah Pierpont.   From that union have descended 12 college presidents, 265 college graduates, 65 college professors, 60 physicians, 100 clergymen, 75 army officers, 60 prominent authors, 100 lawyers, 30 judges, 80 public officers, state governors, city mayors and state officials, 3 congressmen, 2 United States senators and 1 Vice-President of the United States.

Nor is that all.   The direct descendants of this Jonathan Edwards include: Aaron Burr, who was Vice-President; Mrs. Eli Whitney, wife of the inventor of the cotton gin, and the novelist, Winston Churchill.

The oldest daughter was Abigail.   Perhaps the most notable descendant was Robert Treat Paine, one of the signers of the Declaration of Independence.

Then there was Elizabeth, the next daughter, whose descendants include the Marchioness of Donegal, a distinguished woman of Ireland; and the Fairbanks brothers who manufacture weighing scales known all over the world.

The next daughter, Mabel, gave the world Melville W. Bigelow, one of the greatest legal writers of our time, and Morrison R. Waite, former chief justice of the United States. The glorious story of fine blood seems unending.   Other notable descendants are Bishop Vincent, founder of the Chautauqua movement and father of George Vincent, head of the Rockefeller Foundation; Grover Cleveland, Ulysses S. Grant and Edith Carow, widow of Theodore Roosevelt and mother of his five sons, one of whom was killed in the air service in France.   The remaining four are starting upon careers of honour and distinction.   And so this splendid history of great blood continues, invigorating, healthful, making its incalculable contribution to all that is best and noblest in the life of any nation.   I am not surprised that many of the descendants of Elizabeth Tuthill—and they are to be found all over America—wear as a sign of distinction "The Tuthill Emblem"—a golden badge of honour.   Honour, indeed— they are honoured, the nation is honoured by such blood as that of the Tuthills.

Now for the contrast.   We plunge immediately and head-long from national glory to national shame.   Two hundred years ago there lived in New England a vagabond named Max Juke.   The melancholy story of the descendants of this degenerate can soon be told: 1,220 of these social scourges have been traced.   Now you can watch the blood stream of a nation being polluted past all remedy.   Of the descendants of Max Juke, 300 died in infancy, 310 were professional paupers, 440 were wrecked by disease, 50 were prostitutes, 60 were thieves, 7 were murderers, 53 were criminals of some other kind, many were habitual drunkards addicted to every form of vice and depravity.

In the face of the social menace of the Max Jukes of our nation, it would appear but the simplest form of common sense—the only way indeed to save a race of fine people—to insist, as 27 out of the 48 States of the United States of America have insisted between 1907 and 1931, that the mentally deficient shall be compulsorily sterilized.   Of all the unfortunate victims who fill the mental hospitals of the United States no less than 50 per cent. are the offspring of mental defectives. They, and all those across whose lives their pathetic condition falls like an ominous shadow—are but reaping the inevitable punishment, the horror of allowing to continue what should be immediately stamped out.   By sheer weight of numbers the mentally deficient—the most prolific of all mankind—constitute such a threat to the well-being of the state as to imperil its very existence.   Let it not be thought that I exaggerate.   I have already referred to the dire prophecy that 75 years from now half of the population may be working to support the other and imbecile half.

Leaving for a moment the medical or racial point of view and regarding it as an economist, the family of Max Juke—whose scandalous record I have already mentioned—cost the state $1,300,000 in 75 years.   How, indeed is it possible to place too great an emphasis upon a social evil which cries aloud for remedy.

I have intentionally directed your thought to this menace

as it exists in the United States in order that we may recognize, in all its evil potentialities, that same menace of racial degeneration within our own borders. What of Canada? What of Ontario? I shall bring to your attention certain definite facts and quote a few statistics. I wish to present a picture of conditions in Ontario, which I hope will remain continually in your minds until an enlightened public opinion demands legislation to curb this evil.

At present Ontario spends $4,000,000 annually to maintain hospitals for the insane. But the "Max Jukes" of this Province go their way unchecked and unrestrained. Like begets like, and so they propagate their kind at a rate which requires that every twenty months a new asylum be built at a cost of $2,000,000 and with an annual maintenance charge of $300,-000. At the present rate of increase in mental defectives, we shall within twenty-five years be spending $8,000,000 annually in this Province for their maintenance, and we shall have twice as many institutions as we have now devoted to their care.

In the mental hospital at Orillia there are several groups of half a dozen—each group from the same family. You can in imagination trace the course of such unchecked propagation. The seeds of deficiency are transmitted from generation to generation, continuously affecting an increasing number of unfortunates and imposing upon the shoulders of the mentally and physically fit a heavier burden, which, by its economic weight, discourages them from raising large families.

Devastating as a forest fire and all the more terrible that it rages unseen and undetected in our midst, race degeneration takes its insidious toll here as everywhere else. I cannot but feel that this is allowed to continue rather through ignorance than indifference. I feel sure that public opinion, once aware of the magnitude of this menace, will not be satisfied with less than thoroughly effective measures to make it in the course of time only a shameful memory like the dungeons and torture chambers of the past.

Between 1871 and 1931 our population little more than doubled, but the number of insane in our institutions multi-

plied sixfold and the cost of caring for them increased ten-
fold. I repeat the distressing figures—twice as many people,
six times as many insane, ten times as heavy a burden of
cost. Perhaps reference to one family history is all that is
necessary to impress upon you the seriousness of the economic
aspect of this problem. An immigrant, tainted with mental
deficiency, entered this country. He, his son and two daughters, and seven illegitimate offspring in the third generation
are at this time costing a municipality $3,460.00 annually
for support and care.

Records have been kept of one Canadian family which
has provided inmates for mental hospitals at New Westminster, London, Hamilton and Orillia. Of the four known
branches, three are for the most part mentally defective.
Ten Mongolian idiots have appeared in this family and
twelve of its adult members were maniacs.

There are many other family histories which could be
cited, but why spend more time in the melancholy past and
present? Our concern should be action that will mitigate
this scourge in the future.

The remedy, the recourse which can save us from the
horrors incidental to a continued spread of deficiency, is
sterilization for individuals contemplating marriage when
there exists the taint of insanity, mental deficiency or epilepsy
in the family history. Such individuals should be subjected
to thorough psychiatric examinations and sterilization advised if the dangers for their progeny seem great. It is,
above all, desirable that we look to the possibility of social
legislation which will prevent the marriage of mental defectives unless first of all they be sterilized.

Not only would sterilization curtail the increasing demand
for hospital accommodation for defectives, but it would
permit of a restricted class of these defectives, who must
now be confined, being allowed at large in the community.
Thus it would relieve the pressure on public institutions.
It would relieve the pressure on our penal institutions too.
For, as Mr. Justice Oliver Wendell Holmes of the United

States Supreme Court said when upholding the Virginia Sterilization law: "It is better for all the world if, instead of waiting to execute sentence upon degenerate offspring for crime, society can prevent those who are manifestly unfit from continuing their kind." The case of Buck *v*. Bell decided on May 2nd, 1927, has definitely committed the United States to a policy of human sterilization as a means of coping with the socially undesirable in their midst.

Sterilization* promotes both the health of the patient and the welfare of society. It is in no sense a punitive measure. It is protection to the individual, to the state and to posterity. It has no ill effects upon the individual. On the contrary, it results in a better physical and mental condition. In the State of California a law permitting sterilization was adopted in 1909. Investigation has disclosed no serious complaints from the thousands of persons who were treated. Here in Hamilton are some far-sighted people who have been doing splendid work in connection with this matter, though handicapped by the lack of supporting legislation. However, they are courageously creating the public opinion which necessarily precedes the enactment of such measures. Mr. Kauffman of Kitchener has established a clinic in his city to deal with this condition in a practical way and he, as well as your local organization, is making a valuable contribution to the welfare of the race.

May the day speedily come when Ontario will awake, as Alberta and British Columbia have awakened, and as twenty-seven States in the American Union have awakened, to the enormity of this peril and the necessity for prompt action. Alberta and British Columbia and twenty-seven American States have adopted legislation permitting the

---

* There exists much confusion as to the nature and effect of the operation necessary for sterilization. In the male it is a very minor operation. It is only necessary (under a local anaesthetic) to make an incision skin-deep in each groin and to tie a small cord (the vas deferens).

In the female the same operation is performed with the minor difference that it is internal rather than external, and is merely the tying of the fallopian tubes.

Nothing is removed and there are definitely no physical effects and no interference with normal sexual relationships.

sterilization of mental defectives. They realize, as I hope Ontario also will realize, that whereas material wealth can be replaced by man, God's wealth of heredity stored in the germ cells if once lost can never, never be recovered.

I have said on a previous occasion, and I shall always be of the opinion, that moral and religious sense necessarily revolt against the destruction of human life at any stage. But sterilization contemplates no destruction of life. On the contrary, sterilization means the ennoblement of life by damming up the foul streams of degeneracy and demoralization which are pouring pollution into the nation's life blood. No reasonable man would countenance a diphtheria carrier going about communicating disease to many of those with whom he comes in contact. Yet the disease the diphtheria carrier transmits is curable and is incidental only to the immediate period of a few weeks during which it runs its course. But the infection transmitted by mental defectives is incurable. Its victims are the unborn generations. Its potency for misery and for suffering is great beyond all powers of description.

Sterilization of the unfit is not open to objection on the ground that it comprehends race suicide. On the contrary, it is the antithesis of race suicide; for what could be more suicidal, what more destructive to any race than to permit degeneracy to increase at its present rate? It is indeed suicidal for a race, a nation or a province to cast its germ cells, its precious jewels of heredity, into the oblivious, bottomless sea of mental, moral and physical degradation.

Let us pause for a moment and in a spirit not of intrusion but of sorrow and pity gaze into a home—there are many such hopeless homes in this country—where feeble-minded parents are being left to care for their young. You will never forget this sight. Terrible is the plight of these parents and their children, but even more shocking is the apathy of public opinion which has permitted them to reproduce their suffering, yet menacing, kind. Ontario is well to the fore in many forms of social legislation. I am sure that with a full understanding of the problem of race degeneration public opinion will not hesitate to demand action designed to relieve existing conditions and to crush the menace which the future holds in store.   In this Canadian Club and in other Canadian Clubs throughout Canada may leadership be given to such thought.   Then the proud record of forty years will be crowned by still another distinguished contribution to the common welfare.

THE BLIND WE HAVE ALWAYS WITH US

*A Radio Address Delivered on Behalf of
the Canadian National Institute for the
Blind, May 1, 1933*

It is not many years since the plight of the blind seemed
to be almost hopeless. Then their only recourse was to
become either dependents on casual charity or charges upon
the State. Blindness was regarded as equivalent to complete incapacity, and few of the people so handicapped were
able to engage in gainful occupation because they were given
neither encouragement nor opportunity to do so.

But today those who have lost their sight can be and
are masters of their fate. An understanding public opinion
and the devoted work of the Canadian National Institute
for the Blind has lighted the lamp of hope in the darkness,
where once was only despair. Thousands of the blind have
been equipped to lead useful lives and to be independent of
public and private charity.

The Canadian National Institute for the Blind is one of
the few blessings conferred upon us by the war. It had its
inception in the experience of those of our soldiers who were
blinded overseas and who at St. Dunstan's in England, under
the inspired tutelage of Sir Arthur Pearson, found new heart
and new hope. They came back to Canada undaunted by
the handicap of blindness, fired with a zeal to improve
the lot of blind civilians and, perhaps most important of all,
to engage in unending warfare against blindness.

Were the time at my disposal I could speak to you at
length of the Institute's services; of its achievements for
the 7,000 blind people on its register, 2,400 of whom are in
Ontario and 800 in this city of Toronto. I might tell you
how it has provided vocational training to equip so many of

them for useful, gainful employment; of the assistance it renders in solving individual problems; of the financial relief with which it supplements reduced incomes or provides maintenance where other disabilities in addition to blindness make the individual unemployable; of its fine library of Braille books; and above all of its work for the prevention of blindness.   This last effort appeals strongly to me as a doctor, for I know how great a service can be rendered in this connection; how many people are handicapped by blindness today from causes that, with the help of the Institute, will not in the future impair or destroy human vision.

Every day in the year the Canadian National Institute for the Blind carries on its splendid work.   Only one day in the year does it appeal to the citizens of Toronto for the financial support without which it could not exist.   Its annual tag day campaign is tomorrow and is in charge of the Toronto Women's Auxiliary of the Institute of which Lady Baillie is President.   Present economic conditions have imposed a demand upon the Institute that is heavier than ever.   I appeal to you in all earnestness, in the cause of humanity, in grateful recognition of the men who gave their sight in the Great War, and in the interests of future generations, to give to the taggers tomorrow as generously as your means will permit, knowing that whatever you give will be spent in a great and deserving cause.

GREAT MEN OF QUEEN'S

On Receiving the Honorary Degree of
LL.D. at Queen's University, Kingston,
May 10, 1933

Mr. Principal, Ladies and Gentlemen:

This is the first degree that has come to me without hard labour, but none the less I am very appreciative of it. I have to thank you, Sir, and the Senate, on behalf of myself and the other two most recent of your alumni, Dr. Eve and Dr. Race, for the honour you have conferred upon us. However little we have deserved it, we have been impressed today by the beauty of these buildings, by the excellence of the equipment, and by the wonderful spirit of all connected with this University—these have so inspired us that we shall endeavour henceforth to measure up to the ideals of your admirable institution.

Kingston, picturesque and historic, is indeed a fitting home for a great university, because education was prized and sought for here from the earliest days of settlement. One hundred and fifty years ago Kingston was surveyed as a town site for the United Empire Loyalists who began to arrive early in the following year, 1784. Among these Loyalists was the Rev. John Stuart, first rector of Cataraqui, who, in 1786, opened the first school in Ontario. Necessarily it was a private seminary, for there were no public funds then available for education.

The school, which was held in a log cabin, was described by Mr. Stuart as "a select classical school, an excellent place for children." Seemingly in those days there was a bountiful supply of fuel in this district, for the fees were set at so much money quarterly and I can find no record that, as was the case with Dr. Baldwin's school which opened in York in 1803, each scholar was required to bring one cord of wood at the beginning of the term.

From these precincts men and women have gone forth to win distinction in all parts of Canada and in many parts of the world. I am not as familiar as some who are present today with the long and honoured history of Queen's University and with the notable names of its founders, supporters and graduates. But among the names that come readily to my mind are those of Principal George Munroe Grant, and Sir Sanford Fleming, Chancellor of the University and builder of the Canadian Pacific Railway. To them is due a great measure of thanks for this institution which gives Kingston its reputation as a city of learning.

There are others I recall vividly from my own days as an undergraduate at Toronto, when an encounter with the Queen's Football Team was always, and often with good reason, a cause of apprehension. I remember the team managed by Hon. W. F. Nickle, K.C., which won the Dominion Championship in 1893, and which had among its members Senator H. H. Horsey, Brig.-Gen. A. E. Ross, M.P., and Prof. W. C. Baker.

Others who won distinction, both on the field of sport and in the larger affairs of industry and finance, are your honoured Chancellor, Dr. James Richardson, to whom you are indebted for the splendid George Richardson Memorial Stadium, the finest of its kind in Canada and which, I am sure, augurs well for the future of football at Queen's; and the Chairman of your Board of Trustees, Mr. J. M. Macdonnell, who was the first Rhodes scholar from Queen's University.

To my own science of medicine you have contributed very notable figures, as is only to be expected from a university whose medical faculty was the first in Canada to recognize the need for full-time professors. It was in 1904 that the present Dean of your Medical Faculty became full-time Professor of Anatomy, and some years previously Dr. W. T. Connell, full-time Professor of Pathology and Bacteriology.

Time does not permit me to refer to all of the many outstanding Physicians and Surgeons connected with, or graduated from, your medical school, but I should like to pay tribute to Dr. Austen, your Professor of Surgery, who has done such useful work in medical organizations for the advancement of our profession, not only in Ontario but throughout Canada.   Then, in the son of your Emeritus Professor of Hebrew you have supplied us with a leading gynaecologist, Dr. Dennis Jordan, who is one of your trustees.

Naturally I am most conversant with your fine record in the field of medicine, but your achievements are by no means so confined.

In the realm of national affairs we think at once of two of your graduates, Prof. O. D. Skelton, Under-Secretary of State, and Prof. W. C. Clark, recently appointed Deputy Minister of Finance.   The last appointment to the Supreme Court of Canada was that of a Queen's graduate—Mr. Justice Frank J. Hughes.

In the development of important natural resources, due, no doubt, to the work of Dr. W. G. Miller in your Mining Department, Queen's graduates play leading roles.   Only lately I attended the Annual Dinner of the Canadian Institute of Mining and Metallurgy, where a Queen's man, J. J. Denny, was presented by Mr. Stanley, President of the International Nickle Company, with their medal for outstanding contribution to the mining industry.

And so, if time allowed, I might go on and name many others who, at Queen's, were trained to render great and important service to this country and to their fellow men. Before passing from the subject I wish briefly to refer to your contribution in the Great War.   Fifteen hundred men and women and 189 casualties is indeed a proud record of service.   Gen. A. E. Ross, a South African veteran, crossed with the first contingent and served to the end of the war, practically always in the front line.   That is a better tribute than mere words to courage and endurance.

Under Col. Alexander MacPhail you had an engineering corps available for service in the first week of August, 1914. In connection with my duties in France I was privileged

to see the excellent work of No. 7 (Queen's) Canadian
General Hospital, which was commanded by the Dean of
your Medical Faculty, Col. F. Etherington, with Lieut.-Col.
W. T. Connell in charge of medicine, Lieut.-Col. J. F. Kidd
in charge of surgery, and Matron Willoughby as head of
the nursing staff.

Now, Sir, it is no mere chance that this University has
sent out so many men and women to render useful and
distinguished service; nor is it any wonder that there should
be such a spirit of proud loyalty among Queen's graduates.
Your present Principal, that distinguished Oxonian, Dr.
W. H. Fyfe, adheres to the high ideals of his predecessors.
Continued devotion to the principles that brought honour in
the past, together with resourceful and skilful handling of
present problems, will assure you a brilliant future.

After all, the function of a university is to train men
and women to know how to live. It may produce great
scientists, great teachers and great thinkers, but, above all,
it must produce great men and great women, and even humble
men and women, who live lives that are true to the ideals
taught here, will be great in the best sense of the word.

I admire not alone what is accomplished in your halls of
learning but also what is achieved in your arena of sport.
For I am an advocate of manly sport and believe, like the
ancient Greeks, in "a healthy mind in a healthy body"—as
revealed and developed on the field of sport.

It has been my experience all through life that a young
man reveals his character very plainly in the field of sport.
I do not mean that the best tennis player will prove the
most intelligent worker, but one cannot play three sets of
tennis with a couple of young men without at the end forming
a definite opinion as to their respective qualities of courage,
perseverance, intelligent anticipation and sense of honour.
And these, after all, are what one needs to know about any
youth in whose career one is interested. There is no better
school for character than sport. A man can learn to be a
sportsman, just as he can learn to be a doctor or a lawyer.

You here in Queen's realize, as the British people always have done, the importance of athletics in which a spirit of emulation, a strict sense of duty and a habit of unremitting industry may be taught and learned.

The graduating class is to be congratulated upon the opportunities they have had here to develop mind and body, to prepare themselves so that they may be of service to their country and, in the interest of their own happiness and the happiness of others, practise the art of living.

It is difficult for one who almost exactly forty years ago today was in the position of you young men and women—it is difficult for such a one to resist the temptation to give advice. It is a privilege which we older persons claim as a compensation for our advancing years. A French wit defined education in this way—"Education is what remains when you have forgotten everything you ever learned." That was a clever way of saying that true education is the building of character. Knowledge is only a means of attaining wisdom. You are going forth today with knowledge which can guide you into the rich and contented fields of wisdom. I urge you to use it for that purpose.

Institutions do not make men or women; but such institutions as this University provide the instruments with which persons so inclined may fashion themselves into men and women of real worth. Even this University will be but a superior piece of mechanism unless each student trains himself to estimate true values and true worth. This ideal has never been better expressed than by the great poet Goethe:

"Wouldst shape a noble life?   Then cast
    No backward glances towards the past;
    And though somewhat be lost and gone,
    Yet do thou act as one new-born.
    What each day needs, that shalt thou ask;
    Each day will set its proper task.
    Give others' work just share of praise;
    Not of thine own the merits raise.
    Beware no fellow man thou hate;
    And so in God's hand leave thy fate."

YOUTH AND EDUCATION

*On Receiving the Honorary Degree of
LL.D. at a Special Convocation at the
University of Toronto, May 26, 1933*

Mr. President, Ladies and Gentlemen :

Almost exactly forty years ago I received at the hands
of our distinguished Chancellor—then Vice-Chancellor—my
Doctorate of Medicine. I am doubly honoured to stand again
before Sir William Mulock to receive the degree of Doctor of
Laws.

If I am not more worthy now than I was forty years ago,
your revered President, Dr. Cody, must bear some measure
of blame because during most of the period, as Rector of
St. Paul's, he was my spiritual adviser. I know of no greater
privilege than to be chosen for honourable recognition by
the University at which I received my early training in the
profession of medicine. I am grateful to Dr. Cody for the
assurance that it is not alone because of my office but as a
member of the Board of Governors and as an alumnus
of this University that I am being so honoured. I am particularly grateful to be in the distinguished company of men
of such outstanding attainments.

In this great seat of learning we have two mighty forces
that can mould the world more nearly to the heart's desire.
These are education and youth. Youth with its high hopes,
its courage, energy and enterprise; and education, the wise
counsellor and trustworthy guide.

The task of setting order where there is now confusion,
and of directing the world into prosperous channels of goodwill demands all our wisdom. So in a very real sense our
happiness, and indeed the fate of civilization, is dependent
upon education—education which can safeguard us from the

53

pitfalls of social and economic error and point the way to an era when we may cast off the fetters of weakness, jealousy and folly, and acquire new strength through renewed faith in old and simple truths. Education is a means of achieving that balance, of effecting that intelligent compromise from which the greatest good of the greatest number will result. The function of this University, and I trust of all universities, is to give youth inspiration and equipment for the greatest social usefulness, so that we may attain the serenity and joy of which Wordsworth spoke:

> "Serene will be our days and bright,
>   And happy will our nature be
> When love is an unerring light
>   And Joy its own security."

I gladly make way for that distinguished economist, Sir Josiah Stamp, who so strikingly exemplifies the achievements of education and whom we are all so anxious to hear.

CHEAPER CONVALESCENCE

An Address Delivered at the Annual Banquet of the Ontario Medical Association, Hamilton, May 31, 1933

Mr. President, Ladies and Gentlemen :

As your Chairman has suggested, I am pleased that my appointment as Lieutenant-Governor should be considered a compliment to the profession in which I have worked for forty years. At all times I shall endeavour to discharge my duties in a way that will bring credit to my calling, and I am sure that whatever success I have in this connection will be due to the training I have had, for I believe that in the practice of medicine a man has unique opportunities to prepare himself for the responsibilities of any career. To be a successful practitioner he must have sound judgment, he must be versed in the humanities, he must be patient yet resolute, and must combine an understanding of the frailties of human nature with a true love for his fellow-beings. With such qualities a man may be expected to serve creditably in most fields of endeavour.

The honour you have done me in inviting me here tonight is one of which I am deeply sensible. I welcome this opportunity to meet with my associates who, like me, are interested in organized medicine. I have always felt that doctors should pool their ideas and opinions for the common good. As a past President of the Ontario Medical Association I have sufficient knowledge of its work to know that it has proved its worth, and I believe that every doctor in Ontario should belong to the Provincial organization. The problem in our profession is not that there is insufficient knowledge to go around but rather that our days are so short, our tasks so arduous and the advancement of learning and technique so rapid, that very real effort and sacrifice are required to keep reasonably in pace with the progress which results from the work of thousands of devoted students in laboratory and clinic. It is quite impossible for any one man to make all the benefits of our extraordinary advancement available to the people, and it therefore becomes the duty of such organizations as this to facilitate a free interchange of knowledge and experience.

A little while ago a man who had been a resident of Toronto for about one year asked me if there was in that city such a thing as a family doctor. He had at intervals tried to find a family doctor to treat the illnesses common to a family of wife and four children, but he had succeeded only in finding specialists. In the course of the year he had had six specialists attending his family. He claimed that in England one general practitioner would have rendered all the services needed.

In common with others I have for years deplored the fact that so few men were willing to undertake the responsible role of family physicians and that, as a consequence, the latter were fast disappearing. It is estimated that in the United States fifty per cent. of graduates in medicine immediately take up a specialty. In my opinion it would be much better for these young men and women to have a few years of experience in general practice. In the first place I am sure that many of them would become enamoured of the opportunities thus afforded them to serve the largest possible number of people in the community. In the second place the experience of a general practice seems to me to be a very desirable qualification of a thoroughly competent specialist.

What every community requires more than anything else, especially at the present time, is a good family doctor. A good family doctor can attain the great dignity of being regarded as a super-consultant, as Prof. Langdon Brown has suggested. He will have the responsibility of saying when a specialist should be called in, and of advising who the specialist should be. With his broad general experience and his intimate knowledge of the history of the individual case he can assist the specialist to render the best possible service.

The unit of practice, regardless of how medical services are organized or how social organization may change, will continue to be the individual patient. If the individual is to obtain the most helpful counsel it is important that there be available to him a family doctor who is acquainted with the social, economic and other environmental factors which influence him and his health. To serve in this capacity of general practitioner is a great responsibility, and I urge that the medical men of this Province by post-graduate work, by the reading of journals, by attendance at medical meetings, keep abreast of the advances that are being made in medicine, so that they will be able to render the service to their patients that is demanded of them.

I have no hesitation in advising the public to pin their faith on the family doctor, and allow him to act as a final "clearing house" to secure for the patient any and every assistance that can be provided through specialism.

About $700,000,000 is spent in the United States each year for medicines, and 75 per cent. of this, or more than $500,000,000 is spent for self-medication, largely in the form of patent medicines. This suggests that the public are specializing in treating themselves, which may in some measure be due to the confusion inevitable when the patient lacks the understanding guidance of a general practitioner. May I give a case to illustrate the dangers involved in self-medication.

A few months ago a patient came to me suffering from advanced cancer of the rectum. He informed me that he had had constipation for two years and that the medicines he had procured from a drug store, although taken in increasingly large quantities, had failed to relieve him. Having had no bowel movement for nearly a week he had for the first time consulted a doctor the day before. The doctor, on examination, recognized the trouble and referred him to me for operation. Unfortunately, it was too late.

The annual expenditure of the people of the United States for tobacco alone is about twice the total gross income of all the physicians in the country. The public buys what it is taught to buy, and manufacturers spend between one and two billions of dollars a year on that instruction in the form of advertising. When the public is convinced of the value of proper medical care it will readily seek it. There is abundant evidence on all sides that the public is giving more thought to physical well-being and is more concerned than ever with the improvement of the race, the protection of health and the provision of adequate medical attention for all in need of it, so we may expect a growing demand for, and an increasing reliance on, our professional services.

Hospital care for the sick is at the present time imposing a heavy charge upon all large municipalities, and I feel that they will therefore be interested in any suggestion to relieve the strain. Our profession alone is in a position to know and to advise municipal officials on the requirements for hospitals for the sick, and we should therefore urge upon them the desirability of their taking advantage of our experience in order to gain greater efficiency and to reduce the cost to the tax-payer. From an experience of many years as a surgeon to a large general hospital I have long held the opinion that considerable money could be saved by some modification of the provision made for the caring of the sick.

The cost of patients in a modern hospital is due to the necessity of providing expensive facilities, i.e., X-ray departments, pathological laboratories, operating rooms and a highly-trained staff. While all these facilities are necessary for a patient acutely ill, or one who undergoes an operation, they cease to be necessary when the acute condition passes and are not needed for many chronic cases. These patients can then be equally well cared for in a "convalescent home".

This "home" could and should be provided in the country on a small farm, where most of the supplies necessary for the feeding of the patients could be produced, and where the patients could get out in the fresh air and undertake some light employment which would materially assist their convalescence. I venture to say that the entire cost of patients in such a "home" need not exceed $1.00 a day, whereas it now costs municipalities $1.75 a day, and the Government an additional 60 cents.

I wish to make it clear that I do not submit this suggestion on economic grounds alone, for I am confident that it would be greatly to the physical advantage of the patients themselves to convalesce in new and more congenial surroundings.

If such a "home" were provided, from 30 to 40 per cent. of the patients now in our hospitals could be immediately removed there. This would not only make an immediate saving possible, but would at once increase the accommodation in all the hospitals for active treatment cases, and in this way postpone for many years the necessity for increased hospital accommodation.

Without distinction between rich and poor, the medical profession has always done its duty by the State, and the position which it enjoys in the public esteem is the fruit of its long devotion to high ethical standards and its zeal in expanding its usefulness by continuously adding to its resources of skill and knowledge. It must always be alive to its great responsibility to give leadership and direction to society in respect to health preservation. As a university-trained group, its members can, in addition, exert a great and beneficent influence upon the body politic. As citizens, as well as professional practitioners, they can merit the highest esteem of the community.

No difficulty is experienced in demonstrating that physical and mental health is the greatest asset of a nation as well as of an individual. It is one of the necessities of everyday life. The prosperity and happiness of a people are largely dependent upon mental and physical vigour. Ill health and its effects are recognized widely as one of the major causes of indigence and unemployment. The most pressing need is to devise a permanent and comprehensive programme of conserving health and treating illness and disability which will become an essential part of the co-operative endeavour known as civilization.

THE CANADIAN MANUFACTURERS' ASSOCIATION

A Welcome to their 62nd Annual Meeting
Extended at a Luncheon in the Royal York
Hotel, June 6, 1933

Mr. President, and Gentlemen:

The morning press speaks of this meeting as "Canada's Parliament of Industry" and I presume it is on this account that you thought it necessary to have your Parliament opened by the representative of His Majesty; but you have not been as considerate as Mr. Henry, for, when I open the Ontario Legislature, he carefully prepares a speech for me.

I have been interested to see the extraordinary growth of your Association from 32 in 1900 to 3,700 and also that one-quarter of your membership is west of the Great Lakes, a territory that we have for years regarded as chiefly agricultural. The fact that you have territorial divisions extending from coast to coast means that industry is playing a steadily increasing part in the affairs of our country.

I appreciate the advantages which come from organized effort. We doctors have medical associations for the interchange of ideas and opinions, which we have found, as I am sure you are finding in your Association, most helpful.

You are meeting today in an atmosphere of greater cheerfulness and confidence than we have had for years. Today's press announces that 1,300,000 more men returned to work in the last three months in the United States.

I consider it a great privilege in my official position to have the opportunity of extending to you a very hearty welcome, and may I express the hope that your deliberations may result in much benefit to the industries which you represent and to the country as a whole.

THE AMBITIONS OF YOUTH

Before the Canadian Club at a Luncheon
in London, June 7, 1933

Mr. Chairman, Ladies and Gentlemen:

To one who for many years has enjoyed membership in a Canadian Club the invitation to address you today came like a request from old friends, and it was with real pleasure that I accepted. I have looked forward to this meeting with you and I am particularly pleased that I have been introduced by my valued friend and distinguished predecessor, Colonel Henry Cockshutt, whose devoted services have won him the deserved gratitude of the people of Ontario. It is a pleasure to greet him now as Chancellor of Western University. He honours and is honoured by that important office.

Your presence here, Sir, is good reason why, at the very beginning of my remarks, I should digress for a moment and say a few words about the university whose graduates have won distinction in many places and in many fields of endeavour. Your predecessor in office, Hon. Dr. W. J. Roche, has a fine record of public service and will long be remembered for his administration of the Department of the Interior in Sir Robert Borden's cabinet. His responsibilities in his present office as Civil Service Commissioner are great, but I am of the opinion that the honour he cherishes as dearly as any is his status as the first graduate of your medical school. Mr. Justice Sutherland, who also won distinction in public life as Speaker of the Federal House, was the first graduate in Arts, and this year that first class of Western University graduates celebrates its fiftieth anniversary.

Mr. Arthur Little, Chairman of your Board of Governors, is deserving of special mention for his faithful work on behalf of the University.

It is also a privilege for me to refer to a former Chairman of the Board, the late Mr. C. R. Somerville (not only because of his son Sandy's eminence in the grand old Scottish game of golf), and to the truly remarkable growth of the University under his regime. I learned with surprise and delight that within the relatively brief period of the past sixteen years your student body has increased from 120 to 1,800 in all departments and affiliated colleges. This sound growth reflects great credit upon every member of the Faculty and Staff, and especially upon your President, Dr. W. Sherwood Fox.

Though young as Universities go, Western's record is such that any seat of learning might well be proud of it. The granting of its Charter in 1878 as educational centre of an area of fourteen Western Counties has proved to be a memorable event in the history of education in Canada. Yours is the lasting glory of having established at Western, in 1912, the first Public Health Department of any University in the world.

I was interested, while being shown through the new Rockefeller building in which is housed the School of Hygiene and Tropical Medicine of the University of London, England, in 1931, to hear a statement from the Dean, Dr. Jamieson, that he regarded the course for graduate nurses given in the Western University as the best in the world and as the model which he and his colleagues followed.

I understand that the Ontario Government's programme for dealing with the cancer problem contemplates the establishment of a "cancer centre" in London. This seems in every way desirable, as London is the centre of a population of 1,000,000 people and has a University which has the facilities to provide the necessary scientific personnel to ensure the success of such a "centre". For if we are to succeed in stamping out this disease we must not be content with the present therapeutic means at our disposal, viz., surgery, X-ray, and radium, which only enables us to do the best for the afflicted according to our present imperfect knowledge both of the disease and of the "rays" used for its destruction; but such a centre must be controlled and dominated by a spirit of research based on scientific knowledge. This, unquestionably, is the most important thing to bear in mind in the development of such a "centre".

It would be admitting defeat if we were to assume that the present methods of treating cancer were final. Much valuable work is being done by the British Empire Cancer Campaign, a branch of which I have been asked to organize in Ontario.

Many interesting facts have been elucidated about cancer which warrant the confident expectation that we are within measurable distance of discoveries that will effectively deal with this disease, just as typhoid fever has been practically eliminated and tuberculosis controlled.

As I came to London today I recalled that one hundred and forty years ago Governor Simcoe and his party travelled through here en route from Niagara to Detroit, and so enamoured was the Governor of this particular territory that he declared he had found an ideal location for the capital of Upper Canada. Mrs. Simcoe wrote that "the Governor found his expectations perfectly realized as to the goodness of the country on the banks of La Tranche" (which Simcoe re-named the Thames). She went on to say that, "in the Governor's opinion the fork of the river at this point is the most proper for the capital of the country to be called New London". However, Lord Dorchester was not in agreement with Simcoe, and Toronto was selected.

If Governor Simcoe did not succeed in his plan to give you the status of a capital, at least he conferred upon this municipality a great name, unparalleled perhaps in the associations it calls to the minds of all who have British antecedents.

It is not my purpose to draw a close parallel between the two cities, identical in name, one rich in historical associations, the other relatively so young and on the threshold of its greatness. I would rather refer briefly to such of your sons as Sir Adam Beck, whose memory is so fittingly commemorated by the splendid Queen Alexandra Sanatorium here, and to congratulate you upon the contribution London has made to the increasing greatness of Ontario and Canada.

You have here two essentials for fine achievement. These are youth and educational facilities.

All great men are educated men. By this I do not mean that they are all products of formal education such as is provided in schools and universities, but where such formal education is not available they always set about to find ways and means of educating themselves.

Less than fifty miles from here as the crow flies is the village of Vittoria, and there in the autumn of 1817 came two wandering teachers and announced a course of lectures on English grammar. A boy of fourteen working on his father's farm near the village eagerly attended, and was fascinated by the lessons which must have seemed dreary enough to some of the youths who were there under compulsion. Night after night, the farm lad hung upon the words of the teachers, and by day in the fields he recalled and fixed in his mind the wonders he had heard. He borrowed books and devoured them by the light of the fire in the old farm kitchen. When the next year the lecturers returned he was again a pupil, but before the term had run its course one of the lecturers fell ill and the student became an instructor. He left home and became an assistant teacher in the Vittoria Grammar School, working for a mere pittance. Then duty called him back to the farm, where he worked until he was twenty-one, but gave every spare moment to study. Then he set out again seeking more instruction, and before he was twenty-five he was known throughout Upper Canada as one of its most learned and able men. Though he had never attended college as a student he was founder and first principal of Victoria College, and at the age of forty-one became chief superintendent of education for Upper Canada and organized the Ontario system of free schools. His name was Egerton Ryerson.

What is the power and the fascination that could influence this untutored youth and, in spite of all difficulties, make him for us a figure of great historical importance? I believe it is the instinctive abhorrence which all fine minds have of ignorance, blind prejudice and unworthy superstition; it is the incentive to banish these enemies of progress that are eternally hostile to true happiness; it is the will to break the shackles of reasonless instinct and unfounded opinion and to liberate the mind from the doubts and fears that have enslaved unnumbered generations. In my opinion, nothing finer could be said of education than that it leads to a richer freedom. Thomas Huxley has said that one condition of national success is the moral worth and intellectual clearness of the individual citizen, and while he maintained that education could not give these, he did believe that it can cherish them and bring them to the front in whatever station of society they are to be found, and that the universities ought to be and may be fortresses of the higher life of the nation. People, he believes, are divisible into three sections; an immense body who are ignorant and speak out; a small proportion who know and are silent; and a minute minority who know and speak according to their knowledge. It is from this last class, which must be principally the product of our universities, that real leaders will be recruited.

These leaders must take command in the continued assault upon the dark citadels of ignorance.

And so we turn eagerly toward youth, educated youth. Youth frets at restraints, is impatient of the importunities of custom, and reserves reverence only for that which is worthy of reverence. In youth you have an active, restless, searching mind that is quick to analyse all those things, whether they be customs or arbitrary laws, which age comes to accept as unchanging and unchangeable. Youth is an intelligence thirsting after righteousness and knowledge. It is an exalted privilege and duty for schools and universities to encourage young minds and to direct them wisely.

It is customary with some people to measure wisdom by length of years and to admit little in the way of achievement from young people. History does not warrant such

an attitude.   May I give you a few examples.   Sir Francis
Drake, while yet in his twenties, was the most famous sailor
of his time and in his early thirties he circumnavigated the
world.   Captain John Smith, the true founder of Virginia,
was a soldier of fortune at sixteen.   At twenty-five we find
him prominent in England, after having been captured by
the Turks and sold into slavery.   The Pilgrim Fathers were
not a body of embittered and discontented adults.   One-
third of the one hundred and two passengers on the *May-
flower* were under twenty-one and only nine were over forty.
Robert Clive was only twenty-two when he destroyed forever
the designs of the Frenchman, Dupleix, for an Indian empire.
General Wolfe was commissioned in the Marines at the age
of fourteen, and when thirty-two, disregarding the counsels
of older and more experienced generals, stormed and captured Quebec.   James Cook was a young man when he
discovered Australia and New Zealand.   George Vancouver
took part with Rodney in the West Indies expedition, surveyed the south-west coast of Australia, explored the Pacific
Coast of Canada, discovered the Gulf of Georgia, wrote his
journals describing a full and active life, and died while still
in his thirties.   Nelson was a captain at nineteen.   William
Pitt became Prime Minister while in his twenty-fifth year.
Disraeli was famous as a novelist while still in his twenties.
The Marquis of Wellesley, brother of the Iron Duke, was a
Lord of the Treasury at twenty-four.

> "How soon hath Time, the subtle thief of Youth
> Stolen on his wing my three-and-twentieth year,"

said Milton.   But youth is not measured solely by the number of our years.   My experience in forty years of practice
teaches me that youth, in its essence, is pre-eminently
a state of mind, and as for myself, I feel that I can speak
as a man still young, and therefore still apt to say things
that do not meet with ready acceptance from those who are—
shall we say—growing mentally old.   Youth has an open
mind, quick to receive impressions, new truths and fresh

advances in knowledge; whereas the mind that is old is too often tightly closed around opinions which no power of man can change. I am convinced, too, that it is the precious purpose of education to keep the mind young, eager and hungry—as healthy youth is always physically and mentally hungry—for that knowledge which ripens into wisdom.

The mind of youth awaits guidance into channels of greatest social usefulness. The mind of age tends to become static, rather than dynamic. You will remember, of course, that at all times I am comparing youth on the one hand with uninformed or uneducated age on the other hand. Proverbially, there is no fool like an old fool, but it is also true that some of the youngest men I have ever met had the snows of winter as a halo about their brows. We want more of these young, old men, and fewer old, young men.

It is in education that the elixir of youth is to be discovered. Education—with all the fine qualities that it nourishes—is possibly the only thing in life that we cannot have too much of. In speaking to you of youth and education I am—however inadequately—discussing the two things on which the future of Ontario, Canada and the world depend. Without education we cannot contemplate the future with any sense of security—it holds nothing in store for us individually or collectively. Yet education is more than training and more than preparation for the future. It is an end in itself. The real purpose of education is to produce happiness—the happiness that comes from an interesting and cultivated mind, well-stored with ideas. A man or woman with an interesting personality not only finds life well worth living, but is a source of charm and inspiration. For this reason the acquisition of knowledge, the strengthening and enrichment of the mind, are goals in themselves. As long as life lasts they contribute dividends of happiness and satisfaction.

A liberal education is an education which has not only prepared a man to avoid the great evil of disobedience to divine and natural laws, but has trained him to seek and prize the rich rewards which Providence offers with so free a hand. The only medicine for suffering, crime and all the other woes of mankind is wisdom. Wisdom is the proper use of knowledge and knowledge is the fruit of education. Educate a man and you have given him the key to the Pandora's box of wisdom. Whether he opens it or not is another matter and has no bearing upon the importance of education.

Huxley, so many of whose views on education have stood the test of years, asks us to suppose it were perfectly certain that the life and fortune of every one of us would, one day or other, depend upon his winning or losing a game of chess. Don't you think, he asks, that we should in that event consider it a duty to learn at least the names and the moves of the pieces? Do you not think we should look with a disapprobation amounting to scorn upon the father who allowed his son to grow up without knowing a pawn from a knight? And then he says: "Yet it is a very plain and elementary truth that the life, the fortune, and the happiness of every one of us, and, more or less, of those who are connected with us, do depend upon our knowing something of the rules of a game infinitely more difficult and complicated than chess. It is a game which has been played for untold ages, every man and woman of us being one of the two players in a game of his or her own. The chess-board is the world, the pieces are the phenomena of the universe, the rules of the game are what we call the laws of Nature. The player on the other side is hidden from us. We know that his play is always fair, just and patient. But also we know, to our cost, that he never overlooks a mistake, or makes the smallest allowance for ignorance. To the man who plays well, the highest stakes are paid, with that sort of overflowing generosity with which the strong shows delight in strength. And one who plays ill is checkmated—without haste, but without remorse.

"What I mean by Education is learning the rules of this mighty game. In other words, education is the instruction of the intellect in the laws of Nature, under which name I include not merely things and their forces, but men and their ways; and the fashioning of the affections and of the will into an earnest and loving desire to move in harmony with those laws. For me, education means neither more nor less than this. Anything which professes to call itself education must be tried by this standard, and if it fails to stand the test, I will not call it education, whatever may be the force of authority, or of numbers, upon the other side."

Ladies and gentlemen, we live in a country bountifully endowed by Providence. But let us not fall into the error of thinking that greatness is measured in material terms alone. Size is not grandeur and territory does not make a nation. The great issue, about which hangs a true sublimity, and the terror of overhanging fate, is, what are you going to do with all these things? What is the end to which these are to be the means?

Education is the instrument by which we can fashion these means to a worthy end. No human being, and no society of human beings, ever did or ever will come to much unless their conduct is governed and guided by the love of some ethical ideal. With education we can set up such ideals and, with them as beacons, steer a course through life that will bring us happy and unafraid into that port where all earthly voyages end.

> "Must hopeless man in ignorance sedate
> Roll darkling down the torrent of his fate?"

asked Juvenal. In the two thousand years that have passed since that question was put there has been ever-increasing reason to believe that man need not do so. Our great hope in this connection today is the fine quality of our youth and the splendid devotion of those men and women to whom the precious mission of education is entrusted.

A UNIVERSITY'S LOSS, THE WORLD'S GAIN

An Address on Receiving the Honorary
Degree of LL.D. from the University of
Western Ontario, June 7, 1933

Mr. President, Ladies and Gentlemen:

May I, first of all, express my hearty thanks to the Senate and Chancellor and President of this University for the great honour you have done me today. The honour is doubly appreciated because it has been conferred upon me by my good friend, Colonel Henry Cockshutt, a predecessor in the office I now hold. I can only hope that in giving me this Degree today he has transmitted some of the fine qualities of mind and heart which enabled him to fill this high office so acceptably to the people of this Province. I am not unmindful of the important part played by Mrs. Cockshutt and, although I know my wife will strive to live up to the high standard set by her, she will suffer the handicap of not having two charming daughters to assist her.

The high position attained by the graduates of Western makes her worthy to be classed as one of Canada's great Universities. Dr. Banting's idea, which led to the discovery of insulin, had its birth here whilst he was instructor of Anatomy in your Medical School, and was completed at the University of Toronto. The discovery of insulin is one of the finest accomplishments in the history of medicine and is properly a matter of great pride for Canadians generally and for the Canadian medical profession in particular.

You may say, "What a pity that Dr. Banting did not work out his problem here", but it was a glorious loss, and the story exemplifies that singular devotion to the principle of serving humanity which is inculcated in medical men.

While yet associated with your University in London, Dr. Banting awoke one morning with the idea which ultimately led to the discovery of insulin. The new medical laboratories here were at the time in course of construction and only some three months from completion. Dr. McKibben, the Dean of the Faculty, fully realized what it meant to have the glory of such a discovery for Western University, but people were dying of diabetes every day and he could not contemplate doing anything that might delay the discovery. The measure of Dr. McKibben's great and unselfish devotion to the advancement of science and the welfare of the public is the decision which he unhesitatingly made when Dr. Banting discussed his project with him. He advised Dr. Banting to go to another university where he would have facilities to proceed at once with his great work.

Now, just a word to the young men and women who are graduating today. Opportunities to live well are still abundant in this third decade of the twentieth century. Opportunities mean, in the long run, a chance for men and women to make good in the world. Though realities may be stern, they may be overcome by faith and hope, if only the will to win keeps strong.

Look upon the future with an adventurous spirit, but with it think respectfully of the past. These are days when there is a tendency on the part of those by whom experience has yet to be gained, to chastise the experienced, and this is a common error. So, in addition to the many other bumps you may have, may you develop yet one more—that of veneration. Remember, whatever the future holds for you, whether you become a leader or one of the "also rans", that you are part of a great brotherhood known as the British Empire. You can all make some contribution to the civic strength of your nation; this in a sense is leadership. Apply what you have learned here in your college, the value of team-work, but apply it in its larger sense to your country, remembering always that

> "The game is more than the player of the game,
> And the ship is more than the crew."

HOUSEWIVES

*At the Graduation Exercises of the Mac-
donald Institute, Ontario Agricultural
College, June 16, 1933*

Mr. President, Ladies and Gentlemen:

In my several capacities: as the representative of His
Majesty, as the practitioner of a science that concerns itself
so intimately with the welfare of the race, and as a farmer
engaged in extracting wealth from the soil; in all these I
stand in great admiration of this institution which renders
such splendid service to the people of Ontario. It is a privilege to address the young ladies who are being graduated today
and to meet the distinguished men and women who direct
this organization, and to compliment them upon the skill
and faithfulness with which the good work is being carried
on. It is an honour to speak in this beautiful memorial hall
which immortalizes the supreme sacrifice made by one hundred
students of the Ontario Agricultural College in the Great War.

I note that in your curriculum of studies an opportunity is
provided for instruction in public speaking, and I take this
occasion to complain to my Minister of Education that this
privilege is not extended to the Lieutenant-Governor and
that there does not seem to be a course of instruction in his
other duties.

I take some pride in considering that this institution,
dedicated originally to training helpmeets for men on the
farms, has, by public insistence, I presume, extended its service
to those who dwell in the cities and towns. After all, that is
just as it should be, for in all my long and intimate contact
with people in the cities I have never seen or heard anything
to suggest that the toiler in the busy marts of commerce or
in the mighty manufactories is less in need of a devoted and
competent mate than is the worker in the fields.

I am dealing, of course, only in obvious facts when I say

that the home is the very foundation of society; that it is the treasure-house of the State; the sacred precinct in which all the fine emotions have their truest expression, and the realm in which womanhood is exalted to its greatest dignity. Yet, perhaps, such thoughts will bear repeating. I think that the late Sir William Macdonald, whose wise and generous benefaction made this institution available to our young womanhood, would be indulgent to me when I say these things, and I should like to pause for a moment to pay respectful tribute to the memory of the man who, thirty years ago, perceived the possibilities of the fine public service which has been developed through the conduct of your work here.

Now, since it was my great—and I hope deserved—good fortune to find the help and solace of a devoted and unselfish wife, I have often wondered that the career of home-making should, for so many centuries in the history of our civilization, have been one upon which women must enter without any schooling other than that provided by the magnificent instinct to consecrate herself to the happiness and welfare of some oft unworthy man. For centuries we have had organizations to train men for the arts and sciences. But for that great art and that very recondite science of making and maintaining a home there was, until recent years, no organized curriculum. I think that of all the tributes I might pay to womanhood there is none more commendable of woman's enterprise, ingenuity, high-heartedness and courage than that our social system—whose keystone is the home—overcame this deficiency.

I think compassionately of the young bride who confessed tearfully to her adoring husband that although she had boiled the eggs for hours she could not make them soft. I think also of the little boy in kindergarten who in his piping voice, interrupted the class when his teacher was showing them a picture of a western wheat field to say: "My daddy, he says 'Shredded wheat again! Shredded wheat for breakfast! Shredded wheat for dinner! Shredded wheat for supper! Ain't there never nothing but shredded wheat!'"

Now these may be extreme examples—though none the less

valid—but may I say in passing that I recognize in your home economics course here an enemy of my medical profession; for in your research in the realm of food values and your training in the selection, preparation and portioning of foods you are preparing to avert many of the ills of the human system which, once established, demand medical and surgical care.

As I have said, I wonder with thousands of others that for so many years the race survived the lack of an organized system of teaching how to make a happy and contented home. Surely it could not have been because man failed to appreciate the services of a good and competent helpmeet? As long ago as 1637 an anonymous "G.M." wrote a book entitled *The English Housewife*, and the "blurb" beneath the title presented it as:

> "containing the inward and outward virtues which ought to be in a complete Woman. As her skill in Physic, Surgery, Cookery, Extraction of Oils, Banquetting stuff, Ordering of great Feasts, Preserving of all sorts of Wines, Conceited Secrets, Distillations, Perfumes, ordering of Wool, Hemp, Flax, making Cloth and Dyeing; the knowledge of Dairies, office of Malting, of Oats, their excellent uses in a Family, of Brewing, Baking, and all other things belonging to an Household."

You see, even in those benighted days something was expected of the housewife and, as you all know, the longer he lives the more exacting man becomes! And, seemingly, even then the need for some scientific instruction in the household arts should have been apparent. I find a suggestion of this in the failure of Margaret of Cavendish to attain in housekeeping the proficiency which won her some current renown in the realms of literature and the drama. She, a contemporary of Charles I, writes in one of her letters about a resolution to do something useful: "My thoughts," she says, "*although not my actions*, have been so busily employed about huswifry these three or four days, as I could think of nothing else." Then she goes on to tell of the efforts of a well-meaning lady to make herself useful in the house and manage it efficiently. She was sorely in need of the very type of training given by Macdonald Institute. But she lived in less favoured days, and the story of her attempts at house management ends with these words, "At last I considered that I and my maids had better be idle, than to employ time unprofitably, and to spend money idly."

Of course there is a reason for all things, and the reason why our social system survived the deficiency of an organized curriculum in home-making is because the valiant woman-hood of earlier generations was content not alone with making good homes but also trained its female children to do likewise. I might paraphrase Kipling by saying that "Woman's glory is the home." I do not suggest that the home is her only field of achievement. What I do hope to convey to you is this, that because our widening intellectual horizon has opened up so many more fields for useful and distinguished service by women, the work of this institution is all the more import-ant. John Evelyn, the celebrated diarist, writing towards the end of the seventeenth century said:

"Men courted and chose their wives for their modesty, frugality, keeping at home, good housewifery, and in other economical virtues then in reputation, and the young damsels *were taught all these in the country in their parents' houses.* The young ladies of that golden age put their hands to the spindle, nor disdained they the needle; were helpful to their parents, instructed in the management of a family, and gave promise of making excellent wives."

As we progress in other arts and sciences we must, of course, progress in this very important science of home economics, and so it is a splendid thing that we should have here at the disposal of the housewife of tomorrow, equipment and organization and resources of knowledge and experience which will enable her to achieve the utmost proficiency and to render the greatest service to the State.

Some few minutes ago I referred to the anonymous "G.M.'s." book entitled *The English Housewife* and his very modest summary of its contents. I hasten, of course, to assure you young ladies that it will not be necessary to become proficient in the sciences of Physic and Surgery, and to pledge on behalf of my profession our best and most conscientious effort in time of need.   But I do appeal to you not to neglect the science of cookery, and not to exalt too highly that instrument which in some cases becomes the principal implement of the kitchenette.   I refer to the can-opener.   I appeal to you more particularly to attain proficiency in the science of selecting and portioning of foods.   In the medical profession we fully appreciate the importance of dietetics.   I think the general public is accepting our views today, although in the time of Samuel Pepys we might have been exposed to ridicule, for here is Mr. Pepys' idea of a good dinner:

"Home from my office to my Lord's lodgings, where I found my wife had got ready a very fine dinner—viz: a dish of marrow bones, a leg of mutton, a loin of veal, a dish of fowl, three pullets and two dozen of larks all in a dish, a great tart, a neat's tongue, a dish of anchovies, a dish of prawns and cheese."

A very fine dinner, indeed, proving that Pepys was one of the great carnivora.   I am afraid that at best he had but a rudimentary understanding of vitamins.

I am so impressed with the value of proper cooking and a properly balanced diet that, were I privileged to make suggestions to my Prime Minister, I would propose that legislation be enacted whereby a course in home economics would be a compulsory qualification for marriage.   For instance, I note that you have a course in experimental baking, and how very much better it seems to me that such experiments should be conducted in your model kitchen here rather than upon some young husband.   Kingsley very justly observed that, "The secret of thrift is knowledge, knowledge of domestic science saves income," and he might have added, temper.   I am glad to learn that you are giving instruction in the principles of genetics, and that on the theoretical side attention is directed to Mendelism and to the proof of the chromosome theory of inheritance.   The principles of genetics can be applied to human affairs in eugenics and, of course, to plant and animal breeding.

I am happy that in addition to instruction in all the essentials of home-making, including household micro-biology, provision is made to carry out important research work whereby you have added greatly to our knowledge of the food values of many vegetables in common use. In this connection I wish to mention the splendid work of E. Jean Millar and Mary M. Darby of your Department of Home Economics, which has proved that the Canadian green leafy lettuce is much richer in minerals and vitamins than the pale, blanched and more expensive imported iceberg lettuce. During 1931 the value of lettuce imported into Ontario was $453,766.

These same young ladies, with their investigations of the food value of honey, have shown that honey is not only a good food comparing favourably with bread, potatoes, jam, and so forth, but that it is a better sweetener than ordinary sugar. It contains the two sugars, dextrose and levulose and small amounts of protein and mineral matter, so that we would be better off if we used honey exclusively as a sweetener. A number of recipes have been tested in your institute by Dorothy Hewitt, and these have been issued in the form of bulletins. I was very interested and pleased to know that Miss Hewitt is a graduate of the Wellesley Hospital in Toronto. I am sure she will make a valuable addition to your staff, in dispensary, clinic and home nursing, first-aid and mother-craft work.

It is a source of much satisfaction to me that research and investigation play such an important part in the duties and work of the O.A.C. I have personally benefited from the assistance which your College gives to any farmer requiring advice on the nature of the soil and the kind of crops for which it is best suited.

There is so much here to commend that I must neglect many important things, but I cannot refrain from reference to the splendid opportunities for recreation here provided. The beautiful Cutten Fields which adjoin your Campus and which were so generously given by Mr. Arthur Cutten, one of Guelph's most distinguished sons, provide exceptional opportunities for winter and summer sports.

This beautiful city of Guelph was founded on St. George's Day, 1827. The site was selected by John Galt, administrator of the Canada Company, who surveyed some 40,000 acres before choosing this location. Mr. Galt was not only a man of astounding energy and ability, but he was blest with a most delightful literary gift. One marvels that relatively few people know his novel entitled *The Annals of the Parish*, which deals with the earthly career of the Rev. Mr. Balwhidder, Minister of Dalmailing, a purely fictitious character, of course. It seems to me a coincidence of the greatest significance that Mr. Galt, who founded the city which was later to become the home of Macdonald Institute, should have expressed through Mr. Balwhidder so keen an appreciation of the services of a good helpmeet. In his first choice of a wife, Mr. Balwhidder did not seem to be exceptionally blessed, but listen to what he had to say about the second Mrs. Balwhidder, née Lizzy Kibbock:

"Well may I speak of her with commendations; for she was the bee that made my honey although at first things did not go so clear with us. For she found the manse rookit and herrit, and there was such a supply of plenishing of all sort wanted that I thought myself ruined and undone by her care and industry. There was such a buying of wool to make blankets, with a booming of the meikle wheel to spin the same, and such birrings of the little wheel for sheets and napery, that the manse was for many a day like an organ kist. Then we had milk cows, and the calves to bring up, and a kirning of butter, and a making of cheese; in short, I was almost by myself with the jangle and din, which prevented me from writing a book as I had proposed, and I for a time thought of the peaceful and kindly nature of the first Mrs. Balwhidder with a sigh; but the outcoming was soon manifest. The second Mrs. Balwhidder sent her butter on the market-days to Irville, and her cheese from time to time to Glasgow, to Mrs. Firlot, that kept the huxtry in the Saltmarket; and they were both so well made, that our dairy was just a coining of money, insomuch that, after the first year, we had the whole tot of my stipend to put untouched into the bank."

MEDICINE ACKNOWLEDGES NO NATIONAL BARRIERS

A Speech of Welcome to the National Tuberculosis Association at a Dinner in the Royal York Hotel, June 28, 1933

Mr. President, Ladies and Gentlemen:

To welcome you, to wish you, and therefore all the world, profit from your deliberations is a pleasant privilege.

I may claim a three-fold interest in the work of your Association—(1) As a representative of His Majesty the King, who has always been so devoted to the welfare of all his subjects. (2) By virtue of my office as Lieutenant-Governor of Ontario, I am Honorary Vice-President of the Canadian Tuberculosis Association. (3) As one who has practised surgery for thirty-six years, I have not only a knowledge of the great need for an organization such as yours but also an intimate understanding of the splendid way in which it is functioning.

I congratulate the Canadian Association on having honoured us by bringing the National Tuberculosis Association here for its meeting. We have reason to be proud that your first gathering outside of the United States should be held in Canada. Perhaps there was some little hesitancy about taking that first step away from your own country. If so, I hope you are now glad of your decision, and I think you will all agree that it was only a step across an imaginary line.

Between your meeting here and the momentous conference* now proceeding in London one may discern a striking dissimilarity and several interesting analogies. At London they are discussing means of removing certain impediments to the flow of commerce, which are believed to have contributed a great deal to our existing difficulties. Happily there are no

*The World Economic Conference.

79

obstacles to the free interchange of scientific knowledge in the medical profession, and every addition to the store of learning, every improvement in technique, is immediately available for the benefit of every man and woman of every race and creed. However, the motive actuating those in attendance at the two meetings is the same high motive: to improve the lot of our fellow-beings. You are meeting here in a friendly country to carry on your work. Your compatriots are meeting in another friendly country to carry on their work. There, they are seeking to solve problems of the utmost complexity and all of an economic character. You are joined in combat with a scourge that has its own important economic aspect, for each year it wastes thousands of lives and dissipates untold wealth. We all pray that your efforts, like those of your compatriots abroad, may be successful. We realize, of course, that success abroad will promote the cause so near and dear to your hearts, for as privation and hardship are lessened the world over, the fortresses of the white plague are the more readily invested and the more certainly overcome.

On behalf of the people of Ontario, I welcome you to our Province and wish you continued success in your noble work.

MILESTONES OF PROGRESS

At the Official Opening of the Central
Canada Exhibition, Ottawa, August 21,
1933

Mr. President, Ladies and Gentlemen:

The Exhibition which I have the great honour and pleasure of declaring officially open today, embraces many beautiful productions of the manufactures and the arts, and a variety of exhibits of craftsmanship in its various forms. I hasten to congratulate the officials of the Exhibition, both upon its excellence as a whole and in detail. But since I am a farmer myself, I feel more competent to discuss that phase of the Exhibition which has to do with agriculture in all its forms.

And it is natural that I should discuss agriculture upon this occasion, for it was General Simcoe, the first Lieutenant-Governor of Ontario, who made the earliest serious effort to help agriculture in Upper Canada in 1792 after the close of the Legislature held at Niagara. He organized an agricultural society at his headquarters. So it seems appropriate that I should be asked to open this, your 46th Exhibition, in which livestock and agricultural products take so important a place. There comes to my mind another early association between Lieutenant-Governors and fairs of this kind.

The First Provincial Exhibition held in Toronto in 1846 was housed in the old Government House at the corner of Simcoe and King Streets. It happened that the three other corners were occupied, one by a church, another by a school and the third by a saloon, and accordingly the intersection was referred to as salvation, education, legislation and damnation. The small grounds of the old Government House provided ample space for the display of agricultural implements. This brings forcibly to mind the contrast between the exhibition of those early days and of the present day as exemplified by the splendid grounds and fine large buildings necessary to accommodate the Central Canada Exhibition.

An interesting psychological process, which recently has been becoming more apparent to me, is that mother Nature never permits her children who spring from the soil to suppress their love for the soil. A youth may quit the farm-house and the little red school to try his fortune in the great centres of population. He may become successful to the extent that all the luxuries and attractions of a large city are at his command, but no material success he achieves is strong enough to overcome the love of the land that was born in him. Rough and laborious as his boyhood may have been, many a man looks back upon it with longing and is unable to overcome his craving for contact with mother Earth again. And so, scattered through this Province we have the spectacle of hundreds of farms conducted by men who have never lost the longing, but who, in most cases, have utterly forgotten the technique of farming operations. Their services to the cause of agriculture lie perhaps not so much in the success they attain as in the mistakes they can afford to make. But the effect of their effort is generally good because they go in for breeding stock, for instance, which the ordinary farmer is unable to afford, and perhaps they are pioneers in labour-saving devices; possibly too, they serve as a medium of exchange of thought between the rural population and the city bred man.

I belong to the class of those who have embraced the first opportunity to seek the communion with nature which they knew as boys. I have never aspired to what is often called a "show farm", upon which wealth is lavishly expended; my ambition has been to make a good farm and, if I can, a good farmer out of someone else. So my acres are my chief pride, and the source of one of the greatest gratifications in the life of my wife and myself is that we have a son who has inherited his parents' love of rural life, and who is never happier than when he is caring for the cattle or leading an animal of his own breeding timorously, but confidently, into the show ring.

He is more of a farmer now than I am and I rejoice that he seems to be desirous of attaching himself permanently, not to the overcrowded ranks of city dwellers, but to scientific methods of farming and improvement of breeding stock.

It is this love of the land that has done so much to make exhibitions such as this an annual event of great importance and interest. Even among those who do not live on the land there is keen interest in agricultural and exhibition associations which are devoted to the advancement of our basic industry. Agricultural associations were the earliest foundation of exhibition enterprise, and as long ago as in 1828 the Northumberland County Agricultural Society held a fair in Colborne at which premiums were offered totalling the sum of $77.00. When we look at your prize list today it is interesting to recall that at Colborne in 1828 there were 14 prizes for livestock, 2 prizes for cheese, 2 for field rollers and 2 for essays on the culture of wheat. Even at this early period your predecessors in exhibition enterprises showed a remarkable foresight by recognizing the need to encourage scientific research. Seventy-five years later, Dr. Charles E. Saunders* began at the Dominion Experimental Farm here in Ottawa the researches which led to the development of Marquis wheat, whose benefit to western agriculture may be conservatively estimated in terms of many millions of dollars yearly. Who shall say that these early essays on the culture of wheat did not play their part in developing that trend of thought which ultimately guided Dr. Saunders in his historic work?

At that first fair in Northumberland County, fourteen of a total of twenty prizes were awarded for livestock. This exemplifies the interest which has always been taken by the British people in the development of fine farm animals. Northumberland was largely settled by Britishers, and this no doubt accounts for the predominance of livestock prizes.

It would be interesting and not unprofitable to trace a little further the accomplishments of agricultural societies in the development of agriculture in this Province. Societies for

*Now Sir Charles Saunders.

the exhibition of the products of the farm and for friendly competition among growers and breeders played so important a part in the life of the community that in 1830 the Government, recognizing their value, decided to assist them by an annual grant. This wise policy resulted in an increase in the number of agricultural societies, and a corresponding improvement in the quality of field crops and livestock.

Horses, sheep and milch cows increased rapidly. The first Ayrshire cattle can be traced to the Scottish settlers who came out in sailing vessels and brought with them their food, often including a good cow to provide fresh milk for the voyage, which lasted from four to six weeks. The cow was sold either on landing at Montreal or in the eastern part of Upper Canada, and this accounts for the early predominance of Ayrshires in Eastern Ontario and Quebec.

It is just a hundred years since Rowland Wingfield, an Englishman farming near Guelph, brought a small herd of choice animals across the ocean. He landed them at Montreal, took them to Hamilton by way of the Ottawa River, the Rideau Canal and Lake Ontario, and then drove them on foot to Wellington County.

I have already referred to the love of the early British settler for pure-bred stock. One has only to look over your prize list to see the predominance of animals originating in the British Isles. In horses—Thoroughbreds, Clydesdales, Hackneys, Shetland ponies; in cattle—Shorthorns, Herefords, Jerseys and Ayrshires. In sheep—Leicesters, Southdowns, Hampshires, Oxfords, Cheviots. In swine—Yorkshires, Tamworths, Berkshires.

Although the foundation of our livestock industry is largely due to importation from the British Isles, I am not unmindful of the contribution made by our French-Canadian fellow-citizens, many of whom are unsurpassed as agriculturalists.

Not only has progress in agriculture been stimulated by Government grants to Agricultural Societies, but scientific methods in farming have been inculcated by the educational facilities provided by our splendid Ontario Agricultural College, by the Experimental Farms conducted by the Federal Government, by the Federal Research Council, and by our own Ontario Research Foundation.

All the knowledge of agriculture possessed by many city dwellers is the farm-house and barns seen through the window of a train or a speeding car, but the economists and those who study farming problems realize that any deterioration of the buying power of the farm is immediately transmitted to every bank, to every factory, and to every occupation in which the nation engages. Agriculture is the largest purchaser of everything we make, and when the farmer receives only a tithe of their value for his own products his resultant inability to buy produces stagnation in all channels of trade.

We often speak of agriculture as our basic industry, and while this is probably true, we are fortunate in this Province in having two other primary industries—viz., mining and forestry. In a sense mining may be considered as complementary to agriculture, for prosperity in the mining field means a very large market for the products of the farm. There is a population of approximately 100,000 people in the mining area of Northern Ontario, all of whom are consumers of products of the farm.

In production of gold, Canada stands now only second to South Africa, and Ontario provides 75 per cent. of the Dominion's gold output. The nickel mines of Sudbury supply 90 per cent. of the world's demand.

Our Ontario forests have an annual output of over $100,-000,000 in pulp, paper, lumber and other products. They are also vital to the life of the Province in their effect on the production of water-sheds, their relation to the conservation of fish and game, and the influence they exert in giving us an equable climate. I think we all realize the importance of reforestation, which is taking place to the extent of 10,000,000 forest trees a year.

Exhibitions should be regarded as history of a very definite concrete kind. An exhibition is nothing less than a page of history, a visible, tangible record of human achievement.   It tells the most interesting story in the world, the story of progress made and deeds accomplished.   You will recognize, then, with what pleasure I come to you today and what profound significance I attach to this apparently simple act of opening the Central Canada Exhibition.   For, once the real meaning of an exhibition is fully understood, it is impossible to consider such a gathering as this as, in any sense, a formality. In the past it was the old world fairs, today it is an Exhibition which records, periodically, the story of the progress mankind has made and is continuing to make.

At the very moment, then, that I formally declare this Exhibition open I shall have done a great deal more than is immediately apparent.   I shall have turned to a new page of that history of Canada in which we all take just pride.   In the name of the people of Ontario I shall not merely be placing on view a "display of goods", but I shall be turning over a new leaf of the unending story of Canadian achievement—a page on which is inscribed for all to read, the answer to the question "What has been happening in Canada during the past year? What crops have been harvested?   What minerals have been mined?   What livestock has been reared?   What manufactures have been marketed?"—and a thousand similar questions which concern us all so intimately.

I consider this exhibition as, in a very real sense, a historic landmark, a milestone on the highway of Canadian advancement, or better still, a monument that commemorates the end of another year's progress and the beginning, I am confident, of far greater progress in the years to come.   And here let me say that what I have chosen to regard as Canadian history of a most vital kind would not have been made accessible to the people of Canada but for the labours of those responsible for the gathering together in the Central Canada Exhibition of all that is most significant of the times in which we live.   I desire to express my appreciation of the singularly important service they have thus rendered to the citizens of this Province.

WHY MUSEUMS?

At the Official Opening of the Royal
Ontario Museum, October 12, 1933

Mr. President, Ladies and Gentlemen:

We are gathered this afternoon on the meeting ground of past and present, those two forces which mould the future. Somewhere I have seen the words, "sombre treasure house", applied to the British Museum. I think that in this connection poetic licence was over-indulged, for neither in the British Museum, nor here or in any museum I have visited, am I able to justify the word "sombre". "Treasure houses" they undoubtedly are, and the treasure is beyond computation in material terms. It is a treasure intellectual, historical and cultural.

Nor is a museum, as someone has said, a tomb of the dead past. I think of it rather as a theatre in which is presented a vivid and colourful pageant. It is a pageant sometimes poignant, sometimes exuberant, but always interesting, instructive and inspiring. In this pageant, "sets" and players change from time to time, and the significance of the tableaux and the relative importance of the roles change, too, for new figures are always appearing against new backgrounds. This is so because the present is at most only a moment ahead of the past, and because we live in a world of accomplished fact. The clothes we wear, the houses we live in, this morning's breakfast and today's newspapers are no longer things in the making, and as backgrounds or accessories they take their places, from day to day, in the pageant of history.

Huxley has said that a museum is a consultative library of objects, and in this he has accurately estimated the function of a museum in educational and research work where, I believe, it is no less important than the reference library.

Moreover, a library is a place where we may go to ascertain the views of others about things and events; a museum is more properly a place in which we may examine factual records and form our own opinions. Every day in the great museums scholars are delving into the past and modifying, sometimes only in detail, sometimes in important principles, our understanding of the history of man through the ages.

Although the first museum of which there is record—it was established at Alexandria 300 years before Christ—was not a museum as we use the term today, it was nevertheless consecrated to the same cause as our great modern museums, for it was devoted to the cultivation of learning. Our modern conception of a museum is of comparatively recent origin. It was not until 1682 that the first surviving scientific museum was established. This was the Ashmolean Museum at Oxford. Its nucleus was the private collection of Elias Ashmole, who wrote in his diary on February 17, 1683: "The last load of my rarities was sent to the barge, and this afternoon I relapsed into the gout"—an entry interesting both historically and medically.

From the dawn of the Renaissance there were collectors of articles of artistic and historic interest, but most collections were dispersed at the death of their owners, as must almost inevitably be the case failing the existence of some public museum to inherit and treasure them. Ashmole, of course, collected as a student and scholar, but some others of this time were actuated by motives more in keeping with the character of the late Mr. Barnum, for seemingly a museum was considered poor indeed if it did not possess a unicorn's horn, giants' bones and other exhibits of somewhat debatable scientific value. The printed catalogue of a London museum of the early eighteenth century contains this advertisement:

"Monsters of all sorts here are seen
    Strange things in Nature as they grew so.
Some relics of the Sheba Queen
    And fragments of the famous Bob Cruso."

However limping the metre of these verses it is probably an accurate measure of the educational worth of the museum it advertises.

Although the founding of the Royal Society in 1660 gave a great impetus to learning and stimulated collectors in English-speaking countries and foreign lands, it was not until the eighteenth century that the idea of a state museum was first entertained. This idea was the result of recognition of the educational value of museums, and all here today may be proud that educational value has been fully recognized by the Royal Ontario Museum Act. This Act provides that three of the Governors of the Museum shall be appointed by the Board of Governors of the University of Toronto, and furthermore, the general by-laws and the regulations regarding admission make very specific provisions to encourage the scholar and to stimulate attendance by classes not only from the University, but from the Public, Separate, High and Private Schools. I refer to these regulations because they are clear evidence that advancement of learning is the foundation upon which the Royal Ontario Museum has been so well built.

It gives me three-fold pleasure to be present at this ceremony today. First, as His Majesty's representative in this Province I rejoice that the people of Ontario can claim a museum that ranks among the finest in the world; secondly, as a Governor of the University of Toronto I am happy that the Provincial Government has made such an institution as this available to the Faculty and student bodies; and thirdly, I am greatly pleased that scientific research has at its disposal such a splendid instrument as this Royal Ontario Museum.

I am leaving it to others more intimately connected with this museum to pay tribute to the part played by individuals in making this magnificent storehouse of priceless treasures possible and available to the citizens of this country, but I cannot close without expressing gratitude to all those who have made such a splendid contribution to the life of Canada.

THE IMPORTANCE OF GUIDANCE FOR LEISURE

A Radio Address on Behalf of the Community Welfare Council of Ontario,
October 14, 1933

We have all met people who ask us to suggest something—anything—that will help them to pass the time. We have heard others complain that they do not know how to kill time, as if time is an implacable enemy to be dispatched outright.

These people deserve our pity. In their state of mind they are ready to do violence to the most precious thing they possess. To them, leisure is a burden too heavy to bear. They are showing the symptoms common to all people who don't know what to do with their leisure. Certainly it is only when time hangs heavy upon us that we want to kill it.

"Not to be occupied and not to exist", said Voltaire, "amounts to the same thing . . . . . One must give *oneself* all the occupation one can to make life supportable in this world." He continues: "The further I advance in age, the more I find work necessary. It becomes in the long run the greatest of all pleasures and takes the place of the illusions of life . . . If you do not want to commit suicide, always have something to do."

The Community Welfare Council of Ontario is to be congratulated, therefore, upon the determination with which it is setting about the task of showing how, by ourselves creating a wide diversity of interests, we can transform our leisure time from dead loss into infinite gain.

It is a fact that many of us are not interested in a sufficient number of things—nor indeed sufficiently, in any one thing. We leave it to others to plan our lives, and, if they fail, we are too often utterly lost. Even our work interests us only in so far as it is our means of livelihood. And when that is done, we want somebody to entertain us, somebody to amuse us, somebody to suggest ways of passing the time or of killing it offhand.

What a pathetic confession of futility! In a world of inexhaustible interest, where the beauty and mystery of nature and the works and thoughts of men, where science and art, medicine and engineering and all the branches of knowledge await our leisured interest, we shall miss the whole purpose of living if we do not seize every opportunity for that development of our mental and physical faculties which leads to a fuller and more joyous life.

The remedy for all the brooding resentment, the hatred of life, the bitterness which wells up in the heart of a man as he contemplates his own seeming uselessness in times of enforced idleness, is to *do* something. If you reply, "But what can I do?", then I know that you need just the guidance that these lectures will give.

Leisure is too frequently associated with the possession of wealth. True, leisure is a commodity that can be bought. But whether you can afford to buy it, or whether you have it thrust upon you, the problem remains: What are you going to do with your leisure now that you have it?

If you want to deteriorate physically and mentally you will do nothing, and sink to the depths of misery. If, on the other hand, you preserve your health by exercises, if you cultivate any one of the interests which I shall briefly mention, and if you allot a portion of every day to those little personal ministrations which add so greatly to your self-respect by making you feel better and look better, then you will be doing a great deal to offset the evils of idleness.

First of all, then, maintain your physical fitness. Keep healthy. So important is this that I do not propose to regard it, in such times as these, as a personal problem to be solved by the individual, alone and unaided.

So keenly indeed do I feel the necessity of concerted action by all communities for the alleviation of avoidable mental distress and physical degeneration, that I shall make two suggestions which I trust will be followed by every community where the question, "What shall I do with my time?" faces many citizens and urgently demands an answer.

My first suggestion concerns this extremely important matter of health—always the first consideration. It would be an excellent plan if in every community a Sports Committee could be elected whose duty would be to devise and arrange for a set programme of physical exercise for those who have the empty and unpleasant prospect of a wholly unoccupied leisure. Nothing so completely banishes morbid thoughts as the afterglow of healthy physical exertion. For the younger folk, sports could be arranged, and for those who can no longer indulge in the more arduous pastimes, physical drill would have a splendid tonic effect. All communities should set aside ground and public halls for this purpose.

My second suggestion is that in the less populous rural districts where loneliness and despair frequently go hand in hand, such halls could be made the centre of a healthy, invigorating community life that would benefit everybody.

The splendid work that is now carried out by the Public Welfare Department would thus be advantageously supplemented. For, while the satisfying of material needs may be left to the care of that Department, there remains the problem of leisure for the individual to solve. That solution would be most easily arrived at if every community assumed responsibility in some such manner as I have suggested—ably seconded, of course, by the Community Welfare Council, who have courageously come to grips with this important problem.

But to return to the problem of leisure as a personal problem. I have stressed the importance of regular physical exercise to maintain the well-being of your body—which is the basis of all happiness. What else can you do with your time? What occupations are there for you to engage in?

Has it ever occurred to you that you can make the most entrancing, romantic and informative voyages in a library? A library card is actually a travel ticket which takes you to any part of the world at any time and—in no time at all! It will do more than that. With it you can travel not only through space but through time, to any period of the world's history. You can open wide the doors that lead into the lives of great men; you can sit with them and enjoy their wisdom and their wit.   Books are true friends—friends who never desert you.   Read for pleasure, read for entertainment, read for instruction—but above all *read*.   You will develop an appetite for it.   You will cultivate a taste for it.   "Reading", said Sir Francis Bacon, "maketh a full man."   A healthy, well-balanced mind needs the nourishment that books alone can give.

You live in an age when more avenues to self-development are open than at any other time in history.   There is not only the library, there is the museum.   Like the library, the museum holds something of interest for us all. We need no special training or knowledge to enjoy its treasures.   The will to know and the will to see are all that you require.   Mr. O'Brian, Chairman of the Royal Ontario Museum, told me recently of a woman who earns her livelihood as a cook in a Toronto home.   At every opportunity she goes to the Museum.   Recently, she remarked that she had completed her study of palaeontology and was beginning the study of geology.   Now palaeontology and geology may sound formidable, but if you approach them in the right frame of mind you will find them as fascinating as detective stories.

But you may object that indoor pursuits are not adaptable to your character.   It is perhaps the most priceless quality of leisure that it can be made to suit all tastes.   Long ago, a man who said many wise things described one of the many uses of leisure as "The purest of all human pleasures.   The more you develop it", he said, "and the more you know about it, the more absorbing is its interest."   He was speaking of gardening.   And if you have never tasted the delights of this "purest of all human pleasures" you have missed all that tranquility of mind, that absorbing, healthful interest which is to be found in a garden.   I would assert as one of the most certain things in an uncertain world that gardening never fails to give pleasure—a pleasure which follows the law of increasing and not of diminishing returns.

If you will keep physically fit, and if you will set out to

discover the indescribable pleasures of the proper exercise of the mind—pleasures which cost nothing and never satiate—you will notice a surprising change in yourself and your whole outlook on life. Actually a new life will begin for you. For it is a fact that the appetite for knowledge grows with what it feeds on. Your own mind will propound riddles to you, and you will not be satisfied until you have yourself solved them. The vast realms of thought will be yours to wander over. You will find yourself clamouring for information, for enlightenment on a multitude of questions. But above all, you will find a new happiness—for the mind like the body demands exercise and must have exercise in order to be healthy. Instead of being enervated, listless, apathetic and indifferent to the wonder and beauty of the world about you, you will have found, as it were, a secret passage to a life transformed by thought—and by those great instruments of thought—books.

But life isn't all serious, methodical and studious. There should always be time for gaiety, for companionship, for all those light-hearted, laughter-laden hours spent with your fellow men and women. And although what we habitually call entertainment or amusement has been very thoroughly commercialized, there is no reason why you should not become more and more independent of mass-made methods.

Entertainment is perhaps never so delightful as when the unsuspected talent of friends and acquaintances is discovered and enjoyed. I urge you to develop your own talents, whether they be those of a musician, an actor, a comedian, an artist or any other gifts which atrophy if they are not used. Learn to entertain yourself. If possible, make your own music. If you have a gift for mimicry, for acting, see if with others you cannot rehearse and act amateur plays. A pencil and paper are all that you need if you wish to draw and develop a sense of the beauty of the forms with which this world is filled.

And now in conclusion I want to pay a very sincere tribute to the Community Welfare Council of Ontario, who have undertaken this most important duty of showing how by a proper use of leisure the hopelessness of doing nothing can be altogether changed into those personal triumphs and enduring satisfactions which come from time well spent. The proper use of leisure is of supreme value. The Community Welfare Council of Ontario is determined to aid in the solution of this problem of the proper use of leisure. I can think of no worthier or more important task. It is a great undertaking.

In the lectures which follow, some of the many interesting and profitable occupations which I have but briefly touched upon will be discussed in detail by well-qualified speakers. I would only add a thought which embodies a truth of which poets have sung and great men since the world's beginning have treasured as life's greatest gift.

Of all the joys of life that may fairly come under the heading of recreation, there is nothing greater, more refreshing, more beneficial than a real love of the beauty everywhere about us. Cultivate this feeling and encourage it in every way you can. Consider the seasons: the delight of the spring, the joy of the summer, the flaming colours of the autumn, the stern beauty of the winter. The feeling for beauty is a pearl of great price. It costs nothing because it is part of the joy that is in the world for everybody who cares for it; it is a rich treasure that we all may possess and, possessing it, we deprive nobody. The enjoyment of it excites neither greed nor envy and will take us out of the small worries of life.

Life soon loses all meaning if mind and body are allowed to remain in that state of inaction and idleness which is a pitiful kind of stagnation. Life and motion are inseparable. Only in death is there perfect inactivity. The proper use of leisure is to do something—to interest and to occupy the mind, to care for and to develop the body and to preserve, sometimes in the face of grave difficulties, that co-ordination of all the faculties which is *true* health and which brings an abiding contentment.

A TRIBUTE TO THE SALVATION ARMY

Paid when Introducing General Edward J.
Higgins at a Meeting in Massey Hall,
Toronto, October 15, 1933

Commissioner Hay, Ladies and Gentlemen:

Few privileges could give me so much pleasure as that of introducing General Edward J. Higgins, the Commander of the Salvation Army.

Any man who looks about him must be aware of the work carried on day after day by the brave men and women who have consecrated themselves to the King of Kings and who fight unceasingly against sin, squalor and suffering. Anyone who loves unselfish achievement, who admires heroism, who is moved by suffering, who abhors the degradation of vice and believes in the simple teachings of the gentle Galilean, must in his heart and soul thank the Almighty for the Booths, for their successors and for all the rank and file of this great international army of God. The record of the Salvation Army is a modern chapter of the Acts of the Apostles; its sure inspiration is the answer to that prayer which its soldiers offer every day in their unselfish sacrifice.

As we go about Toronto we see evidences of the Army's fine organization. Its numerous buildings, its Homes for the Aged and for Children, its Rescue Home, its Women's Hospital, its headquarters and its divisional headquarters and training garrison are constant reminders of the devotion and generosity of the Army's friends, and of its own rank and file in providing the funds to acquire these buildings which are concrete evidence of unceasing and unostentatious good work.

I have much pleasure in presenting to you the General of an Army that for more than fifty years has carried on unending warfare against the enemies of all that is precious to Christian men and women—General Edward J. Higgins.

A LITTLE MORE ABOUT LEISURE

On the Prize Day at Upper Canada College,
October 20, 1933

Principal Grant, Ladies and Gentlemen:

When I asked a classmate of yours at breakfast this morning what I should say to you today his answer was "as little as possible." As this undoubtedly represents the feelings of all of you, I will be brief, and at the outset I would like to tell you that I have asked Dr. Grant to be good enough to give you an extra half-holiday.

I am pleased to be here this afternoon, for it is my first visit since the school was remodelled, and I should like to congratulate the Board, the Masters and the students upon the magnificent building and equipment you now have both for work and play.

Last Saturday I opened a series of broadcasts on "Leisure" and stressed the necessity of healthy and well-planned leisure. Apart from the playing-fields and cadet battalion and the gymnasium and the time you require to spend in homework, you will, I hope, find a couple of hours' leisure each day, the filling of which should be carefully planned. It might be devoted to chemistry, botany, reading or art. Such pursuits will soon become a real joy to you and, while you are increasing your knowledge, you are developing something that will grow as the years go on and give you a hobby for later life. You should remember, also, that many of the great inventions of the world were not made during the full working hours of men, but often during their so-called leisure hours. There is a good reason why I should take a special interest in Upper Canada College, because a former Lieutenant-Governor, Sir John Colborne, now Lord Seaton, whose portrait adorns a wall at Government House, as well as one of your walls here, fought strenuously, ably

97

assisted by the Rev. John Strachan, for the establishment of Upper Canada College. How proud these men would be could they return today and see how gloriously Upper Canada College has progressed! What a pride they would take in your war record and in the achievements of the citizens who were educated here. How delighted they would be with the performance of the Smith twins in acquiring scholarships, and I have no doubt they would join Dr. Grant in the wish that they had been triplets!

With a background of more than a hundred years of unblemished history, what a responsibility rests upon the shoulders of you boys today; but remember that not all the tradition, not all the great students who have gone before you can keep up the name of your school unless in each class there are boys who will take the torch from the class that is leaving, keep it bright and hand it on.

The prize-winners today have shown that they have made good use of their time, as I hope all of you may do, so that as you go out into the world you will live up to the splendid traditions of the boys who have preceded you.

YOUTH IS FLEETING BUT EDUCATION STICKS

At the Official Opening of Crescent School,
Dentonia Park, October 21, 1933

Mr. Headmaster, Ladies and Gentlemen and Boys:

It gives me great pleasure to declare officially open Crescent School, transplanted into such a magnificent building and situated in such delightful and promising grounds. I wish to congratulate Mr. Williams and the pupils upon their great good fortune in having such a fairy godmother as Mrs. Massey, who has both the generous heart and the vision to provide so adequately everything that is essential in a Preparatory School.

I think it was the poet Longfellow who was responsible for the assertion that "The thoughts of youth are long, long thoughts." Curiously enough I recall these words principally because this school reminds me all too forcibly that the days of youth, at least, are not nearly long enough. So you will perhaps understand why, at the very moment that I am regretting, as we all do, the swiftness with which school days and youth pass, I find myself envying all the boys who attend Crescent School. Never, surely, were boys able to begin their education in pleasanter surroundings, or to set out upon the life-long exploration of the realms of knowledge in more congenial company. Proverbially there is nothing quite as good as a good beginning—and this is perhaps particularly true in this most important matter of education. Mrs. Massey, in this magnificent and most generous gift, has shown not alone a spirit worthy of all praise but great wisdom in the choice of a gift which will enrich past all computation the lives of boys in this city for many long years to come.

This school will become the great preparatory school of this country. True, you are without the antiquity of a school so old as, for example, the Northaw School in Kent—the ancestral home of the Derings dating back to William the Conqueror. But what of that? The future is all yours—rich with promise. And nearly four centuries ago Sir Thomas Overbury said, "A man who has nothing to boast of but his illustrious ancestors is like a potato—the only good belonging to him is underground." And the same is true of schools.

The great Republic to the south has its Rockefeller and Carnegie, but we, in Canada, have our Masseys. Their name is intimately associated with education through Hart House, that unique University club which promotes every useful activity of youth; Massey Hall, which serves a similar purpose for the music-loving public; the Massey Building at the O.A.C., and the recent addition to and improvement of Upper Canada College. So that Mrs. Walter Massey is following the established Massey tradition.

I have not inspected the buildings as yet, but the grounds afford every opportunity for play, so essential in the development of character; for it is the education received unconsciously that counts for most in the making of a man.

I have read your publication *The Quill* with great interest, and have recognized the names of many past pupils who have made good since leaving your portals. I cannot refer to them all but would like to mention the two Archibald boys, sons of Dr. T. D. Archibald, a very old friend of mine. After leaving here, these boys entered Port Hope School, where Roger won the Governor-General's medal and then went to the Royal Military College, where he became the Battalion sergeant-major and won that much coveted prize—the Sword of Honour. He is now in the second year at Osgoode Hall, and, I am sure, will continue to be a credit to your school. Tommy Archibald's career at Port Hope was interfered with by an operation for appendicitis, but he has been two years at R.M.C. and was the welterweight boxing champion both years. He is now at Cambridge. I gave a general proficiency prize yesterday at Upper Canada College to F. M. Tovell.

So that, although your school is young, it has already produced boys who promise to take a high place in the world, for in considering schools we must remember that the quality of the tradition is of greater importance than its antiquity.   To a school-boy the present and the future are far more important than the past.

While we like to live up to traditions, we should not make them the reason for not seizing the new opportunities that come every day in an ever-changing world, but I like to feel that the boys of Crescent School are cultivating what I might call the forward look, and that they take a lively interest in what is happening all over the world today; for history is now in the making.   The learning of past history should equip you for the future, for we must obey in all things nature's unalterable law—the law of cause and effect. What is happening today is caused by something that happened yesterday or one hundred years ago; and in the same way what you yourselves will be tomorrow, depends largely on what you do today.   It was Shakespeare who put into the mouth of one of his less admirable characters these true words: " 'Tis in ourselves that we are thus—or thus."   So here at school you are actually moulding your own future. You have the opportunity to develop all your physical and mental powers that they may serve you worthily when you go out into the highways and byways of the world.

It is with the greatest pleasure that I declare Crescent School open.

THE STORY OF DENTISTRY

*Before the Academy of Dentistry at their
Annual Dinner at the Royal York Hotel,
October 23, 1933*

Mr. President, Ladies and Gentlemen:

In considering the subject which might interest you this evening it occurred to me that perhaps a brief review of the history and the evolution of your profession and what we may hope from it in the future would be most valuable.

Dentistry is one of the oldest of human crafts. Every archaeologist, in excavating the tombs of long-forgotten kingdoms, comes across evidences of the antiquity of dentistry. The dental art was used for adornment as well as for utility. From the tombs in Egypt, Greece and elsewhere, examples have been found of gilded teeth, teeth adorned with golden bands, with decoration of crown and bridge work and inlays of gold, diamond, crystal and jade, exquisitely fashioned.

The princess of the pre-Inca court on the slopes of the Andes a thousand years ago submitted to long and difficult operations under primitive conditions with crude instruments to have her teeth adorned with golden inlays; in some cases, the enamel of the teeth decorated was entirely removed and then covered by an overlay of gold.

In ancient Mexico and early Hindustan, teeth adorned with turquoise and other precious stones were quite common.

The race was never so young as to undervalue the charm of a row of pearly, white teeth. Oliver Wendell Holmes said that there is no element of a women's beauty which can take the place of even, white, well-shaped teeth.

A great anthropologist has pointed out that the medical problems of the teeth began 100,000 years before we had any history. Sir Arthur Keith says, "Until the discovery of Rhodesian man, this ancient ancestor of ours who lived about 125,000 years ago, we had always believed that caries was a modern disorder, an ailment which civilized man had brought upon himself by the artificiality of his diet. It was therefore a surprise to find that this ancient man, with enormously strong jaws and big teeth, had suffered severely from dental caries. At the roots of the molar and other teeth, abscesses have formed and broken."

Sir Arthur shows that dental caries does not even belong to us but is shared with the great apes, and possibly other species. He says that on examining the teeth of wild chimpanzees, which had lived and died in their native forests of tropical Africa, he found that they also suffered from caries. This disorder, therefore, did not appear for the first time with the introduction of man to civilized life, but there is no doubt that cooking and the artificial ways of preparing food is at least partly responsible for dental caries. The Australian aborigine, living on his native diet, is almost free from caries, but becomes subject to it when he adopts the white man's diet.

Sir Arthur Keith asks, "Is it possible that the condition of the Rhodesian man's teeth represents the first-fruits of the discovery of cooking? Or was it that he, like the Australian aborigine, came into contact with an imported higher civilization which ultimately exterminated him?"

As early as 3000 B.C., the court physician in Egypt also bore the title of court dentist, and an archaeological find of a human jaw of about 2500 B.C. shows indications of a successful surgical operation on an abscess beneath the lower right first molar.

Some years ago, while in Egypt, I visited the Gizah museum at Cairo and saw the mummified body of Ramesis 2nd, who lived 1300 B.C., and I was much interested to see beneath his dried and slightly retracted lips a practically complete and beautiful set of teeth.

In Syria, a physician in the seventh century, B.C.—according to a tablet in gold found in the ruins of Nineveh—

realized the importance of teeth to the general health, because it is recorded that he stated the burning of his head, hands and feet was because of his teeth. He advised that they should be drawn.

It was that excellent anatomist, Leonardo da Vinci, who discovered the correlation of form and function of the teeth, but long before da Vinci, Hippocrates, the "Father of Medicine", recognized the importance of keeping the teeth in good condition, and not only compounded a "dentifrice", but prepared a suitable mouth wash.

Your profession, as well as mine, owes a debt to Hippocrates, the author of the famous oath which has been the basis of ethics for the medical profession for nearly 2,300 years. This code was the first to be adopted by any profession and it is interesting to recall this now when one hears so much about codes in connection with the National Recovery Act in the United States.

For over 2,300 years the medical profession and, I think, also the dental profession, has observed this code because of the correctness of its rules for conduct. Although many changes have happened during all these centuries, the principles embodied in it, based as they are upon honourable dealing and personal morality, have been accepted as the rule of conduct by our profession. No other profession, science or industry has ever been organized upon a code of conduct.

Galen, that famous and learned Roman physician, who was the medical advisor of Marcus Aurelius, also interested himself in dental ailments, especially pyorrhea.

When dentists began their work there was only one operation—extraction, and only one instrument—a pair of forceps, which, legend asserts, was used by Esculapius and preserved in the temple at Delphi.

For many centuries the dentists were content with prolonging the life of teeth by filling cavities and treating pyorrhea, and also became skilful in providing sets of artificial teeth. In Nero's time, the poet Martial speaks of the "belle" laying down her teeth at night just as she does her silken robes, and in another place unkindly remarks on the beauties of the day that "they now have removable teeth and would have removable eyes if they were for sale."

In the eighteenth century, Fauchard, who was really the father of modern dentistry, approached it with the temper and training of a scientist, and published his treatise, *Le Chirugien dentiste ou traite des dents*. To him, dentistry owes the first description of pyorrhea, as well as the first application of orthodental procedure for mal-occlusion. He also helped to dissipate the superstition that a worm or worms within a tooth by ceaseless and insatiate gnawing produced toothache.

The French Revolution contributed to the rise of American dentistry. The famous set of false teeth made in 1790 by John Greenwood for George Washington, now at the Chicago Exhibition, was in all respects similar to that made in France seventy-five years earlier by Pierre Fauchard. Both were retained in position by coil springs. Ten years later, in 1800, Jacques Gardette in Philadelphia, discovered how to apply atmospheric pressure to retain artificial teeth in place. Gardette was a French dentist, who came to the U.S. in consequence of the French Revolution, and he and others from France placed American dentistry under heavy obligations. Even before this time, of course, dentists were practising in the U.S., e.g., in the Revolutionary period we have Paul Revere, who was not only a horseman, but also a goldsmith, a printer and an engraver.

John Hunter is credited with being the first to make a scientific study of the teeth. He was the first to put the danger of infection from dental disease upon a sound scientific basis of cause and effect. He declared that diseases in the teeth are apt to produce diseases in the neighbouring parts. One of the best remembered experiments of Hunter was that of transplanting a human tooth into the comb of a cock, where it took root and grew. He, like Pare and Fauchard, was impressed by the fact that a tooth is a living organism affecting the health of the larger organism of which it is a part, and in turn affected by it.

The money value of teeth is no modern discovery. The Hebrews said, "An eye for an eye and a tooth for a tooth," coupled with the provision that if a master knocked out a slave's tooth he must give the slave his liberty, which indicated a high quotation on teeth in Palestine, 2,000 years ago. It is interesting to note that the Army recognized the importance of a full set of strong teeth in our fighting men. In drafting soldiers for service in the World War, the U.S. rejected for service for defective teeth alone no fewer than 75,000 conscripts.

In 1845, two dentists, Dr. Wells of Hartford, and Dr. Morton of Boston, experimented with nitrous oxide as an anaesthetic in dental operations, but the demonstration arranged by Dr. Wells was unsuccessful. A year later, Dr. Morton, who had been experimenting with ether, persuaded Dr. Warren of the Massachusetts General Hospital to allow him to anaesthetize a patient, which he did successfully on the 16th October, 1846. Thus by the achievement of a member of your profession, my profession and the whole of suffering humanity was placed under a lasting obligation.

There were epochs when dentistry was the colleague of magic and the occult arts. Then followed a period when it stumbled for generations along the dark path of ignorance. In the beginning of the nineteenth century there was no dental profession. A large number of persons practised it in one form or another without having had any training; some were blacksmiths, some goldsmiths, or members of other trades. There is an interesting caricature by Rowlandson published in 1823, of a woman suffering from toothache being treated by a "jack of all trades" with dentistry as a "side line." Displayed in his shop is a sign as follows: "Barnaby Factotum Draws Teeth, Bleeds and Shaves; Wigs made here, also sausages. Wash Balls, Black Pudding, Scotch Pills, Powders for the Itch, Red Herrings, Breeches Balls and Small Beer by the maker. *In utrumque Paratus.*"

Very gradually, however, dentistry has emerged into a

position of respect and competency, and we now see it fully armed, equipped, and accepted as an equal associate of the profession of medicine.

Looking to the future I think that your interests would best be served if you formed a special section of the Academy of Medicine, which would bring you into close and constant touch with the members of the medical profession.

The first dental college was set up in 1840 as an independent preparatory dental school, the first institution of its kind to be established in the world, under the name of the Baltimore College of Dental Surgery. The Harvard Dental School, however, was the first dental school to be associated with a classical university and co-ordinated with its medical school, in 1868. All the men on the first faculty were required to be doctors of medicine, among whom it is interesting to recall were Oliver W. Holmes, and Parkman, Professor of Anatomy and Physiology on the Medical School Faculty, whose attitude towards dentistry is to be found in his following words: "I have a real interest in the welfare of a profession to which so many of us ought to feel grateful with every word we speak and with every morsel we swallow."

A good many have deplored the separate organization of dental schools and have striven not only to bring them within university control, but to make dental training a part of medical training. I see no reason why dentistry should not develop as an oral specialty of medicine and that before this specialty is taken up, there should be a universal basis common to all divisions and specialties of medicine.

Until the twentieth century, the proposition that health in the body and health in the mouth were closely inter-related was not widely accepted. Now, however, health is the foundation upon which the new dentistry rests. In the past, maladies of the teeth were regarded as local ailments and were treated as if they had little or no relation to the general health of the body.

Dental caries still remains one of the great mysteries of medicine. The infection theory has been advanced, and

James MacIntosh and Barlow have isolated an organism which they called Bacillus Acidophilus Odontolyticus, which destroys enamel. Clarke described a streptococcus mutans which he found constantly present in careous dentine. The joint research now being carried on by medical and dental men will, we hope, ultimately lead to the discovery of a way to prevent dental caries.

It is stated that dental caries is sometimes responsible for certain diseases of the intestinal tract, such as gastritis, gastric and duodenal ulcers, colitis, cholecystitis, and possibly, appendicitis. Some experiments have been carried on in this city by Dr. H. E. Paul, a genito-urinary surgeon at Christie Street Hospital, to show the relationship between alveolar abscess and kidney stone. Cultures of staphylococcus aureus were buried in the root canals of a devitalised tooth of a dog, and in a comparatively short time the animal was found to be suffering from stone in the kidney. While this work is in a more or less experimental stage, nevertheless the early results are sufficiently suggestive to be of interest both to the dentist and the surgeon.

It is scarcely necessary for me to stress the importance of research, both for its own sake and as an inspiration in teaching. We have in the Medical Faculty a splendid Research Department headed by Dr. Banting, and I am glad to know that the research work of Dr. Box and others in your Faculty of Dentistry is continuing in spite of the curtailment in the funds for special research, made necessary by the present financial situation.

Certain diseases have their point of entry through the teeth. Notable amongst these are actinomycosis and enlargement of the glands of the neck.

In order to impress upon you the necessity and importance of making a culture of all abscesses I should like to recall an interesting case with which I was associated in London during the War. A distinguished Canadian, living there, had toothache, and when he went to his dentist to have the tooth extracted he took his physician with him (also a Canadian) who, after extraction of the tooth, collected some of the pus on a swab, put it in a test tube and sent the specimen to a bacteriologist, who reported that it contained the actinomycosis fungus. The nature of the lump under his jaw was in this way explained, and appropriate treatment instituted, viz., large doses of iodide of potassium. At the end of six months' treatment all his symptoms had disappeared. It is now seventeen years since and there has been no further evidence of the disease.

Dental caries is also believed to have been responsible for myocarditis and glomerular nephritis. Rosenow, who has propounded the theory of "elective" localization, has demonstrated a connection between dental infection caused by streptococci and the same organisms found in infections of the heart, appendix, gall bladder, kidney, etc.

For the last twenty years numerous general diseases have been traced to some point of focal infection. This is not exactly new, because Dr. Benjamin Rush, one of the signers of the Declaration of Independence in 1801, pointed out the connection between the extraction of decayed and abscessed teeth and the cure of general diseases. It seems curious how little notice was paid to these observations for more than a hundred years.

The World War gave a great impetus to the biological tendency in dental medicine. Dentists restored hundreds of shell-shattered faces and jaws, even, torn beyond recognition, to a presentable condition, and the men to work and service. In this connection I should like to refer to the splendid pioneer work done during the war by Dr. Risdon. The experience he had in plastic and reconstructive surgery during that period has proven to be of immense value to us in civil life, and we are fortunate to have in our midst a man who is confining himself to this limited specialty of surgery.

I should like to pay a tribute to the work of some of the members of your profession in the late war. For the first time in any war dentists have been attached to practically every unit in the Army. Your President, Dr. E. A. Grant, was Dental Officer of the 11th Field Artillery, and I am interested to learn that your President-elect, Dr. Martin, served in the same unit.   Dr. Orville Elliott, who was attached to the 5th Field Ambulance in France, received the D.S.O. and bar, Colonel George Gow and Colonel Mallory were attached to the University of Toronto Hospital Unit. Colonel Gow did splendid work in this unit, and while in Salonika made a denture for King Peter of Servia, for which he was decorated with the "Order of the White Eagle". Dr. Harry Shields gave the anaesthetic, for which he received the Servian Order of St. Savva.   Dr. Mallory also did good work with this Unit, afterwards settling in London, where he enjoyed a large practice until his recent death.

I am informed that the Class in Dentistry of 1923 was composed of 300 veterans who saw service in every branch of the service in the Great War.

Colonel Charles Corrigan left Toronto as a Lieutenant in the C.A.S.C. with the First Contingent in 1914.   He served continuously during the entire war, part of the time on General Currie's staff, ending up by having command of his own Unit and marching with the victorious troops to the Rhine.   He was wounded at Vimy Ridge, received the D.S.O. and the V.D. and was decorated by the French with the Croix de Guerre.   I consider myself very fortunate to have a man with such a record as an Honorary Aide.   I am going to suggest that you appoint an historian to collect and preserve the war records of these men.

Modern dentistry undoubtedly owes a great deal, just as modern aseptic surgery does, to the application by Lord Lister of the researches of Pasteur on the role of bacteria in producing disease.

I was interested to see a statement by Dr. Cotton, Medical Director of the New Jersey State Hospital for the Insane, that he found the extraction of diseased or impacted teeth had had very beneficial effect upon the patients' mental condition, which gives point to the aphorism of the late Dr. Horace Fletcher that all ailments are either mental or dental.

Considerable research has been done by Mrs. May Mellanby of England on the effects of diet upon the teeth. She has shown that both the structure of the teeth and their power of resistance to decay are immediately influenced by changes in the diet.

Dr. Hanke of Chicago found in patients suffering from the severest forms of dental disease that they had diets in which there was a deficiency in vitamins. These cases showed a marked improvement when vitamins were increased. He also found that patients with the healthiest mouths had diets of a higher vitamin content.

When we speak of research in dentistry we are sometimes met with the question, "Is not diet the simple and sufficient cause of all dental ailments?" There is, unhappily, no simple and convenient formula that will make our diet perfectly satisfactory and save us from all further dental troubles.

Investigation of dental education in the United States, undertaken in the 1920's by the Carnegie Foundation for the Advancement of Teaching, attacked vigorously the narrow mechanical approach, and stated that dentistry is a true oral specialty of the practice of medicine; it emphasised the need for scientific research in fundamental phases of dental knowledge.

The Ontario Government through its Dental Department under Dr. Conboy's supervision has instituted a public dental health educational and preventive campaign in the Eastern counties of this Province. Teachers, nurses, dentists and many who have volunteered their assistance are conducting an experiment in the prevention of dental disease by education. Booklets and charts, posters and the cinematograph are all being used to direct public attention to this most important matter—the close inter-relation of the condition of the teeth and the state of the general health of patients. This is true preventive service—the value of which is self-evident.

A man who read Sir Arthur Keith's statements of the anthropologists came to the conclusion that we were doomed anyway, and that we were the inevitable victims of civilization; that with each stage of our development we let one after another of our bones or muscles fall into disuse and atrophy. It is to be hoped that means will yet be found to enable us to preserve our teeth in full efficiency during our lifetime, even should we live to be a hundred. After all, history gives us some confidence. It is 125,000 years since Rhodesian man suffered from attacks of dental caries, and we still have reasonably good teeth. Dental research, which is a preliminary to prevention of dental caries, has been almost wholly neglected, and I am strongly of the opinion that this is the line of progress. Cure must give place to prevention, for only in this way can the great mass of people be served and our social obligations to our fellowman be met.

THE COST OF CONVALESCENCE

At a Luncheon of the Ontario Hospital Association, Royal York Hotel, Toronto, October 25, 1933

Mr. President, Ladies and Gentlemen:

I am glad to know that your Association has the co-operation and support of the Ontario Medical Association, the Hospital Aids Association, the Catholic Hospital Sisterhood and the Provincial Department of Health and Hospitals. For you all have interrelated problems to solve and these yearly meetings give you plenty of scope for free discussion. You have the opportunity of meeting here the representatives of all the Provincial institutions for the care of the sick, and establishing an excellent *esprit de corps*. Enthusiasm is rekindled, your vision is enlarged, and courage revived. Few are aware of the sacrifice of time and energy given by your officers and directors, who, in the intervals between meetings, come to Headquarters in Toronto at their own expense in the interests of your Association.

May I be permitted to say that the Ontario Hospital Association is deserving of the sympathy and support of the public-spirited men and women of this Province, whose help is so much needed during these days of stress.

In order to appreciate the care which is taken in the construction and furnishing of a modern hospital to meet present requirements, it is only necessary to read an account of some of the hospitals existing in Europe eighty years ago. Of the lying-in hospital of Budapest in 1850, it is said that the patients' view from the window was the burying-ground, varied on the other side by glimpses of the dissecting-room, and underneath was an open sewer.

As you are aware, a live subject of discussion at the present time is the relation of the doctor to the indigent sick. This vitally concerns the attitude of the hospital toward the care of the public ward patients who are without means, and should be seriously considered by your Association if it has not already done so.

A number of communities in Canada provide physicians on a salary basis, very similar to the employment of doctors by the Government in Sweden and under the Highlands and Islands Service in Scotland. The employment of physicians on salaries derived from taxation was begun as early as 600 B.C. in Greece, where it was quite general by the end of the fifth century.

Many of you will doubtless remember that in an address which I gave before the Ontario Medical Association in May last I referred to the importance of establishing Convalescent Homes to reduce the heavy charge upon the municipalities for the hospital care of the sick.

I was interested to see that Montreal had realized the necessity and value of such an institution and through the initiative and generosity of Mr. C. W. Lindsay has completed and recently opened a convalescent hospital on the outskirts of north-west Montreal, and will receive patients from the public wards of the Montreal General Hospital, the Royal Victoria Hospital, the Notre Dame and other general hospitals. It is interesting also to note that Colonel Molson, the President of the Montreal General Hospital, stated that already the great benefit of the change from a hospital to these new and more suitable surroundings, has been to reduce very considerably the time it formerly took for a patient to complete his convalescence.

I should like to refer very briefly to two publications whose intrinsic interest is made all the greater by the fact that they present frequently such radically different points of view. One is the report of the Committee on the costs of medical care, and the other is the final report of the Commission on medical education, published in the U.S. in 1932. Of the two, the first, on the costs of medical care, has been received with something very much like a storm, but whether of welcome or of resentment I am unable to decide. It presents a majority and a minority report, and the latter describes the report of the majority as an effort to socialize medicine and reduce it to the plane of a trade. Actually, it seems to be an attempt to evolve and advocate a system already in partial use in other countries.

The Commission on medical education has little or nothing in common with the suggestions put forward by the minority report, but it is full, nevertheless, of suggestions to overcome the faults of our present system of medical care and hospitalization. Undoubtedly, many of you have yourselves read these reports, and the divergency of the points of view are actually a welcome sign of the renewed vigour with which modern community and personal problems are being debated. After all, the medical profession has never been so competent to treat disease as today. Too often, however, the public are led to underrate the service which lies within the power of the medical profession to render every community.

The press and advertisements have combined to foster in the average mind a belief that there is no mystery in the art of healing. Because this is so, and because there exist certain groups without medical knowledge who wish to foist upon the public a wholly new plan of medical economics and practice, I am more than pleased that the Ontario Hospital Association is attacking, as it were, in massed formation, the twin citadels of public ignorance of medicine on the one hand, and public indifference to the benefits of effective hospitalization on the other.

For every great movement requires leadership, and it is by the qualities of the leader that the success or failure of any plan is decided. Today there are many social systems in the world being weighed in the balance; and with the systems, their leaders. In the work that you are doing you are very fortunate in having had the leadership of so many able, far-sighted citizens who find in your work an opportunity of rendering valuable humanitarian public service.

THE WORK OF HEALING AND THE HEALING POWER OF WORK

Before the Canadian Occupational Therapy Association at an Annual Dinner in the Royal York Hotel, Toronto, October 27, 1933

Mr. President, Ladies and Gentlemen:

There are few new difficulties that stand in the way of welfare and happiness. There are, however, new aspects of old difficulties, and so, when we are confronted by predicaments of any kind we may usually find helpful counsel in the wisdom of the ancients. As I was thinking about what I should say to you this evening, I recalled Plato's opinion of the relative importance of the functions and duties of a man. Plato elevated "the poet" to the highest position in the social hierarchy. By the poet he meant the *maker*, the *doer*, the *creator*, which is the literal translation of the old Greek work, "*poeta*".

In this, Plato paid tribute to what, for want of a better term, we call "the common man". For in every man and woman there is born the instinct to make and to do. It has its earlier expression in the infant mind. It is developed delightfully in every normal boy and girl. Deprive a child of the opportunity to exercise his constructive, creative instinct and you plunge him into the depths of misery. The busy mechanism of his mind may not stop except at the cost of mental anguish. The so-called "naughty" child is usually the unhappy child who is compelled by circumstance to substitute destructive for constructive effort.

Vaguely, I suppose, nearly every father and mother realizes that *to make* and *to do* are privileges indispensable to childhood happiness. Plato and other wise thinkers of every age realized that the passion to exercise them persists in the adult;

but it was really only with the genesis of Occupational Therapy in the time of the World War that we began to understand how necessary it is to preserve these privileges for every man and woman.

In 1916 our military hospitals were crowded with disabled men. The homicidal horror had robbed mechanics of their hands, musicians of their hearing, painters of their eyes, labourers of their limbs. In effect, considered in the light of their previous training and experience, these men were dead. How to restore them to useful, independent life was an inevitable question and so vocational training was instituted. Very quickly our military hospital authorities observed that in these efforts to adjust patients to new circumstances they had demonstrated in a practical way the truth of Plato's declaration. Maimed and suffering as these men were, they still aspired *to make* and *to do*, and when once again they were offered the opportunity to make and to do they forgot their sufferings and grew well at an unprecedented rate. And so, from teaching sick men to make or to do in order that they might again be useful members of society we learned to teach these sick men to make or to do so that they might more surely and more rapidly recover good health! In this discovery the men and women who had undertaken the work of reclaiming these poor, maimed victims of war earned a reward greater, perhaps, then they had dared to hope for.

"Not to be occupied and not to exist," said Voltaire, "amount to the same thing. One must give oneself all the occupation one can to make life supportable in this world." He continued: "The further I advance in age, the more I find work necessary. It becomes, in the long run, the greatest of all pleasures and takes the place of the illusions of life. If you do not want to commit suicide, always have something to do."

Here, surely, was a definitely valuable recommendation. Time and again since Voltaire spoke, events have proved the truth of his observation. But not until lately have we realized that lack of occupation and interest are in effect, if not in essence, a disease.

Among my several reasons for gladly accepting the invitation to speak to you today was the welcome opportunity to congratulate you upon the logic and sense of reality which have led you to recognize the malignancy of this disease and its need for therapeutic treatment.

I feel that in speaking to you, I am addressing a gathering of men and women who have rendered, and will in the future render an increasingly valuable service. With the limited time at my disposal, it is difficult to decide whether I should speak of your past achievements or of the even greater possibilities for service which the future holds in store.

I was very interested to read Mr. Dunlop's brief history of occupational therapy, and to learn that the training of ward-aides was undertaken under the direction of Professor Haultain in the University of Toronto's Mining Building in 1916. Some 300 girls were trained and sent to the military hospitals throughout the Dominion, and to their spirit and devotion much of the success of this movement is due. Engineers began the work of occupational therapy and carried it through with the help of doctors, nurses, and these ward-aides, but as the therapeutic value of occupational instruction became more and more apparent, the doctors assumed leadership and subsequently the aides formed an association out of which this organization has evolved.

There were difficulties, of course. I find that one of the greatest of these difficulties was that matrimony thinned out the ranks of the aides at an appalling rate—and still does! Might I suggest to young ladies who seek on opportunity of practising the home-making arts, that occupational therapy seems to offer a splendid opportunity to achieve this ambition!

Lately I have called attention to the need for convalescent homes in which patients who no longer require hospital attention will be able to make the final progress to complete recovery of health and strength. I have stressed the economic advantages of such convalescent homes—the lower capital cost because less elaborate equipment is necessary than in hospitals, and the lower operating and maintenance cost because the only really satisfactory convalescent home would be situated in the country and would have as an important adjunct its farm, which would make it self-supporting to a considerable degree. Practically all the foodstuffs required would be produced on the premises. But in advocating such convalescent homes I have not economy alone in mind. They offer splendid opportunity for occupational therapy. In conjunction with each home there would of necessity be the truck garden and the flower garden. Many years ago a wise man described gardening as "the purest of all pleasures." "The more you develop it," he said, "and the more you know about it, the more absorbing is its interest." Then in addition to the garden there would be the work in the fields, in the barns and stables, and all the delightful interest of raising and tending livestock. Further, there would be the other occupational opportunities of the dairy and creamery and poultry ranch. Many of the patients would find delightful health-restoring occupation in these endeavours.

Much of the neurosis discernable in modern times is due to the fact that machines have robbed man of his birthright, namely, the use of his hands for constructive creative work. We must look to the occupational therapist for relief of this disease.

Four years of war resulted in many thousands of opportunities for occupational therapy to prove its curative value. The war is over. What is the future of this new branch of therapeutics? Peace has its victories no less than war. Peace has also its losses, its defeats, its incapacitated, its maimed and its suffering. Four years of depression have wounded and tortured millions of people. We have a new crop of the anguished and the despondent. In place of shell-shock we have unemployment-shock. Instead of the lost arm or leg, the destroyed sight, the impaired faculties, we have the lost usefulness, the unsuitability to new circumstances—we have the frustrated, the helpless and the hopeless.

The great tragedy of the past four years has not been that men and women have suffered privation because of unemployment—we may say truthfully and thankfully that adequate provisions were made to feed and clothe the needy. The great tragedy has been the destruction of morale, the undermining of spirit, the insidious sapping of the confidence born of a sense of security and usefulness.

With devout thankfulness to Providence we feel today that we have set our feet on the long road to economic recovery. We are determined to travel this road cautiously, yet we shall go forward eagerly. Those of us who can advance must be prepared to help others less able than we. We cannot leave them behind in the morass from which we are emerging. We must equip them for the journey. We must assist them in every way. Although they say to us "we are not able to go any further", we must say, "the goal is worthy of the effort. We will support you with our stouter limbs." And though they say to us that they are of the lost legions whose opportunity was in other and happier times, we must answer, "There are new corps forming in which you may be enlisted and the training that will fit you to serve in these new armies of usefulness is occupational therapy and vocational training."

If I have suggested to you that the challenge of the immediate future is greater even than the challenge of the world war, I am happy, for that was my purpose in speaking to you tonight. I am happy, too, in the confidence that you will not let that challenge go unanswered.

THESE LAID THE WORLD AWAY

At the Armistice Day Service at the Memo-
rial, Public School Grounds, Richmond
Hill, November 12, 1933

Mr. Reeve, Ladies and Gentlemen:

Fifteen years ago men and boys returned to Canada after the most terrible conflict in the history of mankind. To the four corners of the earth the news had been flashed on November 11, 1918, that war was to cease and that the blessings of peace were to come back to a world which, for four long years, had experienced the madness of war and the homicidal fury of nations striving for mastery, one against the other.

On far-flung battlefields lay those who would never again come back to their homeland, those who had made the supreme sacrifice, those of whom Lawrence Binyon has written:

> "They shall not grow old, as we that are left grow old;
> Age shall not weary them, nor the years condemn;
>   At the going down of the sun and in the morning
> We will remember them."

And today we remember those who died, with reverence and with a profound sense of the tragedy of young men cut down in all the pride and strength of their manhood. Not a man whose name is commemorated on this tablet, but went forth with the full knowledge that he was fighting for what he and his countrymen believed to be right, for the liberties of the world, and those who fell, fell in a belief, perhaps hardly uttered by themselves, that somehow or another, their lives might be given to promote the better-ment of the world.

Seven millions perished in Europe, and here we commemorate but a tiny fraction of that vast host. Not one of those seven millions in all the countries of Europe and of the New World, but his death broke some tie of friendship, made a vacant place in some home, and the mourning for them will last with our lives. It is no use our asking that question which has so often come to the lips of disconsolate men and women, "Were their lives sacrificed in vain?" We may justly feel that the world as it is today is a heritage unworthy of these men who died in war, that peace might be made secure for all men to enjoy. And, certainly, such tremendous sacrifices of the youth, the manhood, and the womanhood of all nations made in those tragic days do not appear to be justified by what has happened since. The war to end war seems only to have created new problems, to have fomented new hatreds and to have caused new dissensions among mankind. But I like to think that the peace which has followed the war will yet prove to have its victories. After all, it is in the hearts and minds of men and women that war or peace is born. Although every nation has suffered as a consequence of the war, yet, in Canada, as in other parts of the Empire, we have witnessed a stupendous effort on the part of every class to help their less fortunate brothers who, through no fault of their own, have experienced great hardship. So there has been brought about in a real sense a widespread awakening of the reality of the brotherhood of man.

Of those whose names we commemorate here, "In the sight of the unwise, they seem to die; and their departure is taken for misery and their going from us to be utter destruction, but they are in peace." Peace is theirs and it is a peace that we cannot share. Lincoln said, and I think his words we should take from here today, "We must show an increased devotion to that cause for which they gave the last full measure of devotion." It was for peace they died and for the ultimate ideal of the brotherhood of mankind that they suffered. It remains for us, who yet live, to carry to ful-

filment the high aspirations, the ideals, the hopes and even
the dreams for which

> "These laid the world away; poured out the red
>   Sweet wine of youth; gave up the years to be
> Of work and joy and that unhoped serene
>   That men call age; and those who would have been
> Their sons, they gave—their immortality."

QUACKS V. SCIENCE

*Before a Joint Meeting of the Kiwanis
Club and Other Service Clubs at a Lunch-
eon in the Royal York Hotel,
November 22, 1933*

Mr. President and Gentlemen:

In choosing my subject for this afternoon I have been
influenced, perhaps, by the number of proposals which are
being advanced to remedy existing world-conditions. Hardly
a day passes that remedies are not prescribed, but unhappily,
most of these remedies are suggested by people who lack
adequate knowledge to prescribe. Similarly, on account
of the activities of some people who, without either qualifications or good faith, prescribe for physical ills, it occurred
to me that it might be interesting and not unprofitable to
speak today on the subject of Quacks *versus* Science.

I am addressing a body of men who are united to render
service to the community, and because there are still multi-
tudes of quacks in this age of enlightenment, and quackery
continues to flourish at a time when the qualified, scientific
doctor is equipped, as never before, to cope successfully with
illness, disease and injury you will, I think, be interested by
the quotation of historic example and modern instance of
the serious depredations being made upon public health by
the quack and his too plausible promises of a cure for anything and everything.

Along with the story—the sometimes humorous, sometimes pathetic, but usually tragic story of the frauds practised
upon a too easily deceived public by quacks and quackery—
there is the splendid history of the advancement of medical
science.

Long ago, Samuel Parr perfectly defined a quack: "The
term Quack," said he, "is applicable to all who, by pompous

pretences, mean insinuations and indirect promises endeavour to obtain that confidence to which neither education, merit nor experience entitles them." Properly considered, the quack is a public enemy.

I will endeavour to show the grave evils which attend the powerful machinations, the subtle propaganda, the misleading advertisements which arouse false hopes in the hearts of sufferers, and all those other anti-social activities of quacks who prey on a gullible public by offering spurious remedies.

The story of a most successful "wise woman" named Joanna Stephens proves that quacks find their dupes and devotees in all ranks of society. It was toward the middle of the eighteenth century that Joanna Stephens flourished. One historian refers to her as an "ignorant, vulgar creature", and no doubt she was. But that did not prevent her from deceiving the whole British nation. She proclaimed that she had discovered an infallible remedy for "stone", that most painful malady. Bishops and peers, lords and ladies, bankers and society leaders—all flocked to her. Her fees were exorbitant and she became wealthy.

But those who could not afford her high prices demanded that the remedy be bought outright for every sufferer to use. A public subscription was opened. But Joanna wanted £5,000 for the secret of her cure; and £5,000 was a considerably greater sum then than now, and the money couldn't be raised. Popular agitation then demanded that the matter be placed before Parliament. No matter what the cost, the whole nation wanted Joanna Stephen's infallible cure for "stone", and in 1739, by Act of Parliament, the nation paid the full sum of £5,000 to Joanna that the secret of her cure might be published.

The remedy consisted of egg-shells and snails, soap and honey, wild carrot seeds and burdock seeds, ground and heated and mixed together! Needless to say, every one of her advertised "cures" was a fraud.

We who live 200 years later continue to pay millions to the "Joanna Stephens" and her successors, who fill magazines and newspapers with spurious claims to the possession of remedies which, at their worst, are poisons, and, at their best, do no good whatsoever. Joanna was simply one of the many ancestors of the modern patent medicine vendor.

Joanna Stephens represents one kind of quack. A Mr. and Mrs. Loutherbourg were of a different and subtler kind.

In 1789 Mr. and Mrs. Loutherbourg became famous for curing people without medicine. By the simple expedient of looking upon a patient and touching him, he was there and then and for all time cured. God, this enlightened couple claimed, had endowed them with a miraculous power of healing the impoverished sick—the poor who could not afford to pay.

Such transparent honesty was well rewarded. The Mansion in which Mr. and Mrs. Loutherbourg were soon able to live was besieged by enormous crowds clamouring for cures. The question arises, "How did Mr. and Mrs. Loutherbourg get their money?" As you know, there is nothing altruistic about quacks. Money is their only reason for entering a most profitable, though disreputable and indescribably cruel business.

Well, Mr. and Mrs. Loutherbourg used to issue free tickets amongst the mob at their gates, but, strangely enough, some worthless fellows who had joined the crowds, supposedly from an idle curiosity, used to sell their tickets for sums varying from two to five guineas each to those who were tired of waiting. The miracles of Mr. and Mrs. Loutherbourg ceased with singular abruptness when it was discovered that these strangers in the mob were accomplices of the miracle-working friends of the poor.

Centuries ago there was a certain Sir Kenelm Digby who was the crony of such diverse spirits as Bacon, Jonson and Cromwell—great men, all of them. Sir Kenelm is famous in medical history as the inventor of the "Powder of Sympathy", by which wounds were healed at a distance. But more amazing, perhaps, even than this magic powder is the remedy which he proposed, in all seriousness, for fever and ague.   Here it is: "Pare the patient's nails.   Put the parings in a little bag and hang it around the neck of a live eel and place him in a tub of water.   The eel will die, the patient will recover."

In order that you may not think that the more outrageous forms of quackery are peculiar to the Middle Ages, may I cite an experience I had about twenty-five years ago.   I was called in consultation to see a patient suffering from appendicitis.   His friends had advised a remedy which I had not heard of previously.   It consisted of killing a cat and immediately splitting it open and applying its hot entrails to the patient's abdomen.   In spite of this treatment the disease had progressed so far when I saw the patient that there was no chance of relief by surgery.

In the sixteenth and seventeenth centuries a person mentally unbalanced was commonly described as having "a stone in his head".   Now quackery is nothing if not original, and so the quacks of the time were ready with a unique kind of surgical operation for this distressing condition.   They would make a superficial incision in the scalp of the lunatic, and having palmed a stone or number of stones, would throw them into a convenient basket at stated intervals, during the patient's struggles.   There is, in Rotterdam, to this day, a picture by Jan Steen of a quack incising the head of a screaming idiot who is tied to a chair while an old woman holds the pail into which a giggling boy throws the stones. I may add that history does not record that protests were made against this practice.   I am confident, however, that if objections were made, they were not as violent as those that have since then been advanced against more scientific and humane methods of stemming the destructive tide of depraved and irremediable idiocy.

Hard times for everyone else are boom times for quacks and charlatans.   In days of unemployment and stress, people are uncertain of things and themselves, and, beset by fear and worry, their health suffers.   Sick people, or those who only imagine they are sick, always hope for a miracle.   They look for methods with a touch of the mysterious and the magical. The quack shrewdly offers these things—and prospers!

Typical of this spirit is a case in the city of Limoges, France, where one, Mde. Desbordes, is growing rich on gifts from those who believe she has healed them of disease. Her method is described as "Welcoming into her own body all the ailments of the hundred patients a day to which she limits herself, then, when the last patient has gone, shaking herself loose from all the miscellaneous assortment of human ills she has absorbed." And people believe that! There are today large modern buildings and business corporations with millions of dollars of capital in which even more fantastic doctrines are taught and to which people pay the tribute exacted from them by advertising. Both the buildings and the business corporations prove the fact that the modern quack prospers by committing wild buffooneries in the name of science. Until the public wakes up he will continue to prosper, and he would be the envy of all the quacks of all earlier times were they able to visualize this twentieth century—the golden age of quackery.

When I speak of our own times as the golden age of quackery I speak advisedly. There is more money made by quacks today and more vast corporations built up on quackery, bare-faced and unashamed, than at any other time in the history of medicine.

Dr. Fishbein*, an editor of the *American Medical Association Journal*, states that of all the nations of the world, the United States is most afflicted by its healers. Besides those holding the degree M.D., signifying Doctor of Medicine, and six or seven years of study following high school graduation, a host of queer practitioners pervade the medical field. They have conferred on themselves strange combinations of letters, indicating the peculiar systems of healing which somewhat lax legislation and law enforcement permit them to

* The information which follows concerning various cults and quacks is to be found in *The New Medical Follies* by Dr. Fishbein, to whom I, in common with many others, am greatly indebted.

practise on an unwary public. One of the marks of the charlatan is the use in advertising of such an alphabetic appendage.

The scientific medicine of today is based on the discoveries made in the fundamental sciences. It holds to no single theory as to the causation of disease, and it does not insist correspondingly that the successful treatment of disease depends on the use of any single method of manipulation or administration. The cults may be classified easily into mental healing cults, mechanical cults, electric cults, nature cults and similar divisions since they adhere definitely to single devices.

These cults avoid the fundamental sciences as much as possible. Rather than attempt to correlate the fallacies on which the cults are based with established knowledge, cultist leaders are inclined to deny flatly the facts that have been demonstrated. Of germs and their causation of disease they take little cognizance. Others employ apparatus of such intricacy as excites the ridicule of the humblest tyro in the science of physics.

I propose to give you a few examples of the hundred or more types of healing today offered to the public.

First—"*ALEREOS SYSTEM*". This system of drugless healing is the acme of exploitation of the sweat bath and massage. Ten treatments cost $25, in advance. One cannot complain of the cost, provided one is not fooled into neglecting tuberculosis or ulcer of the stomach, which the promoters claim are cured by this treatment.

Then there is the "*AUTOHEMIC THERAPY*". This is the creation of one, L. D. Rogers, for many years the head and chief owner of the National Medical University of Chicago, a low-grade institution, virtually a diploma-mill. Like many other cultist leaders, Rogers is constantly founding societies of which he is the chief panjandrum. "Autohemic therapy", he says, "consists in giving the patient a solution made by attenuating, hemolizing, incubating and potentizing a few drops of his or her own blood, and administering it according to a refined technique developed by the author."

Playing the game to the limit, Rogers also advertises a $100 mail-order course for other physicians. The appeal is cleverly made to the anti-medical cultists of all varieties by the slogan "Without use of bugs or drugs." A clever and shrewd old fakir is L. D. Rogers! There is not an iota of scientific evidence that his method or his system ever cured anybody of anything.

Then we have the "*AUTO-SCIENCE*", originating in San Francisco by Dr. Feyrer, who presents testimonials from grateful imbeciles who have been cured right away.

Next is "*AUTOTHERAPY*", which is "self-therapy" or "Natural therapy", as the name implies. This little idea grew in the mind of a homeopath, probably obsessed with the slogan "Like cures like." Carrying the idea of the "hair of the dog that bit you" to its ultimate interpretation, Duncan recommends the healing of boils by cooking up and swallowing the matter from the boil; for dysentery he filters the excretions and injects the fluid that filters through; for tuberculosis he filters the sputum and injects the filtrate. He claims all sorts of cures.

"*COUEISM*". Out of France, heralded by such exploitation as was never before given to the introduction of any new system of healing, came Emile Coué, druggist of Nancy. The system that he urged was "Self-Mastery by Conscious Auto-Suggestion". The patient is instructed as follows:

Every morning before you are fully awake and every evening as soon as you are in bed, close your eyes and murmur twenty times: "Day by day in every way I'm getting better and better."

If the patient has a tumour of the spinal cord, an infection of the heart or a cancer of the stomach, and if he is under the care of a competent physician, he can do no harm by occupying his spare moments in the mental exercises suggested.

M. Coué came to the United States and Canada heralded by newspaper publicity planned by a great syndicate, whose managers should have known better. During his tour he was featured by radio, by motion picture, by lecture, and by all the other plans that the publicists use for snaring the unwary.   He died not long after his return to France, and his teachings died with him.

The abrupt relief of hysterical symptoms by suggestion and persuasion is a commonplace in the practice of the average physician.

"*DIVINE SCIENCE*".   This treatment of illness consists in persuading the sufferer that God is good, that disease is the result of man's own foolishness and that God will cure him if he will give him a chance.   These simple doctrines are shrouded, however, in the usual preposterous verbosity. And here in our Province this rather weird cult of curing by the laying on of hands is being carried out at this very time, without, I regret to say, the assistance of prayer.   A certain man happens to be the seventh son of the seventh son of the seventh son.   What mystic or supernatural advantage he thereby possesses over his fellow men I am unable to determine.   But the fact that three to four hundred people visit this man daily at a dollar a time in order that he may lay his hands on them and cure them does seem to show that, in the minds of many, the seventh son of a seventh son of a seventh son possesses powers of healing of a kind denied the scientific doctor of more ordinary parentage—numerically speaking. This man, however, overcomes any scientific scruples remaining in the minds of his patients by demanding a specimen of urine or a few hairs from their heads.   He looks at these.   A glance is sufficient, for chemical laboratory investigation is quite unnecessary for the seventh son of a seventh son of a seventh son.

Such are the advantages of a genealogical accident cleverly capitalized by a quack.   But let me give you an account of another famous modern quack:

ALBERT ABRAMS, who departed this life in 1924 and his "*ELECTRONIC THERAPY*".   For a brief span of years the system that he devised for diagnosing disease and for treating such conditions as he diagnosed caught the fancy of numerous followers, bewildered the ignorant, and amazed even hardened investigators by its superlative chicanery. Electronic medicine embraces the following procedure: One secures from a prospective patient a drop of blood upon a piece of filter paper. This is put in an apparatus called a dynamizer, which in turn is connected with a rheostatic dynamizer from which wires pass to a vibratory rheostat, from which a wire passes to the forehead of some available subject, quite healthy, and employed at a small salary. This person faces west in a dim light. An obliging assistant turns the switch and the electronic therapist thumps on the subject's abdomen. Abrams insisted that areas of dullness in the abdomen of the subject indicate various diseases in the persons contributing the blood. He also claimed the ability to tell the religion of the person submitting the blood and to diagnose disease by this method from the hand-writing.

The Abrams system included the complete scheme of quackery; a special association, a special periodical, a school, travelling lecture-ships, leasing of apparatus with a contract not to open it, and constant charges of persecution against investigators.

On his death, Abrams left an estate of more than a million dollars; his executors continue to promote the cult in San Francisco.

Women are victimized in numerous ways, and the cult of Beauty practises an unending and increasingly bold fraud upon them.

What a vast trade has grown out of the desires of Mr. Babbitt's wife and daughters to enhance the physiognomies and figures with which a none too beneficent Providence endowed them! If one resides in a town in which the trade is backward, the promoters of comeliness may still be found under such old-fashioned headings as Hairdressers, but where the cult of beauty has many shrines they hold forth in all the gaudy glory of Beauticians and Cosmetologists. Estimates place the number of beauty shops in Manhattan at between 1,500 to 2,000. There are at least a thousand in Los Angeles, not counting Hollywood.

Since the profits of the beauty shops are dependent mainly upon the sale of lotions, creams, shampoos, ointments, depilatories, beauty clays, face packs and similar preparations, the number of these increases daily. Preparations similar to most of the beauty clays, selling at from $2 to $10 a pound, may be made by mixing a pound of kaolin, or dried beauty clay, with the same weight of water. Such a preparation costs 20 cents.

Despite the advertisements, it is quite impossible to feed the skin by rubbing in fats or creams of any kind. Nor is cleanliness aided by plastering the surface of the skin with one type of cream after another and then being compelled to wash away the entire mess. There is no such thing as a skin-food. The skin can be soothed, inflamed, or made temporarily more pliable by external applications, but it cannot be fed.

It is a sad mockery of our vaunted civilization and an unanswerable indictment of our standards of education when it is possible for men and women of seeming intelligence, by their millions to entrust their health and their very lives —indeed all that is most precious to them—to men totally ignorant of the structure of the human body, its normal physiological functions, and the nature of the diseases they profess to cure. The secrecy which quacks maintain as to the ingredients of their nostrums is in itself their greatest condemnation. It should cause intelligent people to suspect their value. It is only dishonesty that fears the light. All the great scientific discoveries which have made possible the cure of hitherto fatal diseases have been given freely to the world without cost.

In this connection may I say a word of commendation for the valuable work being done by the national health department. This Department protects the public from the fraudulent claims of nostrum vendors, and by its co-operation with the Radio Commission bans from the air those quacks who seek the Dominion-wide publicity which the radio would otherwise afford them. In this way, the so-called "suggestion" advertisements which create an element of fear and cause people to purchase remedies of no value, have been eliminated.

A few months ago the Radio Commission stopped the advertising of a chewing gum in British Columbia, for which the fraudulent claim was made that it would reduce weight. Since then, a man was refused the air who made the preposterous claim that he could diagnose ulcer of the stomach and other diseases from hand-writing.

From what I have said, it will be apparent that it is easy to impose upon the uninformed laity, and how necessary the Medical Act and the various Drug and Food Acts are to protect this same public from fraud. Laws exist to safeguard your property; how much more necessary is it that your health and your lives should be protected from the cruel menace of avaricious charlatans.

In the short time left I purpose giving you a brief summary of the achievements of science as applied to disease.

Biblical quotations and interpretations formed the basis for the opposition to the use of Anaesthesia. The introduction of anaesthetics to alleviate the pain of surgical operations caused a violent controversy. It was science *vs.* theology, and progress *vs.* stagnation.

Simpson, the discoverer of chloroform, answered these religious objections against the employment of anaesthetic agents in midwifery and surgery in 1847 in this way: "Those who urge, on a kind of religious ground, that an artificial or anaesthetic state of unconsciousness should not be induced merely to save frail humanity from the misery and tortures of bodily pain, forget that most singular description of the preliminaries and details of the first surgical operation ever performed on man, which is contained in the 21st verse of the second chapter of Genesis, 'And the Lord God caused a deep sleep to fall upon Adam, and he slept, and he took one of his ribs, and closed up the flesh instead thereof'—, affording evidence of our Creator himself using means to save poor human nature from unnecessary endurance of physical pain." Thus Simpson conquered.

He showed also that on theological grounds strenuous opposition had been presented against every humane innovation in the past.   For example, vaccination against smallpox was fiercely attacked.   Those opposed to it argued thus: "Small-pox", they said, "is a visitation from God, and originates in man; but the cow-pox (vaccination) is produced by pre-sumptuous, impious man.   The former Heaven ordained; the latter is a daring and profane violation of our holy religion." To lend weight to the objection, one of the ecclesiastical vigilants mentioned "a lady who complained that since her daughter was inoculated she coughs like a cow and has grown hair all over her body".   Another pointed out that vaccina-tion was discontinued in one part of the country "because those who had been inoculated in that manner bellow like bulls!"

Even the Panama Canal was similarly opposed.   In the sixteenth century a cleric by the name of Acosta reasoned thus against it: "I am of opinion that human power should not be allowed to cut through the strong and impenetrable bounds which God has put between two oceans, of moun-tains and iron rocks which can stand the fury of the raging seas.   And, if it were possible, it would appear to me very just that we should fear the vengeance of Heaven for attempt-ing to improve that which the Creator in His almighty will and providence has ordained from the creation of the world."

Certainly such a warning as the "cleric" Acosta gave of the Divine Wrath that would be visited upon those who attempted to build the Panama Canal seemed to be borne out by what actually happened.   To the superstitious it must have seemed as if an angel of destruction did, in truth, guard Panama from the impious desires and blasphemous works of man.   From the first, De Lesseps and his thousands of Frenchmen found the dread plague of yellow fever decimating their ranks.   It is said that there is a Frenchman buried under every tie of the Panama Railway which ran through those miles of tropical country long known as the "white man's grave".

But General Gorgas was not superstitious. He decided to study the problem scientifically, and as soon as it was proven that yellow fever was transmitted by the Stegomyia mosquito, Gorgas succeeded in ridding the Panama of these insects by such means as pouring petroleum on ponds and stagnant pools to kill them. He found that the wings of death that beat over Panama were the tiny silent wings of the mosquito. And the dread plague came not from heaven as a visitation, but from low-lying swamps and pools in which mosquitoes in their billions bred and buzzed their warning of death to the builders of the Canal.

Every period is one of transition, but it may be said that the last fifty years have seen far greater changes than any similar period in the history of medicine. First and foremost is the transformation and enormous expansion of surgery due to Lister's antiseptic methods, and the resulting revolution in technique which made safe many new operative procedures rendered painless by the introduction of anaesthetics. Now surgery which formerly was chiefly concerned with the extremities, could safely invade the abdomen, the head and the chest. Development of abdominal surgery has been phenomenal. The word "appendicitis" does not appear in the first volume of the Oxford Dictionary prepared in 1888, because according to the editor, Sir James Murray, he consulted a regius professor of medicine who informed him that it was not necessary to include it, as the disease was very rare. It was, of course, not *rare*, but was *rarely* diagnosed.

The main advances in treatment have almost all been comparatively recent, and the outcome of laboratory investigation, with the production of serums and vaccines for the cure and prevention of diphtheria, tetanus, typhoid and other diseases.

Insulin, discovered by Banting in 1922, has transformed the treatment and outlook of diabetics.

The same result has followed the discovery in 1927 of the dietetic treatment by liver and gastric mucous membrane of pernicious anaemia.

The names of the heroes of medical science are legion, and here, in the City of Toronto, there are many examples of self-sacrificial devotion to a cause which more, perhaps, than all others, aims at the betterment of men and women by removing every threat to their well-being.

Dr. Wm. Brebner, the son of the late James Brebner, for many years Registrar of the University of Toronto, died on November 9, 1932, from infection due to the bite of a monkey while doing experimental work on Poliomyelitis at the Rockefeller Institute.

Dr. Saddington, a graduate of the University of Toronto, died in New York in February, 1927, from an obscure tropical disease, originating in Kenya, British East Africa. He, too, was on the Medical Research Staff of the Rockefeller Institute, and he, too, took risks which only the enthusiast will take in order that the last barricades of superstitition and ignorance may be stormed and another triumph for medical science be recorded in the story of man's progress.

In the light of the deeds of such men as these how ignoble are the shallow pretences of quacks and how detestable the money-making schemes of quackery by which men and women everywhere are defrauded!

The work of men of science in acquiring control over plague and pestilence is no less valuable to our civilization than the use of steam and electricity upon which all modern industry rests. In comparison with their work, the wealth of patent medicine vendors, the cheap successes of charlatans, the machinations of all those who deal in unscientific quack cures and the preposterous pretences of the superstitious, may justly be regarded as the greatest impediments to that progress of medical science in which lies the only hope of suffering millions.

ON ART AS HISTORY

*On Opening the Exhibition of Early Cana-
dian Art in Connection with the Centenary
Celebrations of the Incorporation of the
City of Toronto, in the Art Gallery, Friday,
January 5, 1934*

Your Worship, Ladies and Gentlemen:

I wish to thank His Worship the Mayor for his kindly
introduction. There is someting singularly appropriate in
the fact that His Worship, who for so long has taken a
prominent part in plans for the celebration of Toronto's
Centenary, should, by the expressed will of such a large
majority of its citizens, be retained to see these plans brought
to a successful fruition.

Exactly one hundred years ago the First Exhibition of the
Society of Artists and Amateurs was held at Parliament
House, which stood on Front Street overlooking the Bay.
But how different Toronto was then!

Here in this Exhibition you will be able to see just how
different Toronto was a hundred years and more ago. For
there were no skyscrapers then to obstruct the view. An
oil painting by Dartnell of Toronto seen from the Island
in the year 1825 shows you the thriving town with none of
the features which the city now possesses. And a lithograph
of Toronto made nine years later in 1834—exactly one
hundred years ago—reveals a town growing and already
changed. For Parliament House had been built in the
meantime—the old Parliament House in which was held
Toronto's First Exhibition of Art, one hundred years ago.
Standing in its six acres of ground, bounded by Simcoe,
John, Front and Wellington Streets, the old Parliament
House was, you may be sure, a sufficiently impressive

building in its day.   Sir John Colborne was then Lieutenant-Governor of Upper Canada and the Patron of the Exhibition. William Lyon Mackenzie was the Mayor of Toronto.

It was with real pleasure that I accepted the invitation to open the Toronto Centennial Historical Exhibition.   For I am convinced that the significance of such a ceremony as this, taking place on the fifth day of the One Hundredth Year since the foundation of Toronto will be apparent to all.

I can imagine no more appropriate method of commemorating the Centenary of the City of Toronto than this Exhibition of Early Canadian Art.   I congratulate most cordially all those responsible for the gathering together from far and near of a collection of such historical interest.   By so doing they have rendered a service to the community, and it may be that I can best express the magnitude of their service by saying that they have, as it were, opened a window into the past of this country, through which all those who visit this Exhibition can see life as it was lived by Canadians a hundred years ago.

For here is something even more significant than what are ordinarily termed works of art; something, too, that touches us even more closely as citizens of a great city than pictures placed on view because of their great artistic merit, their beauty, or their flawless technique.   Here on these walls is nothing less, indeed, than a portion of the history of our country graphically portrayed.

Now since it is impossible, I presume, to open an Exhibition of Art without saying something about Art, and preferably something as noncommittal as possible, and since I have chosen instead to stress the historic rather than the purely artistic importance of this Exhibition, it is reassuring to know that the function of art and history is identical.   For the duty and purpose of both, though in different ways, is to *record*.

And I say this not without high authority in that world of art which is so beset with difficulties for the peripatetic layman.   I am supported, indeed, by no less a guide and mentor than Giorgio Vasari.   In the preface to the Second

Part of his monumental *Lives of the Most Eminent Painters, Sculptors and Architects* Vasari thus describes the historic function of Art: "Art", he says, "exists not in order to make a succinct narration of the events that befell a Prince or a Republic, but in order to observe the judgments, the counsels, the resolutions and the intrigues of men, leading subsequently to fortunate and unfortunate actions; for *this* is the *true soul of history*, and is that which truly teaches men to live and makes them wise, and which, besides the pleasure that comes from seeing past events as present, is the *true end of art*."

The Directors of this Art Gallery and those citizens who have generously lent these pictures to this Exhibition, have placed us under a deep debt of gratitude.   For it is they who have afforded us this opportunity of experiencing that pleasure which Vasari termed the "true end of Art"—"the pleasure that comes from seeing past events as present."

Ask yourself the question, "What was Canada like a hundred years ago?" and see how great is our debt to the men who wrote history with crayon and brush when Canada was still in its vigorous sturdy infancy.

For, ladies and gentlemen, it is a fact worthy of note that the artist who depicts the life of his day makes all posterity his debtor.   He puts the stamp of permanence on all that is, by its nature, impermanent—as life itself is impermanent. He reproduces the scenes about him in order that those who follow may be able to see again what he once saw.   He records those daily incidents in the lives of his contemporaries, those intimate, homely scenes and episodes which the historian in his books can never hope to describe so vividly, and without which the men and women of the past seem too remote to engage our active sympathy and interest.   For the artist can and does paint pictures which speak to succeeding generations far more eloquently than all the history books ever written.   With the passage of time these pictures become the memories of nations—their most graphic and certainly their most realistic history.

I am credibly informed, by the way, that were any young modern artist nowadays to betray a sneaking admiration for a picture painted before, let us say, last year, it would be regarded as evidence of unspeakable mediocrity—or worse— in matters artistic. But the pictures here displayed are to be viewed primarily as historical records of a life that has vanished, never to return; by no stretch of the imagination do they belong to the category of Old Masters. Their value and importance is not in the least dependent upon the artistic quality, although I may add as a purely personal and, no doubt, untutored expression of opinion, that I have gazed on works of art pointed out to me as the very last word in modernity—the last word, I am to assume, in more senses than one—which have seemed to me infinitely less pleasing to the eye than the works of these early Canadian artists.

It may be, however, that it is no longer considered necessary nor even desirable that pictures should do anything so un- exceptional as please the eye of the beholder; and at this point I am reminded of an amusing passage in a book about that brilliant art critic, the late W. C. Brownell, which his widow, Mrs. Brownell, has recently published. Speaking of a skit on modern art which Brownell wrote but never published, she adds "He [that is, Brownell] imagines the majestic Titian being shown examples of the *New* Painting, and listening, respectful but puzzled, to an able exposition of the principles guiding it, and finally exclaiming, with his hand pressed to his brow, 'But the *looks* of it, man! The *looks* of it!' "

Now I think you will agree that the century-old pictures of Cornelius Krieghoff, to name but one of the many early Canadian artists represented here, are certainly not unpleasing to the eye viewed simply as *pictures* and not exclusively as *historical records*. When young Krieghoff wandered into Canada (to visit his brother here in Toronto) after I know not what adventures in Europe and the U.S.A., he would doubtless have smiled at any suggestion that generations later his pictures would be a centre of interest, curiosity and admiration in the Art Gallery of Toronto—the very city in which he, himself, opened a humble studio. As a matter of fact, I believe at that time he thought more highly of himself as a musician than as an artist. Music, at least, did for a long time what his art, at first, failed to do. It brought him his bread and butter, and often, no doubt, a night's lodging. And that was a most important consideration for an itinerant musician, a born wanderer, and a struggling artist like Cornelius. Quite naturally, I suspect too that he was anxious to take full advantage of the prolonged absence from Canada of all those abundant musical facilities and more occasional and fugitive felicities to which the radio has already habituated us.

But to speak for a moment of Krieghoff in his more important aspect as a painter-historian I can mention, from personal recollection, "The Dead Stag" which—or should I say the picture of which?—used to hang in this very gallery, illustrating hunting. And hunting, it should be remembered, was to our forefathers a necessity, not a sport. By hunting they lived.

I can recall, too, a picture in the Galleries of the late Mr. Thomas Jenkins entitled "Early Trading with the Indians". That picture graphically records the beginnings of commerce in this country.

And, thirdly, there is "The Habitant Farm" in the National Gallery of Ottawa in which, more clearly than in any verbal description, is delineated the type of home and home life of the early settlers in Quebec, and, with minor differences, here in Ontario also.

You will now have an opportunity to see a great many other pictures by Cornelius Krieghoff—I believe some seventy in all—portraying varied features of the life of early Canadians, but I would like you to notice that in the three pictures I have mentioned you have Canada's past—made visible for us now—a century later. In these three pictures alone you have life in Canada—hunting, commerce and home life—

a hundred years ago. How little indeed would we know and how difficult it would be for us to visualize our forerunners, to see them as they and all the men and women of that day lived, were it not for these men—amateurs, many of them—whose records of Canada's infancy adorn these walls.

What I have said will, I hope, make us aware of the very considerable debt we owe to these early Canadian artists; to Cornelius Krieghoff, of whom I have already spoken and whose pictures form a separate part of this exhibition; to Mr. Howard, the architect, to whose bounty this city is already indebted for Howard Park (High Park) and who, it is interesting to recall, taught drawing to the boys at Upper Canada College—the college founded by Sir John Colborne (afterwards Lord Seaton), Lieutenant-Governor of this Province one hundred years ago; to Paul Kane, who taught drawing to young ladies of this city—a delightful occupation, I imagine; to Mr. Young, who, like Mr. Howard, was one of our earliest architects; and to all those who a century ago and with all the skill they possessed, portrayed their day and age.

In addition to the water-colours, oil paintings and prints that combine to tell us so much not only of Toronto but of Canada in 1834 and even earlier, I have but to mention the period furniture, the silver ornaments, curios and other objects of interest here gathered together, to show with what care and with what painstaking zeal this Exhibition has been made complete and informative as history, and worthy as a memorial of the past.

I have, I hope, adequately expressed our sense of the indebtedness of this, our generation, to these artists for their historically invaluable pictures of days that will never return. I wish, too, in the name of the Province of Ontario and on behalf of the citizens of this city to thank all those responsible for this Exhibition; the Directors of the Art Gallery; the citizens who have lent their mementoes of the past, without which so fitting a celebration of Toronto's Centennial would never have been possible; the donor of the Collection of

European Paintings, whose generosity is enhanced by his or her anonymity; Miss Burgoyne, who has been good enough to contribute her exquisite miniatures direct from the Baltimore Museum of Art—to this Exhibition's great gain and our added enjoyment; the Royal Ontario Conservancy and the Toronto Camera Club for the prints which are now displayed in the Print Room, so clearly showing the homes in which bygone generations lived; and to all who individually and in co-operation have so worthily and successfully sought to celebrate the foundation of this great city of Toronto.

It is with the greatest pleasure that I declare this Exhibition open.

THE LITERARY PRACTICES OF SOME MEDICAL PRACTITIONERS

Before the Medical Society of the University of Toronto, January 17, 1934

Mr. President and Fellow Students:

It is related that George Gissing, the novelist, being homeless and penniless on the streets of London, used to find shelter in the warmth and comparative security of the washroom of the British Museum. One day, however, yet another misfortune overtook the poor novelist. To his intense embarrassment a hard-hearted and very angry trustee of the Museum surprised him in the washroom when he was in the very act of using the washstand for bath-tub and laundry. And now in that washroom there is this sign, "These basins are for casual ablutions only."

Now, if only for the sake of public hygiene the proper use of a wash-basin—and more especially a public wash-basin—can be clearly defined if only for the guidance of erring novelists and such others as may be driven by necessity to ignore convention. But I feel that no such limitations can be set to the topics considered fit and proper for discussion before medical students. I cannot imagine any group of subjects over which may be placed the legend, "These subjects are for medical students only."

I propose to speak to you, therefore, not as a specialist discussing a special subject, but rather as one who has engaged in most of the multifarious activities inseparable from a busy life in the profession you are now entering. I intend to be discursive rather than particular, while for a short time diverting your attention away from the daily studies imposed upon you by an over-indulgent Faculty, and direct your attention to the Profession of Medicine itself.

And now that you know that for a time at least you are to be delivered from the necessity of listening to a dissertation on some academic subject, I can imagine someone remarking, as Francisco, the soldier, remarked in the opening scene of *Hamlet*, "For this relief, much thanks."

To say of anyone that he is in a profession implies, of course, that he professes something. And if the profession happens to be that of medicine, then we assume quite rightly that a member of that profession knows a great deal more than the average person about medicine and about all those beneficent agencies of health and healing which we instinctively associate with physicians and surgeons.

These assumptions are, of course, correct. But what I wish to point out is, that if you are content to think of a physician simply as a person who has studied medicine, and of a surgeon as one who has practised surgery, then you have a narrow, utilitarian and altogether unworthy estimation of the profession you propose following.

For the Profession of Medicine is not a trade nor is it a business. It is an art which demands not merely knowledge but understanding. It calls for the exercise of sympathy and discretion and that wisdom which enables one to interpret the hearts and minds of men. In the words of Sir James Paget, the Profession of Medicine "offers the most complete and constant union of those three qualities which have the greatest charm for pure and active minds—novelty, utility and charity."

I am aware, of course, that as medical students you see before you examinations which loom like dark portents of troubles to come. It is inevitable, therefore, that you should be led to concentrate upon immediate aims, upon those studies which will enable you in due course to qualify as members of the great Profession of Medicine. But I am anxious that even as students you should cultivate the larger view of your profession—that broad outlook which distinguishes the comprehensive mind. And it is chiefly because of a marked tendency of the day to specialize more and more upon less and less that I hope my few remarks will warn you of the very real danger of a narrowing down of your interests.   For that inevitably leads to a small-mindedness in which prejudice has usurped the place of that wisdom which it will be your duty to cultivate assiduously throughout your life of service to your fellow-men.   The Profession of Medicine is more than a profession.   It is nothing less than a way of life—a broad way of life—a way of life that is second to none when engaged in to the full extent of your powers.

Kipling once exclaimed—"What does he know of England who only England knows?"   And that question strikes at the very roots of ignorance—the very type of ignorance which it is the purpose of all true education to overcome. I might as pertinently ask you what does the physician know of medicine who only knows the component parts of the medicines he prescribes?   Or what does he know of Canada who only Canada knows?

And it might be well to state at this point that the commonest expression of this narrowness of outlook is found in a petty nationalism.   Ignorance is nowhere more manifest than in the bombastic pratings of a parochialism which preens itself on nothing more substantial than its geographical position.

Now, since I have already spoken of the Profession of Medicine as something which is *more* than a profession, I might well describe the men I shall mention as *more* than doctors.   And by that I mean simply that they regarded their profession as something more than a humdrum matter of routine.   They found in it opportunities for that self-development which is true culture.   While conscientiously engaged in their profession and delighting in its practice, they yet contrived to enrich their minds with other than medical knowledge, thus making themselves true citizens of the world.   It is as if they seized and made their own the intellectual spoils snatched by a hungry mind from books during brief intervals of study in the normal busy life of a physician.

In the year 1671, King Charles II visited the city of Norwich in the County of Norfolk.   There he conferred knighthood on a bashful, unobtrusive little doctor who was so very modest that, to quote a gentleman who knew him, "His modesty was visible in a natural habitual *blush* which was increased upon the least occasion and oft discovered without any observable cause."

I must leave it to you to picture the so visible embarrassment of Dr. Thomas Browne on the day that he became Sir Thomas Browne. You may well smile—even as, doubtless, his friends smiled—though affectionately—at thought of the deepening hues of colour blazing pitilessly on the face of this old scholar as he bowed beneath the sword of his King.

And yet this same shy Sir Thomas Browne, the author of the *Religio Medici*, is as certain of an immortality of fame as any of his seventeenth century contemporaries. Coleridge, the poet, describes him as "a fine mixture of humourist, genius and pedant". But he was even more than that. To this day, indeed, the astonishing erudition displayed in his book, the inimitable dignity and polish of its style, its majestic thunderings, its subtleties of phrasing, its wit, its vigour and the variousness of its beauty combine to hold in perpetual homage to Sir Thomas Browne scholars, students and readers of every age and clime.

Modest Doctor Browne, living in Norwich, industriously occupied with an extensive practice and the education of his children, yet contrived to write that great book, the *Religio Medici*.

Now Sir Thomas Browne is but one of those doctors who were more than doctors because they sent their minds far afield on journeys of exploration into every part of the Kingdom of Knowledge. With what they found there they made books—monuments to their enduring fame. But the range of Sir Thomas Browne's knowledge is so astounding, his wisdom so deep and unaffected, that he best exemplifies, even as he transcends all the others.

You must not be led to think, however, that men like Sir Thomas have long ceased to exist. The greatest possession of any University is its great names, and just as Sir Thomas brought undying honour to the city of Norwich, so Sir William

Osler conferred on this city and this University a claim to distinction and high regard in every part of the world.

I recall hearing Sir William Osler speaking of the necessity of a broad, comprehensive culture. He recommended to students what he termed "bedside books", and said: "Well-filled though the day be with appointed tasks, to make the best possible use of your *one* or of your *ten* talents, rest not satisfied with this professional training but try to get the education, if not of a scholar, at least of a gentleman." And among the books he named were none other than the *Religio Medici* of Sir Thomas Browne and the *Breakfast Table Series* by Dr. Oliver Wendell Holmes, of whom I shall have more to say later.

You know, of course, that Sir William Osler graduated from the Toronto School of Medicine, then went to McGill University, later became a professor at Johns Hopkins University, and was subsequently elected to a much coveted position—that of Regius Professor of Medicine at the University of Oxford. He is probably our most widely known graduate—known wherever medicine is practised.

Whenever I think of Sir William Osler I recall the tragic circumstances of the death of his only son in France in August, 1917. He died from wounds in a casualty clearing station near Poperinghe, only a few miles from the clearing station in which I was myself on duty. A few hundred yards from me Dr. Harvey Cushing served in yet another casualty clearing station, and when the mortally wounded boy was carried into a casualty clearing station some miles away, Dr. Finney of Baltimore, Dr. Wm. Darrach of New York and Dr. Crile of Cleveland—all of them famous American surgeons—were there to do all they could to save his life. I recall, too, the comfort and satisfaction which Sir William felt at the knowledge that these men were at hand to help his son. We are happy to possess a copy at the Academy of Medicine of the excellent portrait of Sir William Osler painted by Orpen—the original of which now hangs in Johns Hopkins University.

Let me now tell you of two doctor-authors well known to you. Then I will attempt to show you as clearly as I can why the qualities which a doctor should possess—the qualities of acute observation and accurate deduction—are but the tools of an active intelligence—tools which can operate in every field of human activity and should not be confined within the narrow compass of any one profession or any one field of knowledge to the exclusion of all others.

I want to refer for a moment to a gentleman whose name is familiar to every one of you. You probably know more about his habits and characteristics than you do about those of any but your most intimate friends. He is a man who couldn't venture into the streets of any city in the world in his customary garb without gathering huge crowds about him; his name is known wherever the English language is spoken. Letters continue to be sent to his private address. And yet this man never existed—he was brought to life and created by a young doctor.

Toward the end of the last century Dr. Joseph Bell, F.R.C.S. (Edin.), was a university teacher with uncanny ability as a diagnostician. Dr. Bell was a thin man, wiry and dark. He had a sharp face adorned with a high Roman nose and keen grey eyes, and he walked in a peculiar manner. He had as his out-patient clerk an observant young medical student named Doyle. With youthful awe Doyle used to watch Dr. Bell diagnosing patients the moment they entered the room. He appeared to know all about them *before they even opened their mouths*. This is the sort of thing that Doyle used to observe happen frequently. A civilian patient one day entered the room. Dr. Bell glanced at him. "Well, my man," he observed, "You've served in the army."

"Aye, Sir."

"Not long discharged?"

"No, Sir."

"A Highland Regiment?"

"Aye, Sir."

"Stationed at Barbados?"

"Aye, Sir."

"You see, gentlemen," the doctor explained to his surprised students, "the man was a respectful man but did not remove his hat. They do not in the army. If he had been long discharged he would have learned civilian ways. He is obviously Scottish. As to Barbados, his complaint is 'elephantiasis', which is West Indian and not British."

Is it necessary to tell you that the young medical student's full name was Arthur Conan Doyle—later Sir Arthur Conan Doyle, who, out of his memories of Dr. Joseph Bell, created Sherlock Holmes? Isn't the very description of Dr. Bell—thin, wiry, dark, with a face not unlike that of a Red Indian—the description, too, of the detective of Baker Street, London, England? Here was a man, a famous detective who never existed! Yet he was so very much alive that when Conan Doyle, being no longer in need of cash, killed him by dropping him with his arch-enemy, Moriarty, into a crevass at Reichenbach in the Tyrolean Alps, the shock was too great for the reading public. The catastrophe caused such universal sorrow that Doyle had to bring the detective to life again and start him on new adventures, solving new problems of crime. And the gratitude of the people was so great that Arthur Conan Doyle was knighted—for the resurrection of Sherlock Holmes.

And in the very name of Sherlock Holmes, by the way, there is an interesting link with yet another doctor—a link that spans the Atlantic Ocean. Conan Doyle was a great admirer of Dr. Oliver Wendell Holmes of Boston, Mass., and in the name of the creature of his brain one doctor has conferred yet another type of fame on a doctor already famous. In Sherlock Holmes the name of Dr. Holmes is commemorated by Dr. Conan Doyle.

Oliver Wendell Holmes died in 1894 at the age of eighty-five, and to typify the type of mind which, while centring upon its profession as its main activity and interest, yet finds time and opportunity to encompass vast tracts of learning in its orbit, the author of *The Autocrat at the Breakfast Table* and *The Professor at the Breakfast Table* serves my purpose excellently. Whittier, the poet, said of Dr. Holmes that "his varied qualities would suffice for the mental furnishing of half a dozen literary specialists—he is a Montaigne and Bacon under one hat."

Something of what I can only call the "multiplicity" of mind of old Sir Thomas Browne lived again in this witty, genial doctor of Boston. Perhaps you will regard his books as old-fashioned, though they are of the type which never goes out of fashion. In them he reveals his breadth and sanity of mind—those qualities that have endeared him to countless readers here and in the Old World. He reveals, too, that he was like Sir Thomas Browne in yet another characteristic. Just as old Sir Thomas loved Norwich, so Dr. Oliver Wendell Holmes loved Boston. His books brim over with his love for Boston and his affection for the antiquities and traditions of New England. It was Dr. Holmes, I believe, who first called tuberculosis "the white plague".

I do not intend, when I speak thus of doctors who have become famous as authors, to suggest that you should attempt to do likewise at the first opportunity. By no means. Indeed, I plead with you, above all, to be loyal to the profession of your choice and jealous of its honour. But I want to show you that the frequency with which doctors have deserted their first loves—the medicine bottle and the scalpel, and embraced a pen and a bottle of ink, is something more than a coincidence. And the fact that in so doing doctors have again and again won renown as authors is not as surprising as may at first appear.

Here, you will admit, is a state of affairs that merits examination. Obviously, there must be some reason for this link between medicine and literature, between the type of mind that gazes at humanity through the microscope and the X-ray; and that other type of mind, the literary mind which views humanity through the eyes of imagination and reveals what it discovers with a pen.

If, as Rudyard Kipling avers, "Judy O'Grady and the Colonel's lady are sisters under the skin", then there should also be some discoverable relationship—some affinity—between medicine and literature. Sir Thomas Browne is but one, and not even historically the first, of a long line of literary doctors whose work has from time to time enriched English and—if I must make a distinction—American literature. What is it that the doctor, the scholar, the author, and, indeed, all men of liberal parts have in common? I could answer in a single sentence by saying that they all have a consuming interest in life in *all* its manifestations. But that is not enough. I propose demonstrating to you not only what a broad-visioned profession it is that you have chosen, but also and by inference how intimately it is bound up with and is a part of the world of men and women whom it will be your privilege and duty to serve. I want you at the outset of your careers to realize that medicine is a humanitarian service rather than a doctrinaire science.

You may recollect that in introducing my topic this afternoon I spoke of the rather narrow limits within which convention or pedantry might seek to confine the range of subjects considered suitable for medical students. I stated that I, at all events, would not be restricted in my choice of a subject by any such artificial limitations. I am anxious to impress upon you the wisdom and, indeed, the necessity of this larger view of your profession. And the link I am establishing between literature and medicine is one which may be extended to include all the arts and sciences which legitimately come within the province of the student, whatever may be the particular avenue of enquiry along which he pursues his studies, and no matter what the particular subject he is studying. To know that subject is to possess knowledge, but to be able to correlate it with all other subjects is to possess wisdom.

But to return to our friends the literary doctors. While it is true that the life of a doctor, like that of a medical student, is bounded on one side by medical text-books, scientific and diagnostic apparatus, operating theatres and hospital wards, and all the paraphernalia of the physician and surgeon, yet on the other side it has no boundaries whatever. It extends over the whole life of humanity, touching it at every point, reaching to the heights and depths of human existence. And it is on this side that the writer and the doctor meet. It is here that literature and medicine and, indeed, all the liberal arts and sciences find themselves contemplating the same scenes—the scenes common to all life and to all humanity—scenes that reveal the heroisms of mankind and its follies, its majesty and its idealism and its depravity, its hopes, its perplexities, its fear of death and its joy in life. Pain and laughter, mirth and despair, all inextricably tangled, yet mysteriously woven into the curious, ever-changing, colourful pattern of life, the lights and shades of our mortal existence.

Now ask yourselves this question. Who so closely, so clearly and with such daily intimacy sees this life as a doctor? For literature and the science of medicine may be likened to two roads, along one of which you have chosen to make your way. These roads do not run parallel and they pass through different regions in the Kingdom of Knowledge. Yet they both lead straight into the homes of men and women, to their deepest thoughts and emotions and to all that concerns them most closely.

So much then for your profession in its true relation to the world about you. All that I have sought to show you is that you should never be content with what you know and never confine that knowledge wholly to one subject, excluding others. Go on learning. If you have mastered one subject, master another. Alexander Pope, the poet, says that "a little knowledge is a dangerous thing." But who is there who knows so much as to be out of danger? I do not, of course, suggest that you be like the man in *Alcibiades II*, to whom are applied the words of the poet:

> "Full many a thing he knew
> But knew them all badly."

But by giving you an enlarged and more comprehensive view of your profession I have sought to warn you of the danger of narrow-minded pedantry within the necessarily narrow confines of any profession, regarded in its limited and purely technical sense. Incessant concentration upon immediate aims, too often tends to get you into a rut, to smother your most vital energies with routine. To live wisely is to learn unceasingly. And on the day of your graduation it may be well to remember these words of Sir Thomas Browne: "It is the nimble and conceited heads that never looked a degree beyond their nests (in this case their profession and even their University) that plume themselves on light attainments, but heads of capacity and such as are not full of a handful or *easy* measure of knowledge think they know *nothing* till they know all." And that is, of course, *never*. No man ever knows all.

With all your natural affection, too, for your *alma mater* and the scenes of your youth, remember that knowledge has never yet been given a local habitation and a name. Wisdom is the monopoly of no one country, university or city. It is to be found everywhere.

And now I would like to say something about your profession as a profession, without any consideration of that broader culture which may be yours if you use medicine as the starting point for what I may term cultural attainments.

In the year 1918 I was sent on a mission to the United States with Sir James Mackenzie. And as an apt beginning to what I wish to say to you I cannot do better, perhaps, than quote to you this passage in Sir James Mackenzie's book, *The Future of Medicine*. "As years go by", he writes, "and as physicians become more expert in detecting auricular fibrillations of the heart and all its symptoms, it will be more and more recognized that its discovery forms a landmark in cardiac clinical pathology. I may be excused", he adds—and this is most important—"I may be excused if I insist upon the fact that all the essential details associated with this condition, its symptomatology, its relation to heart failure, its response to digitalis, were all discovered by the simple means available to a doctor in *general practice*." (He refers, of course, to his own discovery.)

"Moreover, and this is the point I wish to make, the recognition of this condition as a clinical entity and all it implies *could not have been made by investigation, however capable, if they had restricted themselves to laboratory and hospital ward*."

Now, very conveniently, the doctors I have spoken to you about divide themselves into three classes. I have spoken of doctors who, while practising their profession, acquired that breadth of culture which, for want of a better description, I described as making them *more* than doctors. Then I spoke of doctors, who, possessing the qualities which the true doctor should possess, yet found need to express themselves in writing to record their observations of humanity, and became writers—often leaving their profession of medicine. And now there is the third class, of which Sir James Mackenzie is a representative. They are the great doctors. Men who have brought honour to their chosen profession, and incalculable relief to ailing humanity. They are men who, by their labours, their persistence and their patience, have left a legacy of new discovery or successful experiment by which medical science has been empowered to battle more successfully against disease and push still further forward the frontiers of medical science. One and all they are men worthy of your emulation.

As if to bear out Sir James Mackenzie's contention that the observations of a general practitioner are of the greatest value, it is interesting to note that Sir James in his new hospital at St. Andrews relied, in his research into the earliest symptoms of diseases, chiefly upon general practitioners.

And the importance of this is that, just as it is necessary for you to direct your attention to the broader implications of your profession in its relation to life in general, so within the profession itself there is every need for a correction of that latter day tendency toward over-specialization.   There should always be a *broadening out* rather than a *narrowing down* of a physician's work, a more *general* practice of medicine rather than a limited *specialization* in a single branch of medicine.   In this way alone are students and physicians alike able to see the different branches of medicine in their proper perspective and be able to correlate them.   The dominant figure in the world of medicine is and will remain the physician—the general practitioner.   It is he who sees disease in all its phases.

Incidentally, in speaking of Sir James Mackenzie I should like to give you his view of the future of medicine.   "Medicine", he says, "has advanced so far that for the study of disease *after the patient has died*, we find institutions magnificently equipped, presided over by men of great experience and training.   For patients suffering from the advanced stages of disease we have great hospitals, with staffs of skilled physicians, surgeons and specialists.   If we seek to find out what are the facilities offered for the detection and cure of disease in the state when it has not yet damaged the tissues *we discover that there is little consideration given to this aspect of the matter*."

The story is told of a gentleman named Abernethy who, seeing a large class of medical students exclaimed, "Good God, gentlemen!   Whatever will become of you?"   And although many of you, no doubt, cherish the ambition of becoming specialists in one or another of the numerous branches of medicine, I can wish for none of you a fuller life or a more laudable career than that of a general practitioner, serving his fellow-men not in one way alone but in every way.   It is a life of responsibility, but it is a full life and almost alone calls for all those qualities of heart and mind which most fully reveal the man behind the physician.   It will lead to the greatest satisfactions and completest fulfilment to which you can look forward when the doors of this University close behind you for the last time and your life as a doctor begins.

But as I conclude, I do so with a very real sense of the importance of what I am about to say to you. I have spoken of great men. I have named men who have immortalized their names by their greatness of mind, their vision—men who have *brought* something to their profession rather than sought to *get* something from it. I have spoken of men of culture—medical men whose scholarly spirit lived again in such men as Irving H. Cameron, for many years Professor of Surgery in this University, who but recently passed away.

You may imagine the pleasure then with which I now speak of one who belongs to this University, who is a Nobel Prize winner and a benefactor of humanity; he has earned by his work an immortality of fame that is as assured as that of Pasteur or Lister, and yet he has the modesty of a Sir Thomas Browne, combined, however, with the capacity for investigation which distinguishes all great scientists—of course, I refer to Dr. Banting, the discoverer of Insulin.

The invaluable contribution to medical knowledge made by Dr. Banting in his discovery of Insulin eleven years ago and the tremendous importance of that discovery has been accentuated with the passing of years. The far-reaching effects of this great boon to mankind have more than realized the most sanguine expectations of those who recognized its possibilities when it was first discovered.

The promptness with which the Legislature of the Province of Ontario made a special grant for the establishment of a Department of Medical Research under the guidance of Dr. Banting was a just recognition of the value of his work, and received universal praise.

On a recent visit I was able to see these great laboratories staffed by eager workers from places as far distant as Victoria in the West and Halifax in the East, as well as from such intervening points as Brandon, McGill and Queen's.

The department has steadily grown and now has three divisions—Biochemistry, Pathology and Physiology—and is thus in a position to attack the major problems in Medical Research, as well as developing and guiding younger students who have a desire to investigate problems which are suggested by their medical studies.

I found that one of the major problems under investigation in this Department is that of silicosis. Silicosis, as you know, is an industrial disease caused by the inhalation of silica dust resulting in extensive fibrosis of the lungs. The investigation has been carried on in co-operation with the Ontario Mining Association and the Ontario Department of Public Health.

Dr. Irwin has studied the tissue changes in experimental animals in which the disease has been reproduced.

Dr. King has devised micro-chemical methods by which silica can be determined in small quantities of body fluids and tissues.

A photometric apparatus has been developed by which an estimation of the number of dust particles in the air could be rapidly made. This method will facilitate a survey of the dust conditions in mines or elsewhere.

Dr. Franks sought to prevent silicosis by cleaning the air of dangerous silica particles. This is done by drawing the dust through an electric field where the particles are precipitated. An apparatus embodying this principle is at present on trial in the McIntyre Mines, and, I understand, with satisfactory results.

Many other problems are under investigation, perhaps the most interesting of which are the growth of tumours and tumour cell metabolism which will undoubtedly advance our knowledge of this difficult problem, and which, combined with investigations going on elsewhere, will, we hope, within a reasonable period lead to the complete elucidation of this subject with benefit to countless sufferers.

I hope such work will be an inspiration to you, and that you will regard the men I have mentioned as exemplars of all that most befits the noblest of all professions.

Let me close with these words of Robert Louis Stevenson:

"There are men and classes of men," says Stevenson, "that stand above the common herd; the soldier, the sailor, and the shepherd not infrequently; the artist rarely; rarelier still, the clergyman; the physician almost as a rule. He is the flower (such as it is) of our civilization; and when that stage of man is done with, and only to be marvelled at in history, he will be thought to have shared as little as any in the defects of the period, and most notably exhibited the virtues of the race. *Generosity* he has, such as is possible to those who practise an art, never to those who drive a trade; *discretion*, tested by a hundred secrets; *tact*, tried in a thousand embarrassments; and what are more important, Herculean *cheerfulness* and *courage*. So that he brings air and cheer into the sick room, and often enough, though not so often as he wishes, brings healing."

THE THEORY AND PRACTICE OF EDUCATION

*At the Annual Open Meeting and Prize
Giving of the University of Toronto Schools
(Parents') Association in the School on
February 23, 1934*

Mr. Chairman, Ladies and Gentlemen:

To address an assembly which includes not a few specialists in the difficult art of public-speaking is to be guilty of something very like presumption. It is with due deference, therefore, to those members of the Students' Literary Society, who number among their cultural activities that of oration, that I venture to speak briefly to you.

Let me say at the outset that it is not my purpose, even though by a happier dispensation of Providence it lay within my power, to deliver what is customarily termed an oration. It is my hope that the informality of my remarks will allay all possible suspicion that I desire to engage in oratorical rivalry either with those public speakers of the Literary Society, for whose exclamatory and declamatory powers I have a very wholesome respect, or with those members of your Dramatic Club who are also public speakers in a somewhat different sense, and who recently presented Sheridan's famous play, *The Rivals*—rivals, I need not say, in a very different matter, although one in which even oratory is sometimes surprisingly effective.

I am not, however, without compensation for my lack in youth of the training in public speaking now enjoyed by a more fortunate generation. I have a certain advantage, for example, over the members of the Dramatic Club; for there is a nice distinction between the public speaker, as such, and the actor, who is also in at least one sense a public speaker;

for whereas the public speaker is free to say what he *wants* to say, the actor must only say what he is *told* to say—and, moreover, must learn it by heart. But even public speakers, I believe, have been known to learn their speeches by heart, and some of you may recall Samuel Rogers' famous epigram on Ward (afterwards Lord Dudley).

"Ward has no heart they say; but I deny it,
He *has* a heart, and gets his speeches by it."

Since I am speaking to representatives of two generations—the boys at school and those who have entered and perhaps have already spent many years in that larger, sterner school—the school of life—I might start with your School's motto—*Velut arbor ita ramus*—"As the tree is, so is the branch."

This motto contains a truth that is universal and immutable, and yet, perhaps for that very reason, unheeded. It is a truth as obvious as that two and two make four, and whether you are studying art or science, religion or philosophy, or simply learning the lessons life itself teaches, you will find that "as the tree is, so is the branch" is everywhere and at all times true.

And in education, particularly, is the truth of this old Latin proverb vividly, almost startlingly apparent. William Wordsworth stated the same truth in the form of a paradox when, in a little poem recording his sensations on seeing a rainbow, he let fall the remark, "The child is father of the man". What did he mean precisely? Perhaps for the benefit of the younger people here I should say that he was, in fact, stating your school proverb in another way. For just as a fine, healthy, well-tended tree will grow up and thrive, and spread great, strong umbrageous branches in its maturity, so a child educated and developed in mind and body will become a man who, by the power of his mind and the vigour of his body, will be the very flower of manhood. And here it would be appropriate to ask in horticultural or arboreal, perhaps, rather than educational terms,

"What sort of tree is the U.T.S.?" For then we shall know what to expect when the students of today branch out into the world of tomorrow. And the answer is one that I am delighted to give.

Since 1913 there has never been a year in which this School has not won an Open Scholarship at the University of Toronto —a record without parallel in the whole of Ontario. During these twenty-one years, U.T.S. candidates have won no less than seventy-six University Scholarships, not even counting College Scholarships. And last year for the third successive year the University Schools led all Ontario schools in the University of Toronto scholarship examinations, securing five University Scholarships and seven College Scholarships.

Velut arbor ita ramus—"As the tree is, so is the branch." Could there be a finer vindication of the manner in which this School has lived up to its motto than the splendid record I have just mentioned? I congratulate you most heartily upon it.

But it was reserved for your Headmaster, Mr. Althouse, to cap the already high pinnacle of your achievement by a most significant remark. And that remark, instead of qualifying the magnitude of your accomplishments, has immeasurably increased it. For, said Mr. Althouse, "this record of achievement would be quite meaningless if it were not backed by corresponding success on the part of the general run of U.T.S. candidates at the annual examinations. There, too, the percentage of success has been unusually high." Similarly, when referring to your sport and athletics and the triumphs of your first football team in the Inter-scholastic Championship of Ontario, he said, "As in the case of scholarships, the proficiency of the ordinary boy is a source of greater pride than the exploits of the few."

"As the tree is, so is the branch"—not one branch, not a few branches, but every branch. I need not, I think, stress the significance of so high an ideal and so admirable an understanding of the whole purpose and duty of true education.

I have not time to refer by name to all of your graduates,

but I should like to mention one whom this School, and I'm sure any school, would be pleased to regard as an ideal type: in scholarship a good average in all subjects, a good all-round sport, a good musician, whose high character and personality made Johnny Copp popular and beloved by his classmates and teachers.

I must also refer to another of your graduates whose untimely death a few days ago, a martyr to science, shocked the whole community, and particularly the medical profession, for Canada can ill afford the loss of such a brilliant scientific brain as that possessed by Dr. Jack Hendry.

No reference to the fine record of the U.T.S. can be made without bringing to mind the names of the late Professor H. J. Crawford, your founder and first Headmaster, and Dr. Thomas Marshall Porter. Their personalities have helped to establish the reputation this School has for so long enjoyed. I should like to quote from an appreciation by J.O.C. in your Xmas "Twig":

"To Professor H. J. Crawford and T. M. Porter may be traced the immediate and continued success of the schools. Thomas Porter is a symbol of what the School represents. He had the unique power of inspiring devotion to himself, and through him to the things that are greater than he. He will always be the embodiment of what is clean and decent and active."

I am glad to say that under Mr. Althouse, your present Headmaster and teacher of Classics, this high educational standard of all-round excellence is being maintained.

And so the great work of education continues, its ideals steadfastly upheld by men with the devotion, the courage and the energy of those I have just mentioned. It is interesting to recall, too, that just as the city of Toronto this year celebrates its Centenary, so, too, it is almost exactly one hundred years since there occurred in England something which literally revolutionized all previous conceptions of education. Those students present who have a flair for history, and particularly for historical dates, will recall that in the year 1832 the Reform Bill was passed. Till then the churches, alone and unaided, had been responsible for education. But the State decided that education was properly one of its most important duties, and devoted $100,000 a year to education. In 1870, Mr. Forster's great Act was passed to provide State elementary schools.

Educational developments in Ontario began earlier than in England, for in 1807 Grammar Schools were established by the Legislature in eight districts of the Province. In 1822 (ten years before the Reform Bill in England) a Board of Education had already been established in Ontario.

The importance of education in modern times will be appreciated when it is known that more than a quarter of the population of Ontario are in schools of some kind today.

I mention these things because they illustrate how comparatively recently has education been regarded as what it is—the most important single thing in the world. After all, it is education which guides the evolution of the boy into the man—of whom, in Wordsworth's words, he is, in a very real sense, the father. And because evolution is so closely associated in people's minds with the Darwinian theory, I am reminded at this moment of a boy who at school had first heard this theory propounded, and had deduced his own conclusions. When he was home once again he asked his father, in the presence of his aged grandfather, whether the theory that we are descended from simian, tree-loving ancestors was true. But before his father could answer, he added, "Because, father, if it is *true* that we're descended from monkeys, then I really don't think Grandpa has descended very far."

I don't know whether the boy was unconsciously parodying your school motto by thinking that "as the ape *was*, so is the man." I can only hope that age had dulled the hearing of the grandfather.

But education as an active factor in the moulding of the mental and physical character of a boy is more than ever important in days like these. Some years ago the

Dramatic Club of this school produced *Julius Caesar*, and whose who have studied this play either as embryonic actors or for the less inspiring purposes of examinations, will recall that in Rome, too, there were days of unrest, uncertainty and turmoil. You will recall that, seeing all those portents of storms to come, Casca—one of the conspirators—mentions them to Cicero. And Cicero's reply is so true that I want to quote it to you.

> "Indeed," says Cicero, "it is a strange-disposèd time:
> But men may construe things after their fashion
> Clean from the purpose of the things themselves."

In other words, in the presence of seemingly unaccountable disturbances, surrounded by fears and doubts, encompassed about by dark clouds that presage storms and even annihilation, prophecy appears to have become the fashion, and every shade of opinion clamours to be heard. But it is only the wise who should be listened to, and wisdom is the full-fruits of education. And it should be remembered, too, that however abstract wisdom may appear to be as an ideal, yet in its practical workings it is very concrete and real. For as Dr. W. Langdon Brown, Regius Professor of Physics of Cambridge, recently remarked, "The last word of evolution is this; the race is not to the swift nor to the strong, but to the wise."

I want to touch briefly on one other point. While education has cultural aims, it also has very prosaic, practical aims. It has been said—I believe, of some types of education in England—that while it teaches a boy how most fruitfully to occupy his leisure, it does nothing to show him how to obtain that leisure. In other words, it teaches him how to live but not how to make a living. There have been, doubtless, many gifted students who have had reason to bewail the fact that while their academic training left nothing to be desired, their training for the practical business of earning a living was totally neglected during their days at school. So that on leaving it they were thrown bodily, as it were, into the tempestuous stream of life without first being taught how to swim.

Now, that type of education isn't fair to any boy, and is positively inimical to his best interests. And while I believe in a good all-round education, I feel that educators should be constantly on guard that cultural education should not prejudice the practical aims of schools by monopolising *all* a student's school hours. Curricula should be so formulated that a boy with a marked and natural bent should have every opportunity to develop that talent and to study in greater detail the subject of his interest, even if by that he has to curtail the time spent on what used to be termed "general form subjects".

For example, a boy embarking on a commercial career should not be deprived of all opportunity of learning something of the workings of commerce until he leaves school. Vocational subjects should always be an important and not merely a subsidiary part of every school curriculum. I am aware that in touching upon this matter I have broached a subject about which there has always been a great deal of debate. But in fairness to boys leaving school, and face to face with the arduous duty of making a way for themselves in a competitive world, I am only too glad to say something on behalf of students who too often are shielded from the realities of the occupation they intend to take up, until the day when the school door closes behind them for the last time.

Finally, in order that I may not be thought to be laying an undue—although I consider it an overdue and most timely emphasis upon the practical aims of education—let me conclude with the words of Rudyard Kipling, spoken before an academic body some twenty years ago. You will find in them that idealism which should be the most potent impulse in all education. I would like you to notice also that he speaks of the *left* hand as the one to be used for the prosaic business of earning one's living. And in saying a few words on behalf of this left hand I have sought merely to strengthen it, in order that the cultural and practical aims of education in this province may be more justly balanced. Kipling says:

> "If you have to earn your living, earn it with your left hand, and keep your right hand free for your proper business in life. If you become immersed in the task of acquiring wealth, some day you will meet a man who is indifferent to worldly gain, and if you enter the contest with him, you will discover that his little finger is thicker than your loins."

Velut arbor ita ramus—"As the tree is, so is the branch"—and the fruit of wisdom is *power*.

LOOKING FORWARD

*Proposing the Health of the City of Toronto
at a Luncheon at the King Edward Hotel
on the Occasion of the Centennial Celebrations on March 6, 1934*

Mr. Chairman, Prime Ministers, Mr. Mayor, Mr. King, Dr.
McQuibban, and Gentlemen:

It is a pleasure to be here with the distinguished men who
have done so much for Canada, for Ontario and for Toronto.
It is also a matter of gratification to find such a degree of
unanimity in the eloquent toasts and responses. It was not
always so. The city's very first mayor—whose only grandson
is with us—knew the bitterness of political controversy. He
was not only the first mayor of Toronto, he was the first—
and up to this moment, Mr. Mayor Stewart—the only
mayor of Toronto to be publicly burned in effigy. Perhaps the
days of such heated denunciation are forever past, although
some maintain that the blazing bonfire of that day has given
place only to the scorching "leaders" of the editorial page.

History tells us that the first mayor of Toronto, Mr. Wm.
Lyon MacKenzie, did not enjoy such friendly relations with
Government House as have his successors. Sir John Col-
borne, then Lieutenant-Governor, once made rather elaborate
preparations to receive him should he call at Government
House. He mounted artillery on the roof of Government
House, and gunners with lighted matches stood by ready
to receive the future first mayor and his supporters. I have
noted that, architecturally, the present Government House
is not suitable for that kind of hospitality, and I assure you
I shall not follow this precedent, at least during Centennial
Year.

Now I am to propose a toast—a toast to the health of
Toronto. The health of Toronto must necessarily mean the

health of its citizens. It must mean, too, the continued progress and development of Toronto along desirable lines. We have a great and beautiful city that has been blessed by honest and efficient government. It is a city enviably situated, a city of fine residential areas, of beautiful buildings, of high standards of citizenship. That is how we see it, but I fear, in all candour one must confess that this city, in common with every large city has acquired the inevitable "slum districts".

These areas of misery and degradation exert an unhappy environmental influence upon many of our citizens. You will probably say: "But Toronto has few such areas and they are not of great extent." I say, and I think you will agree with me, that Toronto wants none of them, and that the Toronto of the future which we like to contemplate *will* have none of them.

It seems to me that the only availing remedy in Toronto is a planned decentralization which will take the outmoded factory away from our congested central areas and substitute for it in the outskirts a new modern building. That would permit workers to establish their homes convenient to their work in surroundings where their children would learn by experience that grass is a green, living and loving carpet, and that there are really and truly other and lovelier flowers than those on the lithographed calendar that hangs on the cracked, crumbling and soiled wall of a murky room into which the sun's rays have never penetrated. It seems to me, also, that as we evacuate those factories and hovels, we must raze them and bury the distressing memory of them in fine central parks and recreational centres. These parks and recreational centres would be devoted to the physical and mental improvement of our people—they would be community centres for ennobling uses of leisure, which today hangs heavy on the hands of thousands of our citizens, both employed and unemployed.

We do not have to look far for evidence of how normal men and women hunger for recreational opportunities. Mrs.

Bruce and I have been pleased to extend our patronage to the Central Ontario Region of the Dominion Drama Festival, whose play-offs take place at Hart House in the near future. One of the competing plays—and I asked that it should be performed on the night we will be present—is being produced by a group of some forty unemployed who are known as the "Miracle Players". There are many other instances to illustrate how eagerly people welcome an opportunity to make constructive use of their leisure.

Time restrains me from expounding my ideas in detail, and there is no need that I should do so. I see here men who have been giving thought to these things—and we have evidence from time to time that our municipal government has given much consideration to city planning. The planning I have in mind is similar to that to which the Prince of Wales has given leadership. In an address on January 27th last, His Royal Highness said:

> "We must not be content until we have good clubs everywhere, so equipped that those who need them can find opportunities for friendship, occupation, and recreation, where the day can be spent with advantage after working hours. Let self-help go hand in hand with mutual service. Let the State do its utmost by political and economic devices, but there is no remedy which will ever replace, or make obsolete, the way of fellowship."

We are celebrating our city's centenary. Would it not be a splendid thing to commemorate this, our hundredth civic year, by the creation of a large and noble plan conceived in a spirit of fellowship? A plan that would mould this city more nearly to our heart's desire, a plan that would recognize the inalienable right of every man and woman and child to decent and dignified and healthful environment.

Gentlemen, I give you the health of the City of Toronto; Toronto of today, of which we are proud; Toronto of tomorrow, of which our children may be prouder still; and Toronto of the centuries to come, whose citizens, I hope, will have in their hearts a feeling of gratitude because we planned nobly, wisely and unselfishly.

THE CONTRIBUTIONS OF YOUTH

Before a Group of Members of the Central Y.M.C.A., Toronto, March 9, 1934

Mr. Chairman and Gentlemen:

More than a century ago—to be precise, on April 10, 1818—a young man in the town of Teignmouth, Devonshire, sat down to write a preface. He had just completed a long poem and doubtless thought, as many have thought before and since, that a preface would be helpful. And then something happened which I consider quite extraordinary. In that brief preface we are suddenly presented with the spectacle of a young man actually apologizing for being young. The fact that this particular young man had genius makes such an apology all the more extraordinary. The young man was 23-year-old John Keats. The poem was *Endymion*. And since it is inevitable one day, if it hasn't already happened to you, that you will hear somebody remark that "A thing of beauty is a joy forever", it may be well to remind you that that is the very first line of the poem young Keats had just written.

Before I quote a few words from that preface, however, I should tell you that not by any means all those who speak of beauty as a joy forever know that they are quoting young Keats. They may even be as unaware of the author of *Endymion* as the delightful young co-ed who, reading on a notice board that her professor was going to lecture that day on "Keats", waylaid the learned man on the campus and pouncing upon him, exclaimed, "Oh, Professor, I see you're going to lecture today on Keats. How thrilling! But tell me, *what are Keats?*"

But to return to the preface; this is what Keats wrote by way of apology for his youth: "The imagination of a boy",

173

he says, "is healthy, and the mature imagination of a man is healthy; but there is a span of life between, in which the soul is in a ferment, the character undecided, the way of life uncertain, the ambition thick-sighted; thence proceeds mawkishness and . . . a thousand bitters."

You see, there is nothing half-hearted in Keats' discontent with being so young. And as I cannot understand why he should have felt so depressed about it, I can only assume that he had perhaps exhausted his energy in writing that poem and had what is called "an attack of the blues".

Now the whole purpose of what I have to say to you concerning the "Contributions of Youth" is to show you how tremendous has been the debt of the world to young men who have contributed throughout the centuries to the progress of the world. I never hear young people disparaged, for no other reason than that they are young, but I feel a desire to come forward in their defence. Youth throughout the centuries has accomplished great things. And I know of no more heartening and certainly no more appropriate message that I can bring to a gathering of young men than this necessarily brief story of the deeds of young men. For I cannot insist too frequently that Keats was wrong. There never has been a time when it was necessary for youth to apologize for its lack of years. Out of the very turmoil of doubt and uncertainty, of vague aspirations and restless emotions of which Keats speaks, there have grown some of the most splendid products of human genius. It is not always true that the greyer the head is, the greater will be the wisdom contained in that head. The value of experience is always proportionate to the individual's capacity to learn by that experience. There are, unfortunately, those who never learn. Now, in the course of these remarks I shall, of course, speak almost exclusively of young men of genius. And that is as it should be. Genius is always in a minority. The creative ideas destined to change the world have always been the possession of the few.

Some years ago a study was made of 400 outstanding men

to determine at what age they gave convincing signs that their minds were developing swiftly and to a quite unusual degree. Every type of human activity was investigated. And, as young men, I know you will be interested when I tell you as briefly as possible at what ages men of various interests and occupations first gave proof of what stuff they were made, first made themselves felt, and for the first time announced to the world that they were rather unusual young men. I want you to notice how young they were when they first showed their greatness.

It seems that musicians begin life very early—very early indeed. And the careers of many musical composers show that they begin their life-work at the average age of 17. Actors follow very closely at 18. Warriors, artists, divines and jurists average 22. Dramatists and playwrights follow at 23. Poets, physicians and surgeons, inventors, chemists and physicists at 24. Naturalists at 25. Explorers, novelists, essayists, historians, astronomers, mathematicians and statesmen began to develop their respective lines of thought at 26. Philosophers at 27. Reformers at 28. And, for some reason or other, humorists and satirists not until they were 32.

So you see that one is never too young to make a beginning. I give you these average statistics, first, because we are living in an age when statistics appear to be the fashion, and when any argument, not supported by pages of figures, in elaborate detail, is regarded as unscientific and therefore unsound; and second, because you will be better able to realize how very young these young men were.

But I should warn you that the popularity of statistics has yet another reason. Statistics can be made to prove almost anything, and juggling with figures is an amusing pastime. It is only fair, therefore, to point out to you that in giving this low average at which great men first showed their greatness, I do not mean to imply that their greatest work was done at such an early age. I shall return to this very important aspect of the question later.

However, when one comes to consider the precocity of

some musicians, one is filled with wonder. It is as if one comes into the presence of a baby who possesses a brilliant grown-up mind. To be precocious, of course, is not always a good sign. Many biologists, for example, consider precocity as a kind of premature senility—babies, as it were, grown old before their time. You may recall the old saying, "A wit at 5 is a fool at 20". And a young French poet named Relief de la Bretonne, who, at the age of 14, composed a poem on his first 12 loves, is an excellent example of degenerate precocity.

Let me tell you of some musicians whose genius, however, accompanied them all the days of their lives after a very precocious beginning. Mozart, for example. At 3, Mozart shared harpsichord lessons with his sister Maria who was 8. At 4, he played minuets and composed little pieces. At 5, he performed in public. At 8, he played before English Royalty, attempted the composition of a symphony, published his *third* set of sonatas and wrote "God is our Refuge" —an anthem for four voices. At 14, he wrote the music of the opera *Mitridate*. At 15, he wrote the serenata *Ascanio in Alba*. At 16, two operas that were brilliant successes. And at 19, he produced yet another great opera, *La Finta Giardiniera*.

I think you will agree that that was a very promising beginning for an ambitious young musician. There are, of course, others. Meyerbeer, for example, was an excellent pianist at 5, and when but 7 years old played Mozart's *Concerto in D Minor* in public, while the mature age of 13 finds him producing his second opera. Or consider Mendelssohn, who played in public at 9. At the great age of 11 years he wrote a cantata and produced nearly 60 pieces of music for at least four different musical instruments, and a little dramatic piece in 3 scenes. That was not a bad year's work at the age of 11! By the time he was 18, young Mendelssohn had produced I know not how many operas and symphonies, including his famous overture to Shakespeare's *Midsummer Night's Dream*. Handel and Liszt, Wagner,

Brahms and Meyerbeer were all precocious children and amazing young men.

But I wonder how many of you know that we have in our midst a young man to whom the description "amazing" applies with just as much force. Dr. Ernest MacMillan, Dean of the Faculty of Music, University of Toronto, began as a concert organist at the age of 10. At 13, he was Associate of the Royal College of Organists. At 17, became a Fellow; graduated the same year from the University of Oxford, as Bachelor of Music, and when the coming of war found him studying in Germany, he took advantage of his four years' imprisonment at Ruhleben to write a thesis for which he was awarded the degree of Doctor of Music of Oxford. Only a few days ago he was spoken of in New York as one of the greatest living orchestral leaders of international fame.

It is rather significant, by the way, that Beethoven, who is probably the greatest of them all, didn't compose anything of importance until he was over 25. So you see how unwise it would be to generalize about the development of genius. Indeed, the one conclusion you can safely make, as I tell you something of the "Contributions of Youth", is that every age of a man can be his best age, and that to dogmatize about such things is to be convicted of ignorance.

There is, of course, no other branch of human activity in which so many infant prodigies have appeared as in music. I don't know why this should be—why it is that at an age when the normal child is learning to walk, the musical genius has already learned to make music, very different, however, to the type of music which young children habitually make, and of which parents are, I am glad to say, very tolerant, if not precisely appreciative. And now, what about other young men in other lines of endeavour who have succeeded brilliantly while still young?

Most of you, when reading history must have been struck by the unusual number of young men who, choosing for themselves a life of action, rather, perhaps, than one of thought, have turned their attention to the murderous art of war. And in that art they were extraordinarily active

I speak of these young men of war only because in any historical survey of the part played by young men—such a survey as I am now making—it is impossible to ignore war which has again and again visited men and nations. It is my hope, however, that just as men may learn by experience so the world will yet learn the essential futility of all warfare and be guided by a wiser generation into the paths of peace and fruitfulness.

Now, as soon as I mention young men of war before an audience of young Canadians you will almost immediately and inevitably think of General Wolfe who captured Quebec at the age of 32. But there are many others. Alexander the Great, for example, who also died at the age of 32, defeated the Theban army at Charonea before he was 18, ascended the throne at 20 and had conquered the world at 25. So that, while still young, this singularly bellicose young man was sighing for new worlds to conquer. Similarly, our old friend, Julius Caesar, commanded a fleet before Mitylene, and distinguished himself before the age of 22, and before he was 40 finished his war in Spain and was made Consul. Napoleon Bonaparte was a major at 24, a General of Brigade at 25, and Commander-in-Chief of the army of Italy at 26. All his victories had been won and he himself had been overthrown at the Battle of Waterloo before he was 44. Lord Clive of India had distinguished himself at 22, was famous at 35, and by the time he was 40 had added India to the British Empire. Then there is Charlemagne, of France, who seemed to have a veritable passion for conquest. He was crowned King at 26, at 29 he made himself master of France and the greater part of Germany; when he was 32 he placed on his head the iron crown of Italy, and 4 years later, at the age of 36, he had achieved the conquest of Spain. Charlemagne evidently was a young man who was not easily satisfied. I might mention, too—since I have already spoken of Wolfe in this North American Continent—that in the South

American Continent also there were youthful conquerors. Pizarro, for example, completed his conquest of Peru at 35, and died at 40; while Cortez, who conquered Mexico, had altogether completed his military career and had put soldiering behind him at the age of 36.

I am telling you all this as briefly as possible, for the story of youth in every human activity is a long story. By directing your attention to these facts of history I think you will recognize, as perhaps you have never hitherto recognized, what an important part young men have played in the making of the world in which we live today.

You will recall that I began what I may call my "defence of youth" by quoting a portion of the preface of young John Keats' poem entitled *Endymion*. Keats, although he insisted to the last that his name "was writ in water", had achieved immortality and died in his 26th year. Curiously enough the poem *Endymion* is inscribed "to the memory of Thomas Chatterton", a young literary genius who died by his own hand of poison in the City of London when only 17, after carving for himself a niche in the temple of English literature. Almost every nation is indebted to young men for some of the most noteworthy contributions made to its literature, but no nation is richer in its young literary genius than England—and, I should add, Scotland. You have only to think of Byron, who died at 36, of Shelley, drowned in his 30th year, of Keats whom I have already mentioned, and of Bobbie Burns, dead at the age of 37—all of them living within the past 150 years—to see how much we all owe to our young men. I could, of course, multiply instances from as far back as the reign of Queen Elizabeth when young Christopher Marlowe, to whom Shakespeare was so indebted, was stabbed to death in a tavern at the age of 29, or more recently, young Rupert Brooke, some of whose poems you probably know by heart, and who died on active service during the War. They illustrate the magnificent contributions to the wealth of literature made by poets and writers of all description while they were still young men. And the only reason why I have not mentioned such writers as Charles Dickens—of whom you have been hearing so much recently—and who at the age of 25 gave to the world *The Pickwick Papers*—is because he was fortunately spared to attain a ripe maturity, whereas the young men of whom I have thus far been speaking, died while still in their first, splendid flower.

I do not propose, by the way, to tell you of young men in *every* line of thought and of work who have done great things; not only would it be unnecessary but impossible in the time at my disposal. For without mention of statesmen, who, like William Pitt, were Prime Ministers at 25, or of inventors like Alexander Graham Bell, who at 29 exhibited the first telephone, or philosophers or playwrights, or, indeed, of young geniuses of any other kind, I have, I feel sure, said enough to show you that there is never any reason for young men to bewail the fact that they are not old. Nature has, herself, of course, decreed a great and sufficient number of reasons why those no longer *guilty of youth* should deplore the deep vale of years which separates them from the halcyon days of their past and their prime.

I cannot leave this discussion of the "Contributions of Youth" without reference—a local reference which is inevitable in any consideration of such a subject—to the incalculable contributions to the health and well-being of not only this generation but all succeeding generations, by a young doctor who upon graduation served in the Great War, and on his return, with but the germs of an idea which was to prove so epoch-making, sought the opportunities which the University of Toronto laboratories afforded him. I am speaking, as you have already guessed, of Dr. Banting, the discoverer of Insulin, who was assisted in this work by a young medical student, now Dr. Best.

And now as a fitting climax to all I have said in praise of youth, and in acknowledgement of the world's indebtedness to its young men, let me tell you of something which happened at the beginning of this century, something which created a furore at the time, but something of which the majority of you, I imagine, can have no very clear recollection. What I shall tell you is all the more apt because it concerns one of the greatest of Canada's sons, and one whose name adds lustre to the name of the City of Toronto, now celebrating its 100th year. I speak of Sir William Osler.

In the year 1905, on February 22nd, which was also the anniversary of George Washington's birthday, Sir William Osler delivered an address at Johns Hopkins University before leaving for Oxford, where he became Regius Professor of Medicine. It was a sad occasion. All Osler's colleagues were loath to take leave of him, and Sir William had chosen for the subject of his valedictory address "The Fixed Period" —a title taken from Anthony Trollope's book by that name, which Sir William had recently read. By "The Fixed Period" he explained that he meant the period during which a teacher is at his best. And this is what he said. "I have two fixed ideas. The first is the comparative uselessness of men above 40 years of age." And he went on to give examples of medical men: "Vesalius, Harvey, Hunter, Bichat, Laennec, Virchow, Lister, Koch—the green years were yet upon their heads when their epoch-making studies were made."

"My second fixed idea", continued Sir William Osler, "is the uselessness of men over 60 years of age, and the incalculable benefit it would be in commercial, political and professional life if, as a matter of course, men stopped work at this age."

I needn't tell you, gentlemen, that something very like pandemonium broke loose after that speech. Did Sir William Osler really mean that men were too old at 40? Was he serious? The sensation-loving newspapers chose to believe he meant every word he said, and implied in their editorials and cartoons a great deal that he did *not* say. "Osler Recommends Chloroform at 60" was a favourite headline, and thousands of people, past life's meridian, sent in letters, abusive letters, threatening letters, letters of every kind, but none of them particularly complimentary. For at least two reasons, quite a storm of disapproval burst on Osler's luckless head.   The first is that he wasn't understood, and the second that the best time in any man's life is, he thinks, the age he happens to be at the moment, and he resents any and every suggestion that perhaps it isn't.   But, quite apart from the incurable vanity of mankind, did Osler mean in all sincerity that men are too old at 40 and should be asphyxiated or painlessly done away with at 60 or thereabouts?   Now, in the first place, I assure you that he didn't mean what the public thought he meant.   And, secondly, if he had been so far mistaken as to think for a moment that he was right, then the records of history from which I have drawn so many illustrations of youthful greatness, prove all too conclusively that he was wrong.

First of all, then, to show that Sir William Osler was perpetrating something in the nature of a joke, let me read to you his words in the preface to the second edition of his *Aequanimitas*, written two years later in Oxford.   "To this edition", he says, "I have added the three valedictory addresses delivered before leaving America.   One of these, 'The Fixed Period', demands a word of explanation.   To interpose a little ease, to relieve a situation of singular sadness in parting from my dear colleagues of the Johns Hopkins University I jokingly suggested for the relief of a senile professorate an extension of Anthony Trollope's plan mentioned in his novel, 'The Fixed Period'."

I won't quote you the rest of what he says because it isn't as complete an explanation of his views on the subject of age as I would like.   He was, shall we say, half joking and half in earnest.

And because thus far I have let youth have all its own way and have even quoted Osler's speech, which would seem to place extremely narrow limits to the period of a man's usefulness, I propose to turn the tables and to show you as briefly as I may that the "Contributions of Youth" are by no means the only contributions, although they have been magnificent, and that it needed but a knowledge of history to have refuted Osler's contention—had he been serious—that any arbitrary limit may be put to a man's time of greatness.

I have already told you of Osler's own age. He himself was 55 at the time when he made the speech, which seemingly condemned himself and others of his years. Osler, by the way, didn't publish his first book *until he was 40*. The speech was, incidentally, made on Washington's birthday. Now Washington was 43 when he was appointed Commander of the Continental Army, and 57 when he became President of the United States. You recall, too, that Osler mentioned Harvey and Lister and Koch among those whom he described as having "the green years yet upon them when their epoch-making studies were made." Yet the fact remains that, considering only these three of all those he mentioned, Harvey, who was born in 1578, published his great work on the circulation of the blood in 1628 when he was already 50. Lister was nearly 50 when he began to convert the world to the principles of antiseptic surgery, and while it is true that Koch was only 39 when he discovered the tubercle bacillus, it was after 1882 that his greatest work was done.

But even without a consideration of the men cited, rather erroneously, by Osler as men in their heyday at 40, and in their dotage at 41, you have only to call to mind any representative number of men known to you, to detect the inherent fallacy of believing that the period of greatest mental and creative activity is by necessity or by any inviolable law of nature, limited to the earliest years of a man's life. The contributions of age balance the contributions of youth, and it is only to preserve this sense of balance that I shall mention but a few who did great work after they were 40, 50, 60, 70, 80, 90 and, in one case at least, even 100.

Columbus, for example, was 46 when he discovered America. Shakespeare, Milton and Bacon and Thomas Cromwell, and a veritable host of others, did their greatest work after 40. But because I can't enumerate them all I am going to take examples not of men merely over 40, but men actually well over 60, the age at which Osler appeared to recommend some nice, quiet, painless way of putting an end to a man's activities.

What, for example, happened to all those musical prodigies whom I mentioned earlier? What happened to that young musical genius Meyerbeer, or to Handel, who, like him, was a prodigy? Well, when he was 74, Meyerbeer produced the greatest of all his operas, entitled *L'Africaine*, and as for Handel, at 72, when he had been blind for six years, he composed his oratorio, *The Triumph of Time and Truth*. Only eight days before he died, this same Handel played the organ at the performance of his *Messiah*. Verdi, also a great musician, was 74 when he produced his masterpiece, *Otella*, which was even better than anything he had ever composed. At 80 he wrote *Falstaff*, which was every bit as good as *Otella*. At 85 he wrote *Ave Maria*, *Laudi alla Virgine*, *Stabat Mater* and the *Te Deum*, which are extraordinarily beautiful and with which you are probably familiar.

And what, you may ask, happens to poets and writers when they are permitted to live longer than 60 years? Do all good poets and writers die young? By no means. William Wordsworth became the Poet Laureate of England at 73, and was over 80 when he died. Longfellow, whom you probably remember from your schooldays, was 75 when he wrote the beautiful *Bells of San Blas* and the meditation entitled *Hermes Trismogistus;* Victor Hugo at 75 wrote *History of a Crime*, and at 80 *Torquemada*. Dr. Oliver Wendell Holmes was 74 when he published his medical essays and *Pages from an Old Volume of Life*. At 75 this wise old doctor published *A Mortal Antipathy* and *The New Portfolio*. At 78 he wrote *One Hundred Days in Europe* and at 79 published *Over the Teacups*.

And so I could continue with the tale of literary men. Washington Irving, for example, wrote his *Life of Washington* when he was over 70; or I could tell you of Humboldt, who settled down at the age of 76 to begin the preparation of his great work, *Kosmos*, which he completed at 90.   I might mention, too, Tennyson, who at 83 wrote that perfect poem, *Crossing the Bar*, and Walter Savage Landor, who at 85 wrote his *Imaginary Conversations*, and at 87 published the last volume of his *Heroic Idylls*, and the poet Robert Browning, who was as vigorous as ever at 76.

There is, you see, no age at which a man may not undertake and succeed in carrying out great tasks. Think, for instance, of actors like Machlan, the Irish actor born in 1690, who performed in England in 1789, being then a mere 99 years old. Or of great artists like Titian who, when only 98, painted his "Battle of Leporto". Or consider Tintoretta, who at 74 painted the finest of all his pictures, "Paradise", on a canvas which was 74 feet by 30 feet in size. He must have been a proud boy when that painting was finished. For those of you interested in history rather than art I might mention, too, the historian Leopold von Ranke, who, at 73 or thereabouts, settled down to write a *History of the World* and at 90 years of age had completed a little matter of twelve volumes.

Now, it isn't of any great consequence into what branch of human activity you choose to peer, you will see there. men well over 60 still busy doing great work. Galileo, whom you will remember in another connection, made yet another telescopic discovery at 74—that of the diurnal and monthly librations of the moon. The philosopher, Kant, didn't really begin his greatest work until he was 70. At 74 he wrote his *Anthropology*, *The Strife of the Faculties*, and the *Metaphysics of Ethics*. Or if you are commercially minded, I could tell you of Commodore Vanderbilt, who, between the ages of 70 and 83, increased the mileage of his roads from 120 to 10,000 and added some 100,000,000 dollars to his fortune. In the worlds of politics and statesmanship I could remind you of Crispi, who at 75 became Premier of Italy, or of Allen G. Thurman, who at the same age was nominated for the Vice-Presidency of the United States; or of William Ewart Gladstone, who at 83 was Prime Minister of Britain for the fourth time, and of Lord Palmerston who was also Prime Minister at 81.   While for those of you who have a scientific bent I could name Chevreul, the great scientist, who discovered so much of world importance in the realm of colour and who was still busy, still keen and still active when death came at the age of 103.

It is important, by the way, that you should notice that the aged men I have mentioned were set apart from their fellows by their energy and their creative capacity.   They were valiant doers of deeds and not mere holders of offices. With them, to live was to create, to *do*.   And only in this way was their old age made fruitful and mankind enriched.

You musn't think, however, that this by any means exhausts the list.   But in naming men who (many of them well past the biblical term of threescore years and ten) have contributed greatly to the sum total of human achievement, I wish only to bring home to you the conviction that it is possible for all men at all ages to render service proportionate to their powers.

The men I have mentioned—both the young men and the old—were, it is true, outstanding men, men endowed by nature, perhaps, with more than their fair share of intelligence and creative energy.

It is, after all, impossible to indulge in airy generalizations about the most useful years of a man's life.   Both when telling you of young men and of old, I have been careful to give you facts and figures—not too many facts and not too many figures, I hope—for that would be burdensome.   I have done this intentionally and for a very good reason. For, although you should always feel while you are yet young that yours are indeed the golden years, that there are in you at this very moment vast potentialities for self-development, and that the story of youth's contribution to the world is a very splendid story—a story which I have told you only in the broadest outline—yet never forget that time and tide wait for no man.   The years pass ever swifter, and one day you will be old.   And just as I would not have you feel as poor young Keats so intensely felt, that youth is an insuperable obstacle to self-realization, so I would not have you believe that life—all too brief as it is—ends even earlier —as Osler was understood to have said.   Life and hope and achievement are inseparable.   Walter Pitkin has written a book entitled *Life Begins at Forty*, and it was Du Maurier who said, "I think that the best years in a man's life are after he is 40. A man at 40 has ceased to hunt the moon."   However, he went on to say, "That in order to enjoy life after 40, it is perhaps necessary to have achieved before reaching that age, at least some success."

Like Sir William Osler these men were, after all, but expressing an opinion.   Neither point of view is wholly right and neither is wholly wrong.   There is so much to be said for every year and decade of man's mortal existence.   The one fact to be grasped is that life can be made a full and rich and diversified experience from first to last.   If, as you grow old, you can exclaim with the enthusiasm of old Rabbi Ben Ezra :

"Grow old along with me, the best is yet to be,
    The last of life for which the first was made."

then you have nothing to fear.   For if life demands the exercise of any one quality, that quality is courage, which is, after all, only a very special kind of high confidence in one's self.

I am tempted to read to you portions of Sir James Barrie's inaugural speech as Rector of St. Andrews, when he said many notable things concerning courage, but faced as you are with the difficulties peculiar to such times as these, with the problems of life made, seemingly altogether and forever insoluble by the strange bewildering daily march of events as reported in our newspapers, and with prophets of doom and disaster seeking to rob even youth of that last consolation of looking forward to better days to come, I would rather conclude with the words of Walter Besant.   They are true words and I leave them with you.   I hope they will encourage you, just as the examples I have given you of great young men and great old men will make you feel that life is in its essence a tremendous undertaking, an almost incredible adventure among mysteries and realities, and, rightly lived, the greatest of victories.

These are the words of Walter Besant.   He is not speaking of geniuses as individuals but of the genius of the human race as a whole.   That is a special kind of genius and one that men too frequently overlook.

> "Prophets of disaster," says Besant—and I might add that in days like these their name is legion—"Prophets of disaster always omit one or two important elements in their calculations, and it is through these gaps that people basely wriggle, *instead of fulfilling the prophecy that the end has finally come.*
>
> "For all such prophets invariably lose sight of the recuperative power of man and the resiliency of his individuality.   He may be full of moral disease, yet such is his excellent constitution that he presently recovers, shakes off his evil habits as he shakes snow from his shoulders, and becomes an altered creature.
>
> "For the individual man is patient; he has strength to suffer and to endure until he can pull through the worst. Difficulties only call forth his ingenuity and his resources. Disaster stiffens his back, and danger finds him brave and still more brave."

What a wonderful creature is man!   Man when he is young and man when he is old!

BRITISH AVIATION

*Introducing Air Commodore Fellowes at a
Meeting of the Toronto Flying Club,
March 20, 1934*

Mr. Chairman, Ladies and Gentlemen:

I appreciate the opportunity which the Chairman has given me of introducing the speaker of this evening. The story of British achievements in the air is one of which we are all justly proud, and there is, at least, one sense in which Air Commodore Fellowes actually needs no introduction, for his fame as leader of the great Houston flying expedition preceded him here, so that although it has not been our pleasure to meet him in person until now, we feel we already know him.

On behalf of all those who are fortunate in being present this evening, and of all those thousands of citizens of the Province of Ontario, who, with us, take pride in the unbroken record of British triumphs in the field of aviation, I extend to Air Commodore Fellowes a most cordial and sincere welcome to the City of Toronto.

The whole science of aeronautics is so comparatively recent a development, and aviation is so essentially modern that there must be many present who can recall reading with youthful incredulity such prophetic works as those of Jules Verne, who staggered an unbelieving world with a novel entitled *Round the World in Eighty Days*. And already I can hear some young aviator asking "But how many times round?"

And since I know of no better way to illustrate the amazing rapidity with which aviation has developed (a fact which we, as contemporaries are apt too frequently to overlook) perhaps you will permit a personal reminiscence. In the summer of 1909 it fell to my lot to be present at the aviation meeting at Rheims in France, the first ever held anywhere, when after waiting for several hours for a slight breeze to subside, Latham succeeded in making a successful flight of seventy-five yards. On February 23rd of the same year a Canadian, J. A. D. McCurdy, made an epoch-making flight at Beddock, Nova Scotia. In the following year the first air meeting was held in Canada when Count DeLesseps flew in a Bleriot machine. In this same year (1910) the development of aviation was stimulated in Great Britain by the *Daily Mail's* offer of £10,000 for the first aviator to fly from London to Manchester, which prize was won by Paulham although gallantly contested by an Englishman, Graham-White.

And in all that has been done since, British aviators have been to the fore. It is unnecessary to remind you that it was Alcock and Brown who first spanned the Atlantic, and because, with you, I am eagerly awaiting the story to be unfolded tonight of the British conquest of Mount Everest, I shall do no more than mention the names of Amy Johnson or should I say, Mollison?—and her husband; of the Schneider Cup winners who flew at speeds that would make poor old Jules Verne turn in his grave; of Kingsford-Smith, who flew the Pacific and who, as an Australian, is linked to us by ties of Empire; and of that innumerable host of men and boys, and not by any means the least, the Canadian men and boys, headed by our own two V.C.'s, Barker and Bishop, who covered themselves with honour and glory in the dark days of the Great War.

And in all this, what one factor, more than any other, contributed to the success of British aviators? The answer is obvious. It was and is the high quality of their machines and the superiority of British aeronautical engineering, without which all the courage in the world is powerless to achieve.

*   *   *   *

And now, gentlemen, it is our honour and privilege to have with us one who has added immeasurably to those British accomplishments which are too numerous and too well known to you to need recapitulation.

I know of no one with a more distinguished record than
that of Air Commodore Fellowes. It was he who, during
the war, flying low over Zeebrugge—only fifty feet over the
German dock—succeeded in smashing the dock gates and so
bottled up and rendered impotent the fleet of German U-boats.
It was a sorely wounded prisoner of war who was fished out
of the North Sea after that most courageous action. But,
as Rudyard Kipling would say, "That is another story", and
is not to be told this evening. It was our guest, again, who
surveyed and mapped out the air route from Cairo to Baghdad
over the desert, and so helped to establish an aerial link which
has been used regularly ever since. And it was he who, as
Chief Executive Officer and as pilot on the second expedition,
as leader, mentor and guide, accomplished the crowning
achievement—in a very literal sense the summit of achievement—by subduing beneath the power of wings the highest
mountain in the world—Mount Everest—*almost five and
one-half miles in height!*

Of that achievement we are now to hear. And in listening
to his enthralling story I know that we, as Canadians, will see
unfolded to us not only a story of adventure and success in
the face of seemingly insuperable difficulties, but also new
vistas of opportunity for this great Dominion of ours. For
it is in no spirit of prophecy, but as a simple statement
of the obvious, that I say that in the development of aviation,
in the closer linking together by aeroplane of the far-flung
cities and provinces of Canada lies our future development.

While air transport between our populous centres was cur-
tailed because of the need to reduce expenditures, it is not
to be assumed that Canada is less air-minded than other
countries. The Flying Clubs are doing a useful work in
training private pilots and in keeping aviation in the forefront. In the northern areas the aeroplane is being used
today to a greater extent than ever, and a large part of the
work that has been done to develop our mineral resources
could not have been accomplished without the aid of the
'plane. The same thing applies to the protection of our

forestry resources and to very important mapping operations that are being carried out by aeroplane in remote areas. The Royal Canadian Air Force and the Department of Civil Aviation have earned the gratitude of progressive Canadians by their splendid services to aviation in this country.

The conquest of the air is at hand, and in the air—or even perhaps at breathtaking speeds in the stratosphere of which we have heard so much recently—lie the roads of the future. These are roads along which mankind will travel to new marvels of transportation of which we, still earthbound, can have but the faintest imaginings, to new methods of communication and commerce, and to those new conquests of time and space toward which men of the calibre, vision and courage of our distinguished guest are forever striving—for the great gain of all mankind.

And, locally, as a means to this end I confidently look forward to the day when the century-old city of Toronto will possess an airport, with all the facilities which the development of air travel and air transportation demands. The Minister of National Defence recently announced that trans-Canada mail and passenger service will probably be inaugurated in 1935. That, surely, would be a happy augury of the future of this city and this province, and a most auspicious beginning for Toronto's second hundred years.

It is with great pleasure that I call upon Air Commodore Fellowes to speak to you.

THE JOY OF CRAFTSMANSHIP

At the Opening of the Northern Vocational
School Exhibition, March 23, 1934

Mr. Chairman, Ladies and Gentlemen:

There is always something singularly impressive in an exhibition such as this and I consider it a great privilege to be present this evening to open the Northern Vocational School Exhibition.

I suppose at no time in the history of the world have exhibitions been so popular. And one of the reasons for this is, doubtless, that exhibitions have never, until comparatively recently, been so necessary a part of our artistic, our scientific, our commercial and our everyday life. But I wonder how many of you have noticed how rarely it happens at any exhibition that you find present not only the product but the producer, not only the thing that has been made but also the person who made it.

At an Art Exhibition, for example, you see the painting, but the painter is nowhere to be seen, and may indeed have passed from the sight of man many centuries ago, if he isn't in Paris or London or the South Sea Islands. At an engineering exhibition you may be fascinated by the intricacy of some piece of machinery, but you will look in vain for sight of the inventor or designer of that machine. And if you happen to be at a Commercial Exhibition of factory products, of course the possibility of your seeing the man responsible for any product will, I fear, be altogether and hopelessly complicated by the fact that probably no one man is responsible—but an army of men. But here at this exhibition are products and their producers gathered together and that makes an exhibition of this kind unique.

And here let me say that the students and the teachers of this school are already making a name for themselves as an

educational body of fine standing.   As one who watched this
building rise from the ground stone by stone I may be said
to have had early interest in the purposes to which such a
great structure would be devoted.   And now, some four years
later, I must tell you how gratified I am (and I speak in the
name of thousands of citizens not present) that the record of
your 2,400 day students and your 2,600 evening students—
your staff of seventy-six teachers and all those who in one way
or another carry on the great work being done here, is a record
of which you may be proud.   You have already achieved success
both in your work and in your sport.   And as an earnest of
what you will yet achieve this exhibition is significant.

I never see an exhibition of work well and truly done but
I am forcibly reminded that such an exhibition is, after all, a
microcosm of the whole world.   What is the world indeed, but
a colossal exhibition, the sum total of prodigious accumulations
of work done by mankind day by day, year by year, decade by
decade and century by century since time immemorial?   And
only in so far as that work is well and truly done has it
endured.   For even the slow-moving centuries haven't time for
rubbish.   That's why it is never allowed to accumulate but
is cleared away, wiped off the face of the earth sooner or later.

But perhaps I should leave for a moment such a very big
matter as the world and tell you of a certain Lady O'Looney.
It is much easier to speak of individuals; and, after all, the
world is only a collection—a rather odd assortment—of
individuals.   Now in speaking of Lady O'Looney I shall do
a rather unusual and seemingly paradoxical thing.   For it is
not customary, I believe, in opening an exhibition, to quote
an epitaph.   But I intend to read to you Lady O'Looney's
epitaph.   This is it:

"Here lies Lady O'Looney
Great-niece of Burke, commonly called 'The Sublime';
She was bland, passionate and deeply religious;
Also she painted in water-colours,
And sent several pictures to the Exhibition.
She was first cousin of Lady Jones,
And of such is the Kingdom of Heaven."

As an epitaph I can only call it stupendous. Lady O'Looney, obviously, was no ordinary person. But what I would like you to notice is that despite her awe-inspiring family connections, despite the prestige bestowed on her by her somewhat distant relationship with the great orator Thomas Burke, and by her being first cousin to none other than Lady Jones, yet the fact that she painted in water-colours and sent several pictures to the Exhibition seems to have weighed with her just as much as her social position. In all this, I am assuming, of course, that the character of Lady O'Looney is accurately described by the obscure genius who wrote her epitaph. I don't know, by the way, whether her pictures were accepted by the Exhibition when she sent them, but that is not important. What is important is that Lady O'Looney tried to do something, to create something, to make something, and that she appears to have found in the results of her own handiwork as great—or even greater—source of satisfaction than the favours she might have enjoyed by the happy accident of her birth.

She illustrates graphically the point which I wish to make, and which I hope will be an encouragement to all those present—to the students and to their parents who must, in their maternal and paternal hearts, be more than gratified that their sons and daughters have so splendid an opportunity to learn in this still young Vocational School how to do, to make, to create by the skill of their hands and the inventiveness of their minds.

For the purpose of education is not merely to teach you how to think, but how to do. Education never aims at turning out a student, who, in the pertinent words of Alexander Pope is

"A bookful blockhead ignorantly read
With loads of learned lumber in his head."

and who is quite unable to put his theoretical knowledge to any practical undertaking.

That doesn't mean, of course, that you should ignore books—which are the instruments of thought. And I know

that the members of your Dramatic Club, who recently produced Shakespeare's *Merchant of Venice*, will be quite horri-
fied by the ignorance of books shown by a young man who
invited his friend to have dinner with him. "I'm sorry I
can't come," said his friend. "But I'm going to see *Hamlet*
this evening." "Never mind," replied the young man,
"bring him along too."

That, you may say, is an extreme case of ignorance of
books.

But I want you to feel the pride which should be yours as
doers, makers, creators, of things of beauty, things of utility,
things which as the years pass and as you continue to produce,
will be added to that infinite number of little and big things
that make possible the rich, various life which is civilization.
There is no finer commendation than to be known as one who
can produce such things as are here exhibited. Thinking is
not enough, it is just as necessary to do. And you can always
lay to your hearts the words of Ralph Waldo Emerson, the
philosopher, who, in one of his essays, says "An action is the
perfection and publication of thought."

And now with no less than 40,000 vocational students in
this Province—all of whom are learning how to do as well
as to think; with 65 day vocational schools in Ontario, of
which Toronto alone possesses 4 Technical Schools, 4
Commercial High Schools and 3 auxiliary schools—that is
11 vocational schools in all—I cannot let this opportunity
pass without voicing the gratitude of the people of this
Province for all that has been done to make this type of
education available to every boy and girl in Ontario.

As far back as 1891 there was a vocational school of sorts
in Toronto. Vocational classes at least were held in old
Wycliffe Hall, facing McCaul Street. In 1900 there was
the Toronto Technical School, occupying premises on College
Street, now taken in charge by the police and used as a police
station. And in 1911 the Government interested itself in
the institution of vocational training in response to the
requests of manufacturers and industrialists when Dr. John

Sneath, then Superintendent of Education, made that outstanding survey of his on education for industrial purposes. He was followed by Dr. F. W. Merchant and Dr. A. C. MacKay, who the one on behalf of the Province, and the other for the City, exerted a tremendous influence upon the development of vocational training from 1914 onwards. And the result was the opening of the Central Technical School in 1915; Danforth Technical School in 1923; Western Technical School in 1928; Northern Vocational School in 1930.

These are all vocational schools, for the only apparent difference between technical and vocational schools is that when technical training is extended to include commercial subjects then that is called vocational education.

In this great development the Government has played a notable part. In 1919 the Federal Government set aside $10,000,000 under the Technical School Act to aid in developing a more practical type of education. And when that Act lapsed in 1929 the Provincial Government undertook to pay the whole cost—that is, fifty per cent. of the building cost and twenty-five per cent. of the salaries paid to the staff. And when you consider that the cost of building and equipping this great building alone was not less than $1,500,000 then that, you will see, was no small undertaking.

And this education is free! See how great then is your incentive to succeed! What opportunities for self-development and self-expression are yours, and how fortunate you boys and girls are to enjoy these advantages. And besides these advantages, you have others—all the advantages of health, the possession of all your faculties without physical handicap of any kind.

I know of no better way by which to illustrate how great are the advantages you enjoy than to tell of a young man who called upon me recently. He is a graduate in Arts and in Law of the University of Alberta. He writes—I have a copy of his autobiography. He designs and sketches. He has won prizes as a singer. He is self-supporting. And yet—from birth he has had no arms. Let me quote you a portion of Mr. W. R. Watson's book: "I hope some day," he says, "to be instrumental in setting afoot a movement to establish Vocational Training Schools in Canada for Handicapped Children, that they may be better able to readjust themselves to their environment and become independent citizens in their community." That, he says, is his desire. I feel sure too that that is the desire of everyone one who has at heart the welfare of his less fortunate fellowmen and women.

In a moment I shall have an opportunity of seeing on display many more of the reasons why the Northern Vocational School has already—in four short years—created for itself such a splendid reputation. I want to congratulate you very sincerely on the fine work that has been done here in preparing you for the very practical business of living. I congratulate the hockey and football teams on their well-merited successes in competition with other schools. I congratulate, also, those students—no less than thirteen of them—who have brought honour to themselves and their School by each of them winning the Pitman Gold Medal for Shorthand. And I know of nothing that so strongly recommends itself to me as your student council or government. For it is never too early for anyone to have practical experience of the duties and responsibilities of Government such as that given here to boys, and I hope, girls too. I cannot but feel that you find in such a record and in the work that was necessary before that record was possible, your greatest pleasure. And since there are so many ladies present it is only fitting, perhaps, that I should quote to you a very wise remark made by a famous woman writer who thought it necessary—it was long before the days of Woman's Suffrage—to write under a man's name. I refer to George Eliot, who in her book *Felix Holt* says, "One way of getting an idea of your fellowmen's miseries is to go and look at their pleasures." I like to think that in this exhibition are the products of pleasure—for in creative work such as you do here is to be found perhaps the greatest of all pleasures, the pleasure which is never satiating to the true craftsman.

As a surgeon I know whereof I speak.   For, when a medical student, I was influenced in my choice of specializing in surgery by the opportunity it offered me to do something with my hands, to repair, to restore and sometimes to reconstruct and to see the result of my own handiwork.   For it is the surgeon who most closely approaches the ideals and practices of a craftsman, who must not only know what to do but do it, not only discover the source of trouble but remove it in a very practical and even manual way.

In all that I have said, therefore, I have been speaking as a fellow-craftsman, as one who chose in youth a vocation— an arduous vocation but one which brings precisely the same pleasures as other vocations—the inexhaustible, never-weary-ing pleasure of making, of doing, of creating.   What I have said will, I hope, encourage you to climb to new triumphs of accomplishment to which this splendid exhibition of your work is but the prelude.

It is with the greatest pleasure that I declare this exhibition open.

THE NATIONAL DRAMA LEAGUE OF CANADA

At the Conclusion of the Performance in
the Dominion Drama Festival Finals at
Hart House Theatre, March 26, 1934

Mr. Chairman, Ladies and Gentlemen:

I am very pleased to be here this evening and to express what must be in the minds of all this audience and of those who have taken part in the performances. That is, a lively appreciation of the fine service His Excellency, Lord Bessborough, whose daughter, Lady Moyra Ponsonby, honours us with her presence this evening, has rendered to Canada by the inspiring and practical way in which he brought about the creation of the Dominion Drama Festival. His Excellency's enthusiasm for dramatic art was known to us before he came to Canada. The contagious quality of that enthusiasm soon became apparent and as he went through the country that enthusiasm infected men and women everywhere. When, a year ago last fall, he called a meeting at Ottawa of people from all parts of the country who are interested in the Drama, the development of the Dominion Drama Festival was a logical result. We were all pleased with the success attending the first Festival. We are delighted with the even greater success this year. I have been happy to learn that you have a larger number of entries in this Central Ontario Region this year than you had last, and I have been gratified by the reports of keen interest and splendid performances which have come to me from Ottawa, London and Kingston, where other Ontario Regional Festivals have been held. I extend hearty congratulations to the committees and to the directors and players who have achieved such fine results.

It seems to me to be a splendid thing that all the people who have worked so hard for the success of this festival are taking part in a work which not only gives them pleasure but affords real pleasure to others. That is indeed a fine use for them to make of their leisure, and it appeals to me particularly because the use of leisure is a matter in which I take a keen interest.

Leisure may be a dead loss or it may be an infinite gain—what decides that is the use that we make of it.

By promoting interest in a National Drama His Excellency and all the members of the various committees and of the playing groups, have advanced a profitable use for leisure. The first record of a drama being performed in Upper Canada is given in the Journal of Montcalm, and took place 176 years ago during a very bad winter—though I doubt whether it could have been worse than a very recent winter—when the French garrison at Fort Niagara was unable to carry on the building of fortifications because of inclement weather. Furthermore, supplies became scarce and soon the men were in an irritable and unhappy state of mind. To offset this, M. Pouchot, the Commandant of the Fort, interested them in dramatics, and Montcalm tells us in his Journal that someone wrote a little comedy entitled *The Old Man Duped* and that the garrison performed it. (I wonder if the "Old Man" did not signify depression, which they hoped the employment involved in the production of the play would banish.)

But Lord Bessborough and those who have loyally supported his project have done more than merely to promote a good use of leisure. They have rendered a further service by advancing the cause of a national drama. The drama is not only a great educational and recreational institution. It is an influence that moulds national character and sentiment. His Excellency has truly said that "The spirit of a nation, if it is to find full expression, must include a National Drama."

Now, I did not come here with the intention of speaking at length. At the request of the Executive Committee I agreed to fill in a little of the time which must elapse between the last of tonight's fine performances and the remarks of the adjudicator, Mr. Rupert Harvey, whom the Drama Festival was so fortunate to procure for the regional play-offs. I understand that the final adjudication of all the fourteen presentations in this Central Region will take place here on Thursday night, and I am sure many of the players from the fourteen groups that have entered will be eager and interested members of the audience. Now the remarks that I have made about the use of leisure, about the importance of being relieved from the unbearable burden of idleness, will explain to you, I am sure, why it is that I am very keenly interested in the Miracle Players—for they are men and women who have suffered more than most of us here from the hardships of these distressing times.

Any remarks I make would be incomplete if I did not refer to the contribution that has been made by the Hon. Vincent Massey and Mrs. Massey to the advancement of dramatic art in Canada. This theatre is a monument to their generous interest.

CONCERNING INFANTILE PARALYSIS

*A Radio Address on Behalf of Crippled
Children's Week Sponsored by the Department of Public Welfare, April 9, 1934*

I am pleased to have the opportunity of taking part in
the Crusade, organized by the Hon. Mr. Martin, Minister
of Public Welfare, in behalf of the Crippled Children of this
Province. I hope that the message which will be brought
to you will awaken such interest in this important work
as to make all parents in this Province recognize their responsibility for the health of their children. Parents should
regard any unusual symptom or complaint as a potential
danger necessitating the calling of a doctor.

There are today 8,000 crippled children in this Province
of whom only fifteen per cent. were born with a disability.
The rest are due to disease or accidents. The principal diseases
causing crippling are infantile paralysis, tuberculosis and
rickets.

Infantile paralysis is the most important cause of crippling in Ontario. This disease occurs in more or less epidemic
form every summer from the middle of July until the end
of October. The germ which causes the disease is so small
that it cannot be seen under the most powerful microscope.
No matter what care is taken of children it is impossible to
prevent them from coming in contact with the germ, and
therefore parents should have sufficient knowledge of the
symptoms of the disease to suspect it at its inception, and
call the doctor.

The germs of this disease attack the motor nerve cells in
the spinal cord, from which the nerves go out to the muscles
in order to carry the impulses which make the muscles move.

Consequently, if the nerve cells are damaged a condition develops which we call "paralysis". Some nerve cells will be permanently destroyed; others will recover under treatment in from three months to two years.

The disease can be successfully dealt with by the use of convalescent serum. This serum is obtained from patients who have recovered from infantile paralysis and who are immune from other attacks. Their blood serum has been found to contain a substance which, when given to a new case, will help the patient to resist the disease.

This serum is distributed free by the Ontario Government all over the Province and is available to any physician. It is most effective if given within twelve hours of the onset of an attack—hence the importance of calling a physician early.

Even when paralysis has developed, a great deal can be done to prevent deformity by means of splints, which will not only relieve the pain, but keep the limb in a good and useful position. This care is required for at least two years, and results in reducing the number of operations for the correction of deformities by one-third.

Unfortunately, it frequently happens that a child urgently requiring treatment is prevented from receiving it by the opposition of the parents. This is both ignorant and selfish; for there is no more cheerful place in the world, or one where greater care is given, than a children's ward in one of our hospitals.

I should like to emphasize these facts: That crippling is preventable if the serum is used at the beginning of the attack. That if paralysis should supervene producing crippling, there are ample facilities to treat and rectify such cases in the hospitals of this Province. There are sufficient hospital beds in all our large centres to accommodate every case. A child of indigent parents will be taken care of free of charge in these institutions. The medical profession will give their skilled service free. This work has the splendid co-operation of ninety organizations, including the Service Clubs, the Junior Red Cross and the Shrine.

It is important that the public should be made to understand how much can be done for crippled children and the necessity for doing it early so that these children may have a better chance of becoming healthy, and, later on, self-supporting citizens.

OUT OF THE WOODS

*Before the Empire Club at a Luncheon in
the Royal York Hotel, April 12, 1934*

Mr. President and Gentlemen:

There is no happier moment in the life of a surgeon than
when he can say to his patient, "Now you're out of the
woods." The patient, of course, shares the pleasure. One
has only to look at him to see that.

Now, this year Toronto is celebrating its CENTenary, its
Cent-EE-nary, and its Cent-ENN-ial. There may be other
celebrations also in progress of which I haven't yet heard,
but, sooner or later, the fact emerges that Toronto is exactly
one hundred years old. And since, in a very literal sense,
Toronto has actually *come out of the woods*—the woods that
for centuries bordered the lake—I think it will be interesting to
pay a hurried visit to the past and see how it all happened.

Where Baby Point now stands on the east bank of the
Humber, there used to be an Indian village named Teieiagon,
in the middle of a forest. Somebody called Joliet marked
it with a pin point on a map he made in 1673. Fifty years
later, French traders came and went. Then they became
tired of coming and going and decided to stay. They built
Fort Rouille. It had 4 guns, 1 officer, 5 soldiers, 2 sergeants
and a storekeeper. For five years all went well. Business
was good. Then in 1759 the English turned up. The
depression had begun. So the French burnt their fort, scam-
pered off through the forest, and left the English to do what
they could with the charred ruins.

For thirty years one might say that X marked the spot.
Nobody wanted ruins. But in 1787 the British Government's
representatives spoke to the Indians about the land stretching
northward from the ruins. Lord Dorchester, the Governor-
General, sent a surveyor to look over the land. It was good

land. The British and Indians had a pow-wow or palaver about it at Carrying Place on the Bay of Quinté. They talked and talked—but it ended in talk. Then another thirty years or so passed—and at last in 1805, on the Credit River, the Indians agreed to sell to the British 250,808 acres—that included York, Etobicoke, Vaughan and King Townships—for £1,700 sterling in cash and goods. The value of land has gone up since then and the value of money has gone down. For all that, I think you will agree that it was a bargain day in real estate.

Meanwhile, many things have been happening. Here and there little townships are springing up. General Simcoe is Lieutenant-Governor of the Province of Upper Canada. Niagara (or Newark) is the first capital of the Province. But just by Niagara is Fort Niagara in the U.S.A., and it is about to be garrisoned by American troops. Simcoe wants to move immediately and make London the new capital. But Lord Dorchester says, "No!" There were already some people—a few settlers—in Toronto. Why not make Toronto the capital? So, willy-nilly, Simcoe came to Toronto with seven officers and camped in tents when the soldiers had cleared away the trees. A few weeks later Toronto was called York by everybody but the inhabitants. Simcoe renamed it "York" after the Duke of York—and Muddy York was born in the marsh, or, if you will, the woods.

And now things begin to move. The Island was still a peninsula. The soldiers began building military buildings and roads. Castle Frank was built—a combined summer residence and Government House for the Simcoes—just beyond the northern boundary of St. James' cemetery—a frame building overlooking the Don Valley. The Simcoes loved it. Mrs. Simcoe cried all day when they sailed away from York on the *Onondaga*, but after they left it, it wasn't much used. In fact, five years before Toronto became a city, a fisherman lit a fire in it, went away and forgot the fire—and when he came back, what was left wasn't worth remembering.

Now, York—no longer Toronto (except to the inhabitants)—was, of course, a military establishment. Two hundred Queen's Rangers did almost all the work. I imagine it was thirsty work. At all events, the Lieutenant-Governor, General Simcoe, signed a warrant authorizing the Commissioner of Stores, Mr. McGill, "to supply from time to time from Government stores such quantities of rum as may be required to be given to the men employed on the wharf and canal at York." And to this day the question, "How much rum did they require?" is as unanswerable as Pilate's famous query, "What is truth?"

However, the York Rangers under General Simcoe did a great deal of valuable work. Yonge Street was opened to Lake Simcoe. They began clearing the highway through the bush in 1794, and in two years the work was completed. Before his term of office expired, by the way, Lieutenant-Governor Simcoe started a newspaper and an annual agricultural show. And the population of Upper Canada rose from 12,000 to 35,000.

And what about York itself? What sort of place was it to live in? Well, at that time it was really quite unhealthy. Mosquitos were a pest and brought intermittent fevers. At no time at the beginning of the last century did the little struggling town extend more than a few hundred feet north of the shore. King and Yonge was not even a cross road, and Church Street was a long, long way from the business district. In 1799 they had a post office, and even before that, a newspaper. It was called *The Upper Canada Gazette or American Oracle*. The name "Oracle", of course, sufficiently indicates that it was the official Government publication. And as for the Post Office, already in 1801 the York Postmaster, Mr. Willcocks, had resigned because "his reasonable charges for the rent of an office, stationery, fire, candles and a servant to attend had been disputed." That was most unreasonable, probably, but the troubles of officialdom had already started. And these weren't by any means the only troubles. Listen, for instance, to this description of York by a traveller in 1798. "A dreary, dismal place", he says, "not even possessing the characteristics of a village. There is no church, school-house, nor, in fact, any of the ordinary signs of civilization. There is no inn", he goes on, "and those travellers who have no friends to go to, pitch a tent."— A shameful state of affairs. But true enough. And sitting here in this great hotel you will appreciate the significance of a letter written by Acting Governor Russell from Niagara to an official in York just before the Legislature met. "Please appraise the inhabitants of the town that 25 gentlemen will want board and lodgings."

As a matter of fact, of course, York was still in the wilds. They say that Bay Street was once called Bear Street because Mr. Justice Boulton's horses attacked a bear in a field nearby. Yes—the horses attacked the bear! A hundred and thirty-four years ago packs of wolves came into the town. One man lost seventeen sheep. And then two bears came to town and ran off with two pigs in their arms, sprinting away into the woods on their hind legs. While nine years later, Lieut. Fawcett of the 100th Regiment killed a bear in George Street by hitting it on the head with his sword.

Exciting days. But I want to hurry on to the days one hundred years ago when Toronto came into being and was incorporated as a city. We'll stop just long enough to see how the population grew. In 1803 there were 456 people in York, and they collected £62 in taxes. In 1812 there were 700. That was the year of the American War. In 1813 the Americans occupied the town twice and burned practically all the public buildings. But the population went on growing. In 1817 it was 1,200, and there were actually three brick edifices in the town. And when the population was no less than 1,336 and everything appeared to be going swimmingly, a Mr. Talbot visited York, looked around him and made these comments: "The situation of the town is very unhealthy, for it stands on a piece of low marshy ground. He who first fixed upon this spot as the site of the capital of Upper Canada, whatever predilection he may have had for the roaring of frogs, or the effluvia arising from stag-

nating water and putrid vegetables, can certainly have had
no great regard for preserving the lives of His Majesty's
subjects.'' The situation of York was, it would seem, not
only pernicious but actually somewhat seditious as well—
a situation which the shocked gentleman viewed with alarm.
But time and tide wait for no man, and even the slow-moving
little town of York didn't wait for Mr. Talbot to finish
speaking. It was, in fact, just getting into its stride. There
were many things to be done. Pioneers are busy people.
And they wanted at least one Police Constable, a Collector
of Taxes, a Postmaster, and all kinds and conditions of public
officials. But nobody had the time and few the inclination.
Very well then, they would have to *make* time. So if you
had been in York you might, on any fine morning, have
received a letter informing you that you were to be the
Town Constable, or the Tax Collector. You would have
objected; you had other things to do. But that made no
difference. You were given two days to find a substitute.
If you couldn't, you paid a fine.

In 1816, for example, the Magistrate appointed a gentleman named John Murchison to be town clerk. He said,
"No, thank you", and was fined for contempt. Then Jonathan Cawthra was appointed. He gracefully demurred, but
paid the fine just the same. Then Jonathan Post was approached, and likewise refused. Likewise, he too paid the
fine. Finally, William Barber accepted, and turned out to
be a lucky fellow, for next month, in addition to his salary,
he received the three fines that had been paid by the three
shy men who shunned the fierce light of publicity which even
then doubtless beat upon such a public position as that of the
Town Clerkship of York.

York, by the way, was undoubtedly unhealthy in its location. It was not for nothing, too, that it was called
"muddy". We shall have time later to see just how muddy
it could be. But we have reached the year 1834. And now
I would like you to have a glimpse of this little town set in
the wilderness. It is a summer day. Suddenly, flocks of

wild pigeons come flying over the town. Let the story be told in the words of a contemporary who was actually present. "A stream of wild pigeons", he writes, "took it into their heads to fly over York; and for two or three days the town resounded with one continued roll of firing; as if a skirmish were going on in the streets—every gun, pistol, musket, blunderbuss and firearm of whatever description was put in requisition. The constables and police magistrates were on the alert, and offenders without number were pulled up—among whom were honourable members of the executive and legislative councils, crown lawyers, respectable, staid citizens, and last of all the Sheriff of the county; till at last it was found that pigeons, flying within easy shot, were a temptation too strong for human virtue to withstand; and so the contest was given up and a sporting jubilee proclaimed to all and sundry." The arrival of pigeons had made it necessary, you see, to proclaim a civic holiday.

And now, it is hardly necessary for me to tell you that on March 6, 1834, the town of York—after a good deal of family squabbling—became the city of Toronto. We haven't time to stay and listen to the quarrel, but many objected, among other things, to what they called the "wild and terrific" Indian name, Toronto, instead of the good old British name York. Even the inhabitants had by this time become accustomed to the name York. And I know for a fact that neither Lieutenant-Governor Sir John Colborne nor Mr. Jarvis, who was Tory M.P. for York, even guessed who would be elected first Mayor of the City when Mr. Jarvis introduced in the House of Assembly "An Act to extend the limits of the town of York, to erect the said town into a city, and to incorporate it under the name of the City of Toronto." But that is another story, and as soon as everything had been settled—more or less—there came a veritable flood of by-laws and regulations to improve the city. Unfortunately, there wasn't much money, but they began laying the first wooden sidewalks instead of footpaths and flagstones, and the main streets were graded and gravelled. A fully incorporated city is not a town. York had been changed in name, said the city fathers, why not change it in appearance? So the new City of Toronto tried its best to forget that it was ever little muddy York. And when fifteen years later the "Great Fire of 1849" began at half-past one in the morning and went on burning building after building along street after street until six or seven o'clock at night—then a whole section of the city had to be rebuilt. New and better buildings sprang up. Muddy York had already changed past recognition.

Just how muddy, by the way, was York? I shall let a gentleman who lived in those days tell it in his own words.

It seems that "while walking on the loose planks forming a sidewalk on King Street he espied a good-looking hat in the middle of the street. Curious to see and pick up the hat, he managed to reach it, and on lifting it discovered to his surprise the head of a man underneath. This individual at once appealed for help and deliverance, urging as a special plea that if prompt assistance was not rendered, his horse which was underneath, would certainly perish. The usual mode of extrication by the use of shovels and oxen was soon supplied, and man and horse excavated. This being the climax of exaggeration on this muddy question, it must now be dismissed."

So much for Muddy York. Now, what of Toronto? We must go forward by leaps and bounds. To travel a century in half an hour is not easy. We shall stay long enough to observe, however, that it was not until the eighties that cement paving came to Toronto. Thirty-nine years ago Toronto's citizens were proud to announce that "many of Toronto's main streets and private thoroughfares are asphalted." Today there are 542 paved streets and 900 miles of concrete sidewalks. All in a century!

Three years after Muddy York became Toronto, the first "cab" appeared. It was called the "City". It was drawn by a horse, accommodated four passengers, and was driven by a negro. It did a wonderful business. In no time there were competitors. Toronto seemed to blossom into cabs. Public street transportation had begun. There were cabs called "Chief Justice Robinson", "Britannia", "Queen", "Niagara", "Princess Royal" and "Transit". The first cabman made so much money that the business was overdone. Servants left their masters to go into the business. There were cabs everywhere. Then came omnibuses and all sorts of horse-drawn contraptions on wheels. And very soon the city had to regulate the duties and charges of all vehicles plying for hire in Toronto. Drivers were told that they must not "wantonly snap or flourish their whips" (I wish we had similar rules concerning motor-car horns), and they were not to use "abusive, obscene or impertinent language of any kind whatever."

In 1861 the first horse-cars appeared on Yonge Street and omnibus proprietors galore went out of business.

With the advent of the new, old things, old customs were disappearing. One hundred years ago a woman in court on a charge of drunkenness threw a muddy boot at the first Toronto Mayor who was reproaching her for her sins. She was sentenced to be placed in the stocks. That was the last time stocks were used in Toronto.

You recall that I mentioned the great fire of 1849. The old frame buildings of Toronto were quick to catch fire. How did Toronto's citizens cope with fires? A hundred years ago the fire-fighters were a bucket brigade. Every house had to keep two buckets filled with water, and every man had to help in carrying the buckets. Every carter had to be a water-carrier when fire broke out. At the scene of the fire eight men with a hand pump did some useful physical exercises, and prizes were offered to "licensed carters and others" who were first to appear on the scene with barrels of water.

Mrs. Jameson, who visited Toronto in 1837, said she was assured by citizens that "a fire was always a public benefit, for a good brick house was sure to arise in the place of a wooden one."

However, Toronto didn't want too many fires. So a

Fire and Water Committee was formed in 1847. Pipes were laid and water pumped up from the lake. Reservoirs were built, hydrants were installed, and so, as the century passed, modern Toronto with its splendid fire-fighting facilities and its hundreds of miles of pipes bearing water to every house, came into being.

I wish I had time to tell you of the work now in progress building a pipeline extending a mile and a half out from the shore at Scarborough Bluffs. Nor have I time to tell of oil displacing the candle and of electricity banishing the gas lamp. Nor will we be able to watch the growth of the Police Force. We can't wait to watch the police deal with surging, window-smashing crowds in the streets of Toronto during such disturbances as the "Circus Riots" in 1855, or the "Sunday Riots" in 1874. It is an interesting story—the story of the development of the Police Force—often an exciting story—and it ends with the 969 men who now compose one of the finest and most efficient of police forces.

I should like to have been able to tell you, too, of the shops and of the inns and hostelries in early Toronto—the precursors of our modern shops and hotels. The cost of this Royal York Hotel, by the way, was 35 *times* the total value of all the property in Toronto one hundred years ago. And I would suggest that on leaving this hotel you go up York Street to Richmond Street. There, on the north-east corner of York and Richmond still stands a frame building which is a hundred years old. It used to be Crispin's Tavern, a popular resort generations ago. Richard Crispin, or "Coachman Dick", who was the proprietor, came to Canada with Lieut.-Governor Sir John Colborne in 1828, to drive the official coach. He and his good wife kept that tavern for years. And if in the act of making comparisons with modern hotels you are deluded into believing Toronto's citizens of old had no first-class hotels, listen to these few words of appreciation written by a visitor to the Rossin House which was opened in 1857 at the corner of King and York Streets.

"Within its walls", he writes, "is congregated every appliance which affluence can desire, every pleasure which luxury can crave. Here are alluring condiments to tempt the most fastidious taste, vinous acidities to lubricate, and gastronomic ponderosities to titillate the palate! The prandial morceau here ceases from troubling, and the sated stomach is at rest. What magical transformations here await human deglutition!"

That is probably unlike anything you have ever heard. Eating in those days was evidently one of the fine arts.

I hope I have given you some insight into the manner in which this hundred-year-old city became an accomplished fact. I haven't spoken of the multiplication of churches in this city of churches; of the activities—public and civic—that centred around old St. Lawrence Hall; of the old-time elections which were so often like small wars and not always bloodless, so that a general election was sometimes also a signal for general uproar. Nor can I do more than mention the libraries and museums which started so humbly and have become centres of enlightenment, entertainment and instruction. The story of all these is an essential part of the story of Toronto.

Life in York was very much like that of an English town in those days. But Toronto began to take on its own characteristics—characteristics which it retains to this day, when to be one of its citizens is to be a citizen of no mean city.

In sentimental retrospect, the thought of living in the days when Toronto was still in its infancy may have a certain romantic appeal. When I recall, for example, that the Hon. Peter Russell, who succeeded Governor Simcoe as Administrator, could make grants of land to himself—"I, Peter Russell, grant to you, Peter Russell"—I am filled with envy. Or when I think of the "Spoon Bill" of the Legislature of Upper Canada, by which a sum of no less than £3,000 was voted to purchase a service of plate for Lieut.-Governor Francis Gore, and when I learn that the Lieut.-Governor took the money to England with him but never bought the plate, when I read that a few days later he called the members of the Assembly—those who voted the money for him—

"rascals" and dismissed them because, as he said, their longer absence from their respective avocations must be too great a sacrifice—then—well, I must hurry on!

Toronto's progress has been very real and so great as to seem at times and in many of its aspects, incredible. For, however glamorous the early days may appear in retrospect, the fact remains that the city of Toronto today far transcends the most sanguine expectations of those past generations who planned and laboured that their vision might be fulfilled. There is much yet to be done in this city of ours, and the difficulties we are called upon to face are, after all, nothing but growing pains.

Toronto is a city of which we may well be proud, and the surest guarantee of its continued progress is the pride of its citizens. For to be jealous of Toronto's honour, to be eternally watchful that the best interests of all its citizens be safeguarded, to be vigilant in the detection of civic and private shortcomings, and to encourage all that will give beauty to the city and happiness and contentment to its citizens—these are the visible, tangible evidences of true pride of citizenship.

A few weeks ago I was very much impressed by the ready enthusiastic reception accorded a few words of mine concerning slum conditions within this city. The response was immediate and active. Today a committee, representing all classes of citizens, is at work on this most difficult problem. The investigations that have already been made show the existence of undesirable dwellings within the boundaries of this great city. And I know that the energy with which this problem has been tackled is but further proof, if any were needed, that the pride of the citizens of Toronto will not tolerate the presence in their midst of any dwellings or districts comparable to those slums which, as long as they continue, will be dark stains on the escutcheons of older and larger cities in the Old and New Worlds. In a press dispatch only a few days ago I noticed that the Government of the United States is combining with officials of many States in a vigorous campaign to rid their cities of slums. Federal millions are being placed behind scores of projects having but one object—the clearing away, the rooting out of those tenement and slum districts which, like a malignant growth, despoil a city of its beauty and rob it of its health. How necessary it is that at the very first indication of the insidious growth in Toronto, or in any city of this great Dominion of any such areas, we should act—and that immediately—so that slums may never grow to be centres of filth and misery for those of our less fortunate citizens, and a terrible handicap to generations yet unborn.

And now, against the background of a few frame houses in a wilderness, set the Toronto of today. No longer a pioneer community but a centre of culture, no longer two score wooden shacks huddled together where lake and forest meet, but a city of homes. No longer a place of darkness where sturdy, toil-worn men and women trudge doggedly along muddy paths toward the dim candle-light or oil lamp that marks their homes, but a city of clean boulevards and broad highways lit by electricity, and where one may walk safe by night as by day; a city of schools; a city, too, of churches and a city which has at its centre the second largest university in the British Empire.

I am glad and proud to recall that it was one of my predecessors in office—General John Graves Simcoe—who first proposed the founding of a university. His dream was realized, for the Legislature in 1798 set aside no less than 500,000 acres for purposes of education. Half of that— 250,000 acres—was for the establishment of a university. When in 1827 King's College was founded—chiefly at the instance of Dr. John Strachan—there was bequeathed to succeeding generations, as the university grew and in 1850 became the University of Toronto, all those tangible and intangible benefits which are the fruits of higher education.

What am I to say, too, of those cultural influences in our midst which give to the name of Toronto prestige, character, and an enviable reputation—a reputation such as can never be based *alone* on material possessions, on the acquisition of wealth or on commercial prosperity. I refer to such forces as are typified in the realm of music by the Toronto Symphony Orchestra, the Little Symphony, the Bach Choir, the Mendelssohn Choir and the Conservatory of Music, over which our own Dr. Ernest MacMillan is, in every sense of the word, the presiding genius. What am I to say, too, of Hart House and the development of Canadian Drama fostered by those enthusiasts who recently sponsored and took part in the Dominion Drama Festival Competition, when no less than fourteen plays were produced in the final play-offs?

In the world of entertainment, Toronto has facilities such as few cities can rival. In the world of sport it has the Maple Leaf Hockey Club and the great Arena, not to mention all those other sports and games—baseball and cricket, skating and football—which give health and joy and not a little excitement to both young participants and to more elderly spectators.

From the little fairs of old has grown the great Canadian National Exhibition—unrivalled anywhere in the world, and the Royal Winter Fair, second only to that of Chicago.

Out of the woods came Toronto. Out of the wild tangle of tree and shrub that for untold centuries was known only to the Indians, the bear, the wolf, and the birds that arrive with the summer—came the little town of York—defiantly planting itself in the heart of a wilderness. By the strength of purpose of the men and women of old, and by ways too devious to trace in so short a time, the city of Toronto came into being.

If at times we are inclined to think that there is yet another wood out of which Toronto has not emerged—the wood in which the countries of the world are painfully groping their way as they seek the open boundless plains of peace and prosperity—there seems now to be every indication that soon the economic undergrowths and the thorny shrubs of international difficulties that delay the feet of progress will have passed away, even as the woods and mud of York have passed out of the sight of men.

OUR HERITAGE OF TOLERANCE

*At the Jewish Gentile Seminar in the King
Edward Hotel, April 24, 1934*

Mr. Chairman, Ladies and Gentlemen:

In the year 1897 I visited Palestine. I saw Jerusalem.
And I suppose there is no city whose name for two thousand
years has been more frequently and more fervently on the
lips of men and women and children than the name of Jerusalem. I went to the Holy Sepulchre. I tried to swim in
the Dead Sea, and I washed off the accumulated salt in the
River Jordan. Bandits infested the country in those days
and we travelled with an armed escort. They were Turks,
those bandits, and they disappeared on the day that Lord
Allenby entered Jerusalem. They have never returned.

But of all that I saw during that visit, the memory of
the worshippers at the Holy Sepulchre remains with me
most vividly. Those devout pilgrims in small self-centred
groups have always had for me a profound allegorical significance. Each group had its own faith, its own ritual, its
own religion. And between each group and every other
group there was an armed guard—for protection, to keep
the peace. It may be that even as I watched, there were
some among those worshippers praying for protection. But
it is an appalling thought that they had, quite literally, to
be protected before they could pray. I felt then, and I still
feel, that I was looking on something which symbolized the
dark story of religious intolerance. It seemed indeed that
where religion most abounded it was most necessary that
armed guards be at hand to enforce "peace on earth, goodwill
to men." I needn't elaborate the moral to be drawn from
such a spectacle. That scene in Palestine was an epitome of
world history. To a young man it was an object lesson.

It would have been rich food for a cynic. It spoke not of the
infinite mercy of God, but of the cruel intolerance of man.
And in the light of subsequent and recent happenings the
terrible implications of those armed guards have become
all too obvious.

Now, gentlemen, this is the last day of your Seminar.
And because it is my hope that as a result of your deliberations
you will face the world of tomorrow with a renewed and a
high confidence, I wish to bring you a message of encouragement. Side by side with the all too well-known and in-
glorious story of the efforts of man to destroy all that is
not made in his own image, you can trace, like a thread of
gold in the tapestry of history, the efforts and triumphs of
civilization—of civilized men—against the onslaughts of a
narrow, vindictive barbarism. I know of no better definition,
indeed, of barbarism than that it is a fierce intolerance, a
hatred of enlightenment and superiority; bigotry—as it
were—run amok.

May I say I am proud to know that in Canada in these
times of stress and anxiety, Jew and Gentile can take counsel
together, as you have been doing. In days like these, this
age-old barbarism of intolerance once again menaces civilization with undiminished virulence. Here and there it has
triumphed. And the thought that in this Dominion, in
this Province, in this City, men of diverse religions and of
varying opinions can and do gather together against this
barbarism as against a common enemy, cements my faith
in the perfectability of this our civilization. For, gentlemen,
to lose liberty is to lose hope; and to lose hope is to lose
everything. It was Victor Hugo who said, "It is through
fraternity that liberty is saved."

More than two thousand years ago, when one of the
characters in Terence's play, *The Self Tormentor*, exclaimed,
"I am a man, and I deem nothing human alien to me", he
brought down the house. For, in literature, at all events, it
was the first clear enunciation of the doctrine of the brotherhood of man.

You will notice that, as befits a layman, I quote from secular sources. I am sure that the Gentiles present will be interested to know that it was St. Augustine who tells us of the thunders of applause which greeted these words.

Now, it seems that the simplest ideas are the most difficult for mankind to grasp. I suspect that the simple things are the only truly profound things. Let me give you an historical example of what I mean. You all recall the lengths to which men and women were driven by their insistence upon their fraternity—their brotherhood—during the French Revolution. It really seems that, failing the actual blood relationship of brothers, they tried, very literally, to seal their brotherhood in blood. The Jacobins, in an excess of brotherly love, set up placards on all the public buildings, "Fraternity or Death". And a witty gentleman named Sebastian Chamfort paraphrased their slogan—"Be my brother, or I will kill you."

There is something in that slogan that reminds me of the kind of brotherhood which is being loudly, boisterously and even ferociously extolled even now. I cannot but feel that it is very different from the real brotherhood expressed politically by such acts as the Magna Charta, and socially, in the attitude of mind and soul so clearly indicated by the question of Wilberforce, the liberator of slaves, when he said, "Am I not a man and a brother?"

The crimes committed in the name of the brotherhood of man are often apt to make one suspicious. A family does not give proof of the family love that exists between its members by murdering its neighbours and imprisoning visitors in the cellar. And the spectacle of nations behaving as no decent family or community of people would behave—and all in the name of brotherhood—reminds me of the truth of a wise old Frenchman's maxim, "Hypocrisy is the homage vice pays to virtue." For even though men or nations may possess none of the true spirit of brotherhood they always find it politic to profess it, to make some pretence of paying homage to that spirit which burns in the heart of every true

man. "Fraternity or Death." "If you are not my brother—
I shall kill you."

How far removed this "brotherhood" is from the traditional hospitality and kindliness of the ancient Hebrew
to the "Stranger within his gates". How different to that
broad tolerance so implicit in the Christian ethic.

The avowed purpose of these meetings is to consider how
relations between Jew and Gentile can be improved; how
mutual understanding can be fostered and made enduring;
how the true spirit of neighbourliness—of a free brotherhood—can be strengthened against that violent, insidious and
altogether detestable form of propaganda to which minorities
have been from time to time subjected wherever liberty is
mocked and freedom held in contempt. As one who throughout life has numbered many Jews as his friends; as one who,
on behalf of all truly civilized Gentiles acknowledges the
indebtedness of the world to illustrious Jews who have entered
every field of endeavour as men bringing gifts with which
to enrich posterity—I seize this opportunity to express the
sympathy of every thinking man, every man of feeling,
with the afflictions that have pursued them and which they
have heroically endured throughout the centuries, and from
which they will continue to suffer as long as brutality masquerades as love of country, as long as hatred is the law,
and as long as injustice is exalted as a religion with warriors
as its high priests. In expressing my sympathy I want to
pay tribute to the part Jews have played in uprearing the
great edifice of this civilization—an edifice whose foundations
will be imperilled only when liberty and tolerance have been
destroyed. May that day never come!

I can begin, but I could never hope to end that long,
long list of the names of Jews of distinction in every sphere
of activity. Of great composers of music like Rubenstein,
Mendelssohn, Meyerbeer and Offenbach. Of modern musicians like Sir Frederick Cowen and Sir Landon Ronald;
Mischa Elman and Jascha Heifitz—those great violinists,
and scores of other musicians. Or I could speak of artists

like Solomon J. Solomon, and sculptors like Jacob Epstein. I would like you to notice, too, how frequently it has happened that Jews have won honour within the British Empire. Only recently it was my pleasure to entertain Sir Herbert Samuel, at one time High Commissioner of Palestine, whose persistent success as a politician in England is comparable in some respects to the brilliant career of yet another great Jew—Benjamin Disraeli, Lord Beaconsfield. Recently, too, Mr. R. D. Blumenfeld was our guest at Government House— a great journalist and the dean of Fleet Street. I could speak to you, too, of the Rt. Hon. Edwin Montague, or of Sir Philip Sassoon, men whom I have known and admired. Or I could name in other parts of the Empire, Sir Julius Vogel, erstwhile Prime Minister of New Zealand, or Sir Paul Samuel, or Sir Julius Solomon, both of whom have, at one time or another, represented New South Wales. Or again, there is Lord Reading, who as Sir Rufus Isaacs was Ambassador to the United States, and later Viceroy of India. There are hosts of others, far too numerous to mention.

In science the contribution of Jews is literally amazing. In mathematics it was John of Seville and Abraham bar Hiyya who first introduced Arabic numerals and the decimal system into Western Europe, and I need but mention that great Jewish contemporary, Albert Einstein, whose crowning achievement in modern analytics has given him enduring fame. I could tell you, too, of Abraham Zakuto, a Jew whose almanacs and charts enabled Christopher Columbus to reach America. Or J. R. Meyer, a German Jew to whom physics owes its great law—the conservation of matter.

The medical profession has been enriched by the contributions of Jews in all ages and countries. In the United States, for example, there is Abraham Flexner, Head of Medical Education, Rockefeller Foundation, who has done more than any individual or group of individuals to elevate the standard of medical education in the States. I recall, too, the splendid work done by Dr. Frederick Forscheimer and by Dr. Richard Weil, one of the founders of the American

Association for Cancer Research. Then there was Dr.
Abraham Jacobi, a pioneer in pediatrics and President of
the American Medical Association, and Dr. Jacob da Silva
Solis-Cohen, the first man to operate successfully on carcinoma
of the larynx. I should mention, also, Jacob da Costa,
a great clinician of the type of Sir William Osler. Dr.
Joseph Ransohoff, Dr. Willy Meyer and Dr. Howard Lilien-
thal are all famous surgeons and Fellow of the American
Surgical Association—an Association to which it is my privilege to belong. There is, indeed, no end to the list of great
Jewish names in every branch of medicine. Cohnheim in
pathology; Freud in neurology; Unna in Dermatology; and
in the science of infection—Metchnikoff, Friedlander, Neisser
and Paul Ehrlich—to mention but a few.

But I have undertaken a task too great to be accomplished
in so short a time. Whichever way one turns, into whatever field of intellectual, social, commercial, scientific, artistic
or medical endeavour one looks, there, among the greatest
names, are the names of great Jews.

An exhaustive list of these names and accomplishments
would be also, I fear, a most exhausting list, but the tribute
I wish to pay is, after all, not to be measured by its com-
prehensiveness but by its sincerity.

How great is the world's debt to great Jews! I have
mentioned, almost at random, but a very few of them—
the merest handful. And I want to take this opportunity
also to say how greatly the life of this city has been enriched
by the presence among us of such men as Rabbi Eisendrath
and Rabbi Sachs, who, by the strength of their idealism and
by the rare power of their eloquence, have made impossible
that ready acquiescence in the condition of things as they
are, which would be the death of progress, but who have
valiantly prophesied things as they might be and should be.

This city, and indeed the whole world, has need of such
men as these and of men of the character, the greatness of
heart, and the public spirit which have for so many years
distinguished the long and honourable career of one of

Toronto's greatest benefactors, the grand old man, Edmund Scheuer. And only last Saturday at an Investiture in Ottawa, His Excellency, the Governor-General, on behalf of His Majesty the King, conferred high honour upon yet another distinguished member of the Jewish race when Mrs. Freiman was presented with the O.B.E. for the splendid social work done by this kindly lady.

It was Disraeli who once remarked that all sensible men are of the same religion.

"What religion is that?" he was asked. "They never tell," was the reply.

But Canada has been and will, I most confidently believe, remain a country in which men and women may be free fearlessly to tell their religion and to worship in their own way without dread of persecution for their faith. This young country has none of the heritage of age-old hatred which destroys but never creates, and which still exists in so many older countries. Canada's spirit is that of youth—generous and tolerant. It is a country over which the flag of liberty is still unfurled, bringing its message of a hope that can never die, where men and women are free.

In the heart of the British Empire is a city where cathedral and church, synagogue and mosque raise their mute graceful spires to the heavens—soaring prayers to the Great God of us all. The priceless heritage of tolerance, the precious gift of freedom which this city and this Dominion, as a part of a great Empire, hold in trust for this and future generations, will, I know, never be betrayed, never be lost. For it is in this freedom, this tolerance, this true democracy that the richest life is to be found for all men.

IN MEMORY OF THE ANZACS

*At the Australian Club and New Zealand
Association Ceremony at the Cenotaph, City
Hall, on the Annual Observance of Anzac
Day, April 25, 1934*

Your Worship, Ladies and Gentlemen:

With gratitude and a profound admiration Canadians today
pay tribute to the memory of their kinsmen from over the
seas who, in the Great War, sacrificed their lives while
serving with the Australian and New Zealand Army Corps.
They came thousands of miles at the call of Empire. They
left all that they held dear. They entered every arena of
warfare, and they displayed a courage, a splendid quality of
endurance and a true manliness that brought to the name of the
Anzacs a fame embedded deep in the minds and hearts of
men and women of the British Empire. The story of Anzac
heroism, indeed, will remain in the memory of future generations as long as the Empire endures and the annals of its
history are read.

As a sister Dominion, Canada deeply sympathizes with
all that is represented by this act of remembrance. For it
was not alone upon the gallant men who fell but upon all
those who were left to mourn their passing that there was
laid the terrible burden of sacrifice.

The memories of Gallipoli and the Dardanelles, of France
and the Near East are redeemed from utter sorrow by our
knowledge that they were the scenes also of the magnificent
valour of the Anzacs—places where the names of Australians
and New Zealanders were covered with glory that can never
fade.

In paying this all too inadequate tribute and on behalf
of the citizens of the Province of Ontario I bring greetings

to the Australians and New Zealanders in our midst. We trust that they find here in Canada those social amenities and that hospitality which will combine to give them a sense of real brotherhood within the Empire.

We greet them as kinsmen. With them we gather here to honour the memory of their gallant countrymen. The years that pass leave undimmed the story of their courage. And as Canadians, as fellow-comrades in arms, we render the Anzacs who passed in the heat of battle, this simple token of our affection and our admiration.

FOR THE BLIND

A Radio Address on Behalf of the Canadian National Institute for the Blind, April 27, 1934

Once every year blind men and blind women and blind children plead with you that they should not be forgotten. All those listening to me will understand me when I say that this annual appeal is such only in name. For the mute appeal of all those of our fellow-citizens—our fellow-Canadians—afflicted with utter blindness, is eloquent every day of every year. While spring and summer and autumn and winter pass them by unseen, only once—only on *one* day—do they ask you to help them.

I hope, for the sake of this great cause, that Tuesday next will be a sunny day. For then, as you see all about you the beauty of the springtime, and above you the blue sky, you will remember those into whose dark night of affliction that beauty never penetrates.

As you pass along the streets of Toronto you will be asked to give. I hope you will give generously. And if for any reason you are tempted to economize—to place a hard or thoughtless curb on your generosity—ask yourself this terrible question: What would *you* do if you were blind?

The question will perhaps frighten you. But it will make your fingers cease fumbling for the coin of small value. It will make paper notes, or, at all events, coins of greater value seem to be the only worthy gifts. It will, I hope, expand your heart and make you happy in well-doing. And it may bring, too, the solemn thought that although *you* can see, although you enjoy immeasurably greater blessings than your blind brethren, yet it is not because you deserve such blessings more than they deserve them.

I am convinced that no one can have such thoughts as these without being conscious of an overwhelming sense of his and her responsibility for the blind. By the inscrutable workings of Providence we have in our midst thousands who are helpless because they are sightless. I am sure that it is not necessary for me to quote statistics in order to prove to you how urgently they need your help. Nor do I intend to emphasize how great a handicap it is to be blind. As you listen to these words of mine you have only to close your eyes to all the familiar things by which you are surrounded and keep them tightly closed. Then imagine, if you can, that never will the power of man be able to open them again. You have but to do this and I know that you will realize more graphically and more poignantly than through any words of mine the pathetic helplessness of all those who cannot see—all those whose eyes will *never* open.

With his sightless eyes fixed on dark vacancy Milton, the poet, exclaimed:

"When I consider how my light is spent
Ere half my days in this dark world and wide . . . "

And you may be sure that at such times his blindness filled the great poet with inconsolable grief. Yet he lived to triumph over a seemingly hopeless handicap and made the world richer by the poems of light that came out of his darkness.

And here I want to sound a note of hope—a hope that depends entirely for its realization upon the generosity of all those to whom I make this appeal on behalf of the blind and the nearly blind. For the splendid purpose of the Canadian National Institute for the Blind is not only "to ameliorate the condition of the blind of Canada", but "to prevent blindness". There is not in the world a nobler work than this. There is none, I know, that will touch the hearts of Toronto's citizens with such power of appeal. And the hope of which I speak is the hope that burns bright in the hearts and minds of the blind. The hope that they may be helped to overcome their difficulties. That they may learn to read by the Braille system and that they may be supplied with books that will entertain and instruct. That by vocational training, the power may be given to them to create things of beauty and utility. And that their lives may be altogether enriched by the generosity of their more fortunate fellow men and women.

On behalf of the citizens of this Province I wish to thank the Women's Auxiliary of the Canadian National Institute for the Blind for their untiring efforts and their enterprise in undertaking this humanitarian service. They have done their part nobly. It now remains for you to respond generously. By so doing, you will not only hearten and encourage them, but you will make it possible for them to carry on without stint, without curtailment, this great work for the blind.

NURSING—PAST AND FUTURE

To the Graduating Nurses of Victoria
Hospital, London, Ontario, May 8, 1934

Mr. Chairman, Ladies and Gentlemen:

It is to be regretted that no poet—nor, to my knowledge any other writer—has left any record of what it is that a young nurse's fancy lightly turns to in the Spring. Whatever it may be, however, I am fairly confident that it is *not* the technical details of her profession. That does not mean, of course, that your minds are not considerably exercised even at this season of the year, about nursing; for, after all, springtime is also graduation time. None the less, I venture to say that on such a day as this—a day that for many of you is the consummation of your student days—you find yourselves taking a somewhat larger, a more comprehensive view of the profession you are entering—or are preparing to enter. I imagine, too, that details don't seem nearly as important now as they do when you are on duty. That is as it should be. For a time, at all events, you have left the silence of the wards and the daily routine of hospital, and you may well forget what I have called the technical details of your profession—which you are doing your best to learn, practise and master. I shall not remind you of them. I promise you that I shall not, as the saying goes, "talk shop", except in so far as it deals with the nursing profession as a whole. I sincerely hope, however, that when the proper time comes you will have no difficulty in remembering the many details of routine nursing I am now asking you to forget—for a time.

Today those dismal and foreboding clouds of final examinations have burst—and I must confess that nobody looks any the worse for it. You are free now to look around you at your profession—your chosen profession—to see it as it is, and as it was.   For it is both a physical and a mental impossibility, of course, to look around you without looking back.   And, as far as we are concerned, that means looking back historically for just a glimpse of what nursing used to be. I could, of course, tell you what nursing used to be in some countries, in a word.   But I'm afraid I would have to choose a derogatory and even defamatory word to describe it.   It was not always what it has become—the noblest and most respected of all professions.

However, like so many other causes and movements, persons and things, that later fell into disrepute, nursing began well.   Indeed, it was the Christian ideal of brotherhood and, of course, sisterhood—a word about which I shall have something to say in a moment—that first made a very few people awaken to their responsibility for the sick.   As you would expect, these people had been converted to Christianity. You have only to think of hospital names like St. Thomas's and St. Bartholomew's in London, or Hotel Dieu in Paris, or such Orders as that of St. John of Jerusalem, to see that nursing was almost entirely religious in its origin.   And one of the results was that fifteen hundred years ago there were already six hundred women nursing in the hospitals of Alexandria.   Egypt, you see, can boast of much more than Cleopatra, the Pyramids and the Pharoahs.   Now it may be that some, at least, of these six hundred women were called "Sisters" just as they were, hundreds of years later, in the secular training schools of Protestant England.   I don't like to think that any of them were designated by a name which has always seemed to me officious even more than official. It is, I admit, an exact name, a true name, but it has no hint of the compliment which such a name should always imply.   The name has always appeared to me to lack something of the fragrance of association, of helpfulness and comradeship which such an honoured title should bear. I refer to the name "Head Nurse".

The amiable practice in England is to honour such nurses with the title of "Sister".   The public understands and affectionately admires such a name. During the War, trained nurses in the Army Hospitals were likewise called "Sisters". I would like to see the day when Head Nurses in Canadian Hospitals will all be called "Sisters". Such a title is rich in friendly helpful associations that are easily understood and are full of a true, sympathetic dignity. I suggest that you set the example here and designate your Head Nurses "Sisters". After all, Victoria Hospital was organized by Sister Florence of the Order of St. John of Jerusalem in 1883. Suppose that kindly lady had insisted upon calling herself Head Nurse Florence, or Superintendent—would she have gained or lost thereby? I think she and all those who might well share with her the name of "Sister" lose by the use of any other name. Don't be content, by the way, with changing only the name of Head Nurse to "Sister". Why not use the title "Matron" instead of "Superintendent"? After all, the time-honoured name "Matron" has precisely the same pleasant and dignified association as "Sister". It is a splendid name. But as for the name "Superintendent" . . . well, I must return to the profession of nursing as it used to be.

You recall that I mentioned St. Bartholomew's Hospital in London. In 1544 it was re-established by King Henry VIII —of whom you have recently been receiving so much mis-information through the cinema. It had a matron and twelve nurses who did domestic work when off duty. Then, I fear that until less than a hundred years ago, the story of nursing and nurses generally is a doleful one—a story that, knowing as you do what nursing is today—would make you exclaim, "Is it possible?" if I had time to tell it to you in any detail.

For example, in 1857—that is only seventy-seven years ago—*The London Times* described the servant nurses in the London hospitals. And this is the description: "Lectured by committees, preached at by chaplains, scowled on by treasurers and stewards, scolded by matrons, sworn at by surgeons, bullied by dressers, grumbled at and abused by patients, insulted if old and ill-favoured, talked flippantly to if middle-aged and good-humoured, tempted and seduced if young and well-looking . . . They were what any woman might be in the same circumstances." As a matter of fact, of course, they were mostly dowdy-looking females of drunken and dubious habits. And that, after all, in view of the lives they were forced to lead, won't, I imagine, surprise you.

Most of you know, too, that notorious pair of nurses, Betsy Prig and Sarah Gamp. About the time that our Chief Justice was learning to read and write, Charles Dickens was actually writing *Martin Chuzzlewit*, in which he told of this precious couple. That was in 1849. Betsy Prig is an actual portrait of a so-called nurse who nursed one of Dickens' friends. Betsy, you remember, was kindness itself—*to herself*. She had a playful habit of stealing a patient's pillow so that she might be more comfortable in her armchair. The immortal Mrs. Gamp—Sarah—was, of course, devotion itself, and could never for long keep away from the tea-pot on her mantel-piece which contained—whiskey. As for her patients, her devotion to them was expressed entirely by her professional fees. Sarah Gamp would condescend to go out nursing at "Eighteenpence a day for working people and three and six [that is more than twice as much] for gentlefolks, night watching being an extra charge."

If you think Betsy and Sarah not precisely the kind of nurses to whom you would entrust the health of a sick friend, I should add that they were typical of the nurses of their time. In fact, they were not nearly as bad as nurses had been! Daniel Defoe, who wrote a great deal more than his most famous book *Robinson Crusoe*, told the story of the Plague of London in his *Journal of the Plague Year* in 1665. If any of you imagine that at such a time nurses were showing themselves valiant in service, working like Trojans to succour the dying, or hurrying with brisk, purposeful strides through the plague-haunted streets and in and out of sick wards, listen to this description of nursing in what many regard as the good old days: "We had at this time", writes Defoe, "a great many frightful stories told us of nurses and watch-men who looked after the dying people, used them barbar-ously, starving them, smothering them, or by other wicked means hastening their end.   The women were in all this calamity the most rash, fearless and desperate creatures, and as there were vast numbers that went about as nurses, they committed a great many petty thieveries in the houses where they were employed.   These robberies extended chiefly to clothes, linen, and what rings and money they could come at when the person died, who was under their care; and I could give an account of one of these nurses, who, several years after, being on her death bed, confessed with the utmost horror the robberies she had committed at the time of her being a nurse, and by which she had enriched herself to a great degree."

To say the least, it seems that nurses in those days had a rather high-handed way of collecting their fees.

But it wasn't only in times of widespread calamity that nurses showed themselves for what they were.   At about the same time John Evelyn, the diarist, lost both his sons through the ignorance and carelessness of nurses.   When his first son died in 1658 he wrote, "In my opinion he was suffocated by the woman and maids that tended him and covered him too hot with blankets as he lay in a cradle near an excessive hot fire in a close room."   Six years later, Evelyn's second son died.   "It pleased God", he wrote, "to take away my son, being now a month old.   We suspected much the nurse had overlain him."

I could tell you much more of nursing and nurses—its history and how very gradually it dawned upon men and women that it was wrong that those afflicted by illness should have the added affliction of such nurses.   But I have said enough to show you how religious conscientiousness had for a time revived that social consciousness which acknow-ledges mankind's duty to the sick, and how, during the centuries, that consciousness had waned until it really didn't exist.   However, about the time that the Betsy Prigs and the Sarah Gamps of the world were in their merry hey-day, a pastor in a small German town turned the garden-house of the Pastorate into a refuge for female prisoners. His name was Theodore Fieldman, and with the help of his wife he trained these women to care for the sick. The work prospered. Three years later he founded a school for nursing deaconesses. An English lady, whose name you all know, attended the school and received her training there. Her name, as you have all guessed, was Florence Nightingale, who, after the Crimean War in 1854, founded a School for Nurses at St. Thomas's Hospital. To omit her name in any story of nursing would be as impossible as to omit the name of London in any account of the most progressive cities of Canada.

With Florence Nightingale, my story of the past must end. For, with her, nursing came into its own. The past was forgotten and the history of nursing since then more than makes amends for all the shortcomings, the ignorance and often the arrant roguery which is so large a part of the story of nursing as it used to be, before the advent of the heroine of the Crimea.

Very quickly, now that we are looking around us at this great profession, and now that we have seen something of its past, let us try to envisage something too of its future. That doesn't mean that I shall attempt to prophesy. Far from it! Even had I the gift of far-sightedness I should be only too aware of one of its penalties—long-windedness. I propose rather for a few moments to hitch my wagon, as it were, not to some far distant star, but to the very concrete and thought-provoking record of a Survey made in 1931 of the nursing profession by Professor Weir. One of his proposals was to reduce very drastically the number of training schools for nurses and to centralize them, very much as was done with Normal Schools several decades ago. He suggests that no hospital with less than seventy-five beds should have a training school. To staff a small hospital with graduate nurses would cost no more than to maintain an

efficient training school.   And if training schools were limited
in this way it would have yet another advantage.   It would
give employment to many graduate nurses and would soon
reduce the graduates yearly to a number that might be
absorbed.

In 1925, Dr. Fred Routley, Director of the Provincial
Red Cross Society, actually studied the operation of fourteen
small hospitals, some of them with and some without a
training school.   He found that the difference in cost was
less than one cent a day per patient.   In the last few years
there has been a growing sentiment against training schools
in small hospitals which, it is felt, might well be operated
by graduate nurses.   The largest of these smaller hospitals—
the Metropolitan General Hospital in Windsor, with 105
beds—is now staffed entirely by graduate nurses.   Indeed,
this trend is so general that Miss Munn, Inspector of Training
Schools for Nurses, states that during the past ten years no
less than thirty-five general hospital training schools in this
Province have been discontinued.   That, I think you will
agree, is significant.

But the public of Canada as a whole will think it perhaps
of even greater significance that 90 per cent. of the nurses
in this country are geographically in a position to serve only
64 per cent. of the population, and that only three persons out
of eight requiring the services of a nurse are financially able
to employ her.   For this unfortunate state of affairs the
socialization of the nursing service is proposed, with the
setting up of Dominion and Provincial Councils.   In making
this proposal, however, Professor Weir overlooks the fact
that the nursing profession is, in itself, a part of the medical
profession's armamentarium.   It cannot function independently as a health agency.   But since we already have Federal
and Provincial Departments of Public Health who are responsible for the preservation of public health, I would suggest
that they might well be given the necessary authority to
evolve and bring into effect a plan whereby the present
condition of inadequate nursing service may be corrected.

This would be to the great advantage of all those to whom the benefits of trained nursing are not at present available.

Now, a word to those of you who are about to embark on the seemingly troubled and uncertain sea of your profession. The economic effects of the depression have been felt, of course, in nursing as in other professions. "What opportunities are there", you may ask, "for a graduate nurse?"

Well, one of the results of the present economic impasse is that for financial reasons people are demanding that patients be treated by doctor and nurse at home instead of being sent to hospitals. In consequence, such visiting organizations as the Victorian Order of Nurses and other voluntary agencies are considering an extension of their work. It has been suggested, too, that the Public Health Department of the various municipalities should include actual nursing care as one of the duties proper to them. At the present time 89 municipalities in Ontario employ about 355 Public Health nurses. To make your future prospects even more hopeful I should mention that one and another of the voluntary agencies in Ontario have 180 nurses engaged in the bedside care of those unable to pay for the regular type of service. In addition, some 50 or 60 nurses are attached to various industries. This is a service that might well be greatly increased for the proper *early* treatment of minor accidents. Such early treatment would not only eliminate further complications of the injury and possible serious illness, but, even from the least altruistic or humanitarian point of view, it would certainly reduce compensation costs.

At this point it would be appropriate to refer to an interesting innovation recently made by those in charge of the Niagara Peninsula Sanatorium. I know that you will be glad to hear that an important field of service has thus been opened for the nurse as a community agent. At Welland it was recognized that responsibility for tubercular patients from any area did not begin and end in the Sanatorium. It was necessary that all persons exposed to infection in the area from which patients came should be examined by a physician for possible infection. So a Public Health nurse was engaged, and one of her duties was to supervise the home care and help the doctor in the care of all cases not requiring sanatorium treatment. The nurse also carried on a public educational campaign. She told the sick how to avoid infecting others. She told the "others" how to protect themselves against tuberculous infection.

This type of service—this extension of the great work being done by nurses—will, if possible, add to the honour and prestige of all nurses, not the least important part of whose work is done in remote places. Think, for example, of the Red Cross Out-Post Hospital Nursing Service where some 50 graduates are working in 24 small hospitals which the Red Cross has been operating for 11 years in Northern Ontario. Magnificent work! It must fire your imagination to think of these fellow-nurses of yours in little hospitals, many of them 150 miles or more distant from any other institution.

The development of nursing has made it necessary, of course, that nurses should specialize. But specialization should be insisted upon only when a nurse shows a natural aptitude for any one of the many branches into which nursing may be conveniently divided. Then and only then a capable girl should be encouraged to follow her inclination and be given every opportunity to develop it. Again and again, I have noticed, for example, how impossible it is to make every nurse-in-training a first-rate operating-room nurse. It is frankly a waste of time for many girls to attempt this highly specialized type of work. In justice to them they should not be bound by the unnecessarily rigid regulations which at present compel all nurses to do an equal amount of operative work. Their time would be better spent in learning and practising work for which they have more marked natural qualifications.

As nurses, wherever you are and in whatever capacity you are called upon to serve, your chief consideration must always be your patient's welfare. Nothing in your patient's environment should be overlooked. Always remember that a patient is in an abnormal mental condition. Be careful what you say in his hearing. Indiscreet remarks overheard can make him despair of recovery. On the other hand, a sick room that is bright, restful and confidence-inspiring, can help him more than even you can guess.

Whatever you do, don't show the utter lack of tact of the nurse who met a lady friend of mine at the hospital door. Said my friend, who was, as a matter of fact, going in to have an operation, "Well, nurse, you see I'm well enough to *walk* in." "Yes," said this nurse, "so I see. But it isn't everybody who walks in that walks out again."

Or take the case of a patient of mine on whom I had operated for goitre. On the third day—although she was doing splendidly—to my great consternation I found her in tears. Till then she had been full of the glad spirit of recovery. I asked her why she was so depressed. "Well," said she, "a friend of mine, Mrs. Brown, called yesterday and asked me how I was. I said, 'I'm feeling fine, considering this is only the second day.' 'Yes,' said Mrs. Brown, 'That's just it. A friend of mine felt just like you do on the second day. She was dead on the third!' "

Whatever you do, nurses, don't forget to protect your patients from such friends as these.

And now one last word. A few moments ago I mentioned the possible socialization of nursing service. Through the Public Health Service the Government already examines and supervises milk supplies, inspects water and performs a great many other valuable functions in the interests of the health of the people. The Government provides research laboratories. The Government distributes toxoids and serums. I am confident that one day all our medical services will be the responsibility of the State. But a little longer—a few more years—and it seems to me that many of the Provinces of Canada will be ripe and ready for the introduction of State Medicine. Such a measure would be of the greatest importance to you as nurses.   For that would mean that the great profession of nursing, which you are now entering, would be placed at the service of all men and all women and all children wherever they may be and whatever they may possess of this world's goods.

THE LOYALISTS OF CANADA

At the Opening of the National Historical
Exhibition of the United Empire Loyalists'
Association, Toronto, May 14, 1934

Mr. President, Ladies and Gentlemen:

There are times in the lives of all people when thoughts of the past come to them with a curious insistence. Such a time is this, when the Loyalists of today honour the memory of the Loyalists of yesterday.

I know of no worthier tribute to the memory of the United Empire Loyalists of the past than this Exhibition. It spans the years that now separate us from our heroic forefathers—the Loyalist founders of Ontario and of Canada. It reminds us not alone of the conditions in which they lived, but also of the admirable spirit with which they overcame those conditions. In that sense, therefore, all that is displayed here is not merely an historical reminiscence. It is a challenge to us to face the problems of today with the same unwearying spirit of courage and co-operation, of loyalty and mutual helpfulness as the Loyalists of old manifested amid the great difficulties—the seemingly insuperable difficulties and dangers by which they, too, were surrounded.

May we profit by their example!

Yet another incidental but extremely valuable purpose is achieved by this Exhibition. It will correct the tendency to indulge in too romantic fancies concerning the days of yore. For it should never be forgotten that the lives of the pioneer Loyalists were hard, uncomfortable lives. The measure of their great achievement is directly proportionate to the tremendous difficulties they had to overcome.

One hundred years ago a gentleman of historic renown (Colonel Thomas Talbot) in a letter to Anna Jameson explained why he had come to Upper Canada. He appeared to blame a certain Pierre Charlevoix, who, said Colonel Talbot, "was the true cause of my coming to this place. You know", continues Colonel Talbot, "he calls this the 'Paradise of the Hurons'. Now, I was resolved to get to Paradise by hook or by crook, and so I came here."

Ladies and gentlemen, you have an opportunity to judge by these relics and portraits of the past the kind of "paradise" it was in which those hardy old Loyalist pioneers lived. I think you will agree that they must have had periods of bitter disillusionment as well as moments when they experienced the joy of personal triumph.

When I noticed that the programme this evening contains a reference to a Loyalist house-warming, I thought of those tiny log shanties in which the early Loyalists lived—palatial residences some ten feet long, eight feet wide and six feet high! I thought of the log houses which were enlargements and slight elaborations of these shanties. I recalled a letter written by John Macaulay to his mother less than a hundred years ago, in which he wrote "we live in a very airy house. The wind blows through it." I remembered, too, a description by Mrs. Traill in 1836 of waking up after a night's sleep in one of the later and much improved houses, such as the Loyalists then lived in: "The sensation of cold early in the morning", she wrote, "was very painful . . . Our breaths were congealed in hoar-frost on the sheets and blankets." Thinking of these things, it occurred to me that in a very literal sense, at least, the problem of house-warming must have been an extremely prosaic and formidable one in those distant days.

With the trees of the great forests, the Loyalists built their little homes and of these trees, too, they built their first roads—corduroy roads—log roads—to link together the small Loyalist settlements. Yet their courage was such that they could laugh at hardships. Consider, for example, this parody of Tennyson's "Charge of the Light Brigade", describing a journey in a coach over one of these log roads:

> "Half a log, half a log, half a log onward
> Shaken and out of breath rode we and wondered.
> Ours not to reason why; ours but to clutch and cry
> While onward we thundered."

At this Exhibition we come face to face with this past. We see it intimately. As nearly as possible it is presented to us realistically. Their lives thus revealed to us make the Loyalist men and women of the past seem closer to us and something more than names. And I think you will agree that thereby none of the true romance of those days is lost—but rather increased.

I congratulate all those responsible for this most fitting commemoration of the courage, the loyalty and the indefatigable energy of the U.E. Loyalists. To realize with what primitive conditions they had to contend, only increases our admiration for them. Their spirit remains. The tradition which they enriched continues with us. May it ever be so.

I have great pleasure in declaring this National Historical Exhibition of the U.E. Loyalists' Association open.

MORE ABOUT THE LOYALISTS

Responding to the Toast "The Empire" at
a Dinner to the United Empire Loyalists in
the King Edward Hotel, Toronto,
May 23, 1934

Mr. Chairman, Ladies and Gentlemen:

In responding to this toast, so eloquently proposed by Mr. Spence, I am confronted by two difficulties. It is not easy further to embellish the theme; nor is it possible in the few moments at my disposal to deal adequately with a subject so great as that of an Empire which girdles the globe and which has given to the world its finest traditions of democracy. Had I pondered the problem deeply I might have been discouraged by the thought of my inability to do justice to the subject. Thus I might have found myself in the predicament of one Patrick O'Brien, hailing, I should judge by his name, from one of the countries of the Empire. Patrick was so unfortunate as to fall into a deep pit, and his companion, whom tradition compels me to call "Mike", cried down to him—"Are ye dead, Pat? Spake to me for the love av hiven." "It's not dead I am," answered Pat, "but I'm knocked intoirely spacheless."

That I should share a similar fate is a fear which has recurred to me several times this evening as I have listened to the eloquent words of the preceding speakers who have developed so well the themes of loyalty and empire. I asked myself: "Now that history has been dealt with so comprehensively and loyalty exalted so worthily, what remains to be said?"

Many of you who have visited London know that it is customary in the summer season to serve tea on the lawn at the House of Commons, and visitors from many parts of the world are regularly entertained there.   The great Labourite, John Burns, who, prior to the War was President of the Board of Trade and thereby a member of the British Cabinet, once remarked to an American visitor whom he met on the lawn, that the river (the Thames) looked very fine that afternoon.   "River!" exclaimed the visitor, "Do you call that a river?"   Somewhat taken aback John Burns admitted that he long had laboured under the impression that the Thames was a river.   The visitor snorted: "You should see our mighty Mississippi, you should see our majestic St. Lawrence, if you want to talk about rivers."

"And of what does the Mississippi consist?" asked John Burns.   "Is it water?"

"Of course it's water," said the visitor.

"And the St. Lawrence, is that water too?"

"Certainly it's water."

"Well," said Burns, who was known to drop his H's when he became excited, "That, Sir," and he pointed to the river Thames, "That is liquid 'istory."

The Empire is history, too—to my mind the most fascinating of histories.   A history that records the development of a philosophy of government, of a spirit of loyalty and of a valiant democracy that may properly excite the admiration of the world at large.   What is it that bred this philosophy, nurtured this loyalty and fostered this democracy?

It is at such moments as this that the mental habits of a lifetime are helpful.   Early in life a surgeon forms the habit of diagnosis.   It is a chronic and incurable habit— but not, therefore, a malady.   Only very rarely does it become such an obsession as in the case of James Smithson—the founder of the Smithsonian Institute—who was dying with five doctors in attendance, none of whom could diagnose his illness. 'My friends," said Smithson, "I desire that you will make a post-mortem examination of me and find out what ails me; for really I am dying to know what it is myself."

I feel that in the behaviour of the Loyalists we may perceive symptoms of something well worth our investigation. Viewed dispassionately, there appears to be no reason in the world why, five years before the year which we are com- memorating, 24 families in New York State had already petitioned the British Government to help them to emigrate and live under the British Flag; and why three whole years before that, 300 Highlanders had already arrived at Albany in New York State, marching hard and fast toward Canada. Why? It appears irrational, to say the least. And again, why did Sir John Jameson sacrifice 200,000 acres of land in the U.S.A. in order to come to Canada, where, during the winter, at all events, his welcome would be the chilliest and most frigid? And what is one to say, too, of those disbanded Regiments—the King's Royal Regiment of New York (or the Royal Yorkers) and the Royal Highland Emigrant Regiment—whose arrival in Canada we are celebrating, and who came that they might be given a location ticket, and live in tents and chop down trees wherewith to build a shelter?

It was, you recall, Sir Frederick Haldimand who showed a truly profound wisdom and a deep understanding of the human heart in settling the Loyalists in groups corresponding to their old army units. Thereby the mutually helpful and companionable spirit which can exist only in such a com- munity, the friendly bonds of which had already been forged, was preserved. The spectre of loneliness which so often preys on the hearts and minds of isolated settlers was effectu- ally exorcised. Therein, I am confident, is to be found the secret of a successful solution of those problems of land settlement which still remain.

But to return to the immediate problem raised by the behaviour of the Loyalists. It would be absurd to say that they hoped to share in the beef bone which four years later— in 1788, "The Hungry Year"—was to be passed from home to home, not many miles from Picton—and which was boiled again and again in order to extract some nutriment. Nor, I firmly believe, were they attracted by the prospect of living a life so lonely and so hard that a Scotch Loyalist, yearning with all his heart for his native land, wrote:

> "If I cou'd see the lane' kirkyard
> Whar' frien's lye side by side:
> And think that I cou'd lay my banes
> Beside them when I died;

> "Then might I think this forest, hame,
> And in it live and dee;
> Nor feel regret at my heart's core,
> My native land for thee."

No, it was for none of these reasons that they came to Canada, and yet, despite the frequent scarcity of food, despite the terrific labour that was necessary before even the simplest needs could be satisfied, and despite the homesickness which must have frequently overtaken them, they remained to lay the sturdy foundations of this great Dominion within the Empire. Indeed, it must have been the knowledge that they, with their kinsfolk at home, were still fellow-citizens of the Empire, that suppressed every consideration of the hardships to be borne. The thought that they were still linked with far-scattered citizens of Empire in other parts of the world, the assurance that they had not lost their birthright, must have made it seem worth while to face and overcome so many difficulties.

So it is that even if in the professional spirit of a habitual diagnostician, one considers the Empire and the part the Loyalists played in its extension here in Canada, one becomes aware that the true reasons for doing as they did are not always the most obvious reasons. The Loyalists were moved by other desires than for personal gain. They were men of vision. And because they were such men, their coming to Canada was symptomatic of much more than can be explained by a simple description of the life—the only life to which they could look forward in Upper Canada, Ontario, or New Brunswick, 150 years ago.

The speakers this evening have most graphically told the story and explained, too, something of the motives by which the Loyalists were prompted in returning to the

Empire. For there existed then, and there still exists within that Empire, a spirit, a quality which is omnipresent, and of which we are all conscious. To say that this spirit, this quality, is a broad tolerance of individual differences would be to describe but a part of that larger freedom which, by reason of the labours of such men as we honour tonight, has been handed down as a heritage—a heritage of which we are the trustees for future generations. It is, I think, this spirit of a larger freedom that binds the people of Empire together. It is a spirit which permits of full self-expression for every citizen and entails the responsibility of the highest type of citizenship. It makes the Empire unique. Because we have free expression of divergent and even contradictory opinions, we achieve a citizenship that breeds the true loyalist. The acid test of democracy is that it should never fear the intelligence of its citizens, however widely separated may be the conclusions to which their personal, individual thinking leads them.

The democratic institutions of the British Empire have long been subjected to this test and are therefore the finer and the sounder.

It was Alexander Pope who defined discord—that is, such differences of opinion as true freedom permits—as "a harmony not understood". He says,

> "Jarring interests of themselves create
> Th'according music of a well-mixed state;
> Such is the world's great harmony that springs
> From order, union, full consent of things."

Or, in the words of that great orator, Thomas Burke, "You have within the Empire that action and counteraction which, in the natural and the political world, from the reciprocal struggle of discordant powers, draws out the harmony of the universe."

Gentlemen, with all my heart I respond to the toast, "The Empire". I could not, if I would, describe what it symbolizes more graphically and pithily than in the words I have just quoted—"Order, union, full consent of things."

CANADIAN CLUBS

At the Biennial Conference of the Associa-
tion of Canadian Clubs, Royal York Hotel,
Toronto, May 28, 1934

Mr. President, Ladies and Gentlemen:

It is most appropriate that this meeting of Canadian Clubs should be held on a Spring morning. It may have occurred to you—but likewise it may have escaped some of those present that Spring and Canadian Clubs possess in common a quality of inspiration that is none the less real because it is somewhat difficult to define. Indeed, it would not be difficult to trace a close parallel—a somewhat romantic but not an unreal parallel—between this pleasant season of the year and the Clubs at whose kind invitation I am here today. I must confess that, for a time at least, the temptation to do so was almost irresistible. Sermons have been preached and speeches made—even after-dinner speeches—about subjects that, to me, at all events, have appeared even more attenuated and almost irresponsibly vaguer and more elusive. But in this case it must be admitted that Spring and the Canadian Clubs are both full of promise and instinct with vitality. They both possess an inspiring, uplifting quality. They are both associated—or should be associated in our minds with the sowing of seeds. And the seeds of enlightenment sown broadcast far and wide throughout this Dominion by the direct agency of Canadian Clubs are assuredly just as certain to bear fruit in the fullness of time as any of those rather more concrete springtime seeds of fruit and flowers, grain and vegetables.

You see how compellingly attractive such a comparison is. It is all the more difficult to resist because it is not merely a pleasing fancy, but has its roots firmly bedded in reality.

You will, I am sure, be able to think of other similarities between Spring and the Clubs to which you belong. Youth, for example, as typified in the persons of your members; or again, the brightness which habitually pervades your meetings. I was impelled to make this comparison only by my desire to pay to the Canadian Clubs the tribute of praise they so richly deserve; I do so whole-heartedly and with a very real awareness of the extremely important part you play in the life of the citizens of Canada, considered as large and small scattered communities of people linked together by a common heritage.

For it seems to me that the Canadian Clubs fulfil a dual function. Not only do you seek to derive every possible benefit from the presence of outstanding men—speakers on whose tongues dwell knowledge, information, entertainment or even the supreme gift of wisdom; but also, and in a very real sense, you are intermediaries between the people of Canada and such men. It is hardly necessary for me to emphasize the great importance of this function so admirably fulfilled by the Canadian Clubs. By thus affording opportunities to speakers to deliver the message that is in them you are able thereby to add immeasurably to the cultural and intellectual life of Canada, and, indeed, to that elevation of mind and spirit in general, which alone has given to man his ascendancy in the scale of nature. That is a magnificent thought—a thought which, I believe, will give to your deliberations at this meeting an added import. I know, too, that it will help you to enter the year that lies before you with not only undiminished but greatly augmented enthusiasm.

No part of a nation's life remains unaffected by speakers who have power to provoke thought even in the unthinking, and the ability to induce even the thoughtful to think more deeply and to greater purpose. To be a member of a Canadian Club is, after all, a splendid way of emulating Nature, which, as you know, abhors a vacuum—in the mind as elsewhere.

May I add this thought.   There are already in Canada many indications that the seeds of enlightenment, of education, of intellectual maturity to which I earlier referred, are already bearing notable fruit.   There was a time when the men and women of this Dominion were content with what they could get of culture.   Books were the monopoly of those who weren't busy.   Speeches and speakers were rare luxuries; not to be criticized, but gratefully and with due humility to be accepted as gifts from an astral plane known as higher education. And higher education itself was in turn the monopoly of other countries.   Not so long ago the prerequisite of any speaker was that he should have enjoyed the quite inestimable privilege of birth and education anywhere but in struggling, pioneering Canada.   This was, after all, but natural.   The people of days gone by—the founders of Canada—were far too busy for such an apparently super-mundane thing as education.

But proverbially, too, "A prophet is not without honour, save in his own country."   And I know that you will join with me in welcoming the more intelligently critical appraisal of speakers everywhere evident.   Canada has grown up.   She is developing her own intellectual standards.   She demands of speakers their message and not their country of origin and such rather irrelevant family details.   Names of far places no longer ring with the old awe-inspiring sound in the ears of our citizens.   The gulf that separated our forefathers from the sources of learning, the imposing seats of culture in other lands, have long been bridged.   The intellectual traffic between them and us is no longer a one-way traffic.   Canada receives—but Canada gives also.

With the disappearance of all possible reason for any further bowings and scrapings of our abject old friend "Inferiority Complex", the task before Canadian Clubs becomes perhaps more difficult, but also and for that reason, even more worth doing well.   It is to such organizations as the Canadian Clubs that Canadians look for guidance in the just choice of speakers from Canada and from abroad who will satisfy an appetite for the acquisition of knowledge and culture which with the years has become far more discriminating and consequently less easy to satisfy with any but the best available.

Allow me then, gentlemen, in conclusion to wish you success in the meetings that are about to begin. May you find in the memorable records of your past that just pride which is a happy augury also of your future. May the very difficulties that may confront you, may the increasing responsibilities inherent in your growth, be but such obstacles as, once surmounted, will place you and all Canadian Clubs yet another step higher in that consistent upward progress which you have made during the years that have passed since your foundation.

It is with great pleasure that I declare the meeting of Canadian Clubs open.

EXHIBITIONS AS STIMULANTS

Opening the Ninth Annual Hamilton Exhibition in the Armouries, Hamilton,
May 28, 1934

Mr. President, Ladies and Gentlemen:

It must be a source of gratification to the citizens of Hamilton that each year the commercial development of this city receives the additional impetus given by this Exhibition. I know you will understand and appreciate the pleasure that is mine at this moment, surrounded as I am by so comprehensive a display of products of Canadian manufacture. To me, as a visitor to this city, it most effectively symbolizes the spirit of optimism which flourishes in your midst, undimmed by the clouds of adverse economic conditions. Those dark clouds are, I verily believe, already dispersing. Here and there the blue sky is peeping through. Little by little, the rising sun of better days to come becomes clearer, visibly brightening the horizon of the future. I think you will agree that the Canadian trade reports recently issued have made pleasant reading. I am confident that you have found in them a very rational justification for believing that we can look toward the days to come with a renewed hopefulness and a fortified optimism.

Most sincerely I congratulate the Canadian Manufacturers' Association, the Chamber of Commerce, and not least, the public-spirited Corporation of Hamilton, who, in conjunction, have made this Exhibition not merely a possibility, but a splendid reality. What we rather depressingly refer to as the "Depression" had already begun in 1930. Yet, in that same year your City Council did not hesitate to sponsor this Exhibition and has sponsored it ever since, with increasing success. Never, I am convinced, was success more difficult to achieve, and time and circumstances less propitious.

Yet, I have only to look about me this evening to recognize the energy and undaunted enterprise of all those responsible for the success of the Hamilton Exhibition. I shall be but expressing the sentiments of those who will visit this Exhibition, and of all those other citizens of Hamilton and surrounding districts, for whose direct and indirect benefit it is being held, when, on their behalf, I thank the City Council and the organizations I have already mentioned. I should add a special word of gratitude to the members of the Joint Publicity Committee. The burden of their responsibilities must have been, to say the least, no easy one. But this Exhibition is sufficient and striking proof of the manner in which they have discharged their duties as representatives of civic and trade organizations.

I can imagine nothing more heartening than the knowledge that ever since 1926 the Hamilton Exhibition has grown year by year; and that despite grave economic handicaps more and more people visit it—the annual attendance increasing yearly. I am convinced that there can be no sounder evidence that the trade and industry of this City is enriched by the unquestionably practical benefits of such an Exhibition as this.

Here on display is indisputable confirmation of the progress being made in Canadian industry. Here, too, is an incentive to increased commercial transaction. But, essential and praiseworthy as these are, this Exhibition serves yet another purpose which should never be forgotten. It is a challenge. It is an encouragement. It will strengthen men and women in the assurance that however great the difficulties by which we are even now beset, such testimonies to the skill of Canadian manufacture as are here displayed, are but earnests of a future for this young country of which we can have no conception, so greatly will it transcend these days of economic dislocation, and so much more satisfactorily will the purposes of true civilization then be fulfilled. The enduring patience which Canadians everywhere have shown through these dark days will yet be magnificently rewarded.

One word more. You noticed, in all probability, that when speaking of what I may call the psychological value of this Exhibition I referred to economic dislocation. That is, perhaps, a somewhat medical figure of speech. However, those of you who have been unfortunate enough to suffer any form of dislocation will, I know, admit the peculiar aptness of such a description. But I have heard yet another description of the condition of the world into which it has been forced by the impediments which have crept into finance and the customary channels of trade and commerce. The description possessed an even more pronounced medical flavour. Civilization was described as having "hardening of the arteries".

As an attempted diagnosis, that is almost incredibly wrong. The difficulties from which we suffer are neither incurable, nor chronic, nor the beginning of the end—as hardening of the arteries always is. They are rather symptoms of flaws which can be set right, of stoppages that can be cleared, of an indisposition, an illness which can and will be cured. This Exhibition itself is designed to improve locally what may conveniently be termed the circulatory system of commerce! Every year since its inauguration it has done so, and I know with what unabated vigour this Exhibition will fulfil the worthy purposes for which it is being held again this year.

I leave it to wiser men than I to prescribe an infallible remedy for the world's ills in which Canada too has shared. I am confident, however, that when the prescription is formulated and the remedy administered—that remedy will be found to be neither the violent cathartics that some recommend, nor the sugary pills of platitude in which others pin their faith, but something that is neither the one nor the other. It has been the courage, faith and steadiness of the Canadian people which has enabled them to keep the flag flying and await with confidence the return of better times. Then, among many other desirable improvements, it will be discovered that it is not an unalterable necessity to attempt to starve ourselves and others into hard-won posperity in a world so abundantly fertile and so continuously productive.

In declaring this Hamilton Exhibition open may I express the hope that it will be even more successful than your last.

A TRIBUTE TO TRUE PIONEERS

At the Annual Meeting of the Canadian
Council on Child and Family Welfare,
Royal Connaught Hotel, Hamilton,
May 28, 1934

Your Worship, Madam President, Ladies and Gentlemen:

I appreciate the very kind words of His Worship the Mayor and your most cordial reception.

The members of the Canadian Council on Child and Family Welfare will, I hope, restrain whatever expressions of incredulity may spring to their lips if I describe them as pioneers in the very vanguard of civilization. It is simplicity itself to prove the unadorned truth of such a statement, for I regard your work as quite literally second to none in its avowed purpose to ameliorate, by voluntary effort, the lot of those who have been overtaken by misfortune within our own borders.

I propose to prove that you may legitimately claim positions of the highest honour in the forefront of humanity's progress onward and upward.

First, then, men and women and children are the greatest of all the riches in the world; for them and by them alone do civilizations exist. Second, the greatest work in the world, the finest and the most valuable, is to protect, to cultivate, to care for this treasure—in a word, to work for its welfare. Need I add the conclusion?—for the inevitable, the inescapable conclusion is that, because you are engaged in welfare work, you deserve the highest honour and the most enthusiastic co-operation of all people. Your work entitles you to be placed in what I have called the vanguard of civilization. But—and I hope this won't sound contradictory—like Good Samaritans who pick up those who have fallen by the wayside, you are also the active rearguard, tending the victims of mankind's own blunders and looking after all those who find themselves seemingly cast aside, unable to keep pace with the restless, wayward, not easily controlled caravan of modern civilization—a civilization moving slowly—at times uncertainly—toward the ultimate goal of universal well-being.

The message I bring to you is a brief message. The length of the programme of which this is but the beginning has not escaped my notice. But by showing why the work of the Canadian Welfare Council and the motives by which that work is prompted are the highest of which men and women are capable, I have, I hope, expressed as adequately as possible my sincere appreciation of the voluntary work you are doing. Times like these are a challenge to the best that is in humanity. You have responded to that challenge most nobly and have earned the gratitude of your fellow men and women.

I fear, however, that gratitude is not enough. The work you are doing is made necessary not only by the more obvious effects of deplorable economic conditions. It is necessitated, also, by ignorance of elementary hygiene, of pre-natal care, of the proper upbringing for children and of much else— ignorance which does so much to nullify the best of intentions, and brings unnecessary, avoidable suffering to great numbers of people. I know you will agree that one of the greatest tasks confronting all those who labour for the public welfare is the dissemination of knowledge. The desire for such knowledge already exists. The anxieties of parenthood are immeasurably increased by withholding it. I look forward to the day when preventive medicine will be taught far and wide—when broadsides of beneficent propaganda will be discharged, as it were, within the hearing and understanding of all people, against man's greatest enemy—disease.

General education of the public will work miracles for public health. How much there is that can be taught! To take a single example—when people know more about children's diseases, when they recognize, for instance, that the common cold is not a simple innocent thing that may be disregarded with impunity, but that it is actually the cause of about half the illness in Canada—then I know they will realize the necessity of instruction in preventive measures, and in its care and cure should it develop. The knowledge that a cold is due to germs and may lead to sinus trouble, middle-ear disease, or disease of the mastoid, should sufficiently indicate its seriousness and impress upon all the necessity of taking every care until it is cured. Perhaps the simplest way of dealing with a cold at its inception is to keep the child in bed for at least two days.

I should like here to refer to a statement which I have heard made by Welfare workers, viz.: that children generally do not receive a sufficient amount of milk. Every child should have as a minimum one pint of milk per day, and would do better with two.

It may be, too, that for this and many other reasons affecting the health and happiness of men and women and children, the pressing problem of adequate housing—fit homes for all Canadians—will then no longer be regarded as a purely monetary or economic problem, but one of far deeper implications, of wider significance, embracing all that we mean by life—the life of this generation and generations to come. When one considers the terrible fruits of neglect and ignorance of all those big and little things which can and will build up a nation of splendid men and women, of robust, happy children, then one cannot but be staggered by the apathy of some, and the indifference of others.

It would be both relevant and proper at this point to anticipate a little the Fourteenth Annual Report of your Council which will be submitted to you this evening. For by so doing I am afforded a most welcome opportunity to express my gratification and to congratulate you most cordially upon the splendid educational work that has already been done by the publication of folders and letters and pamphlets containing information vital to parents and children.

May such good work prosper more and more! Only by such methods, indeed, will the well-springs of health and virility be kept running free and accessible to all people. Only then shall we avoid those destructive landslides of family disaster caused by ignorance of simple rules of health which it is the responsibility of all to know and of the qualified few to impart.

In conveying to you the thanks of all your fellow-Canadian men and women (for there can be none who would withhold so well-merited a tribute to the great voluntary humanitarian work you have done), I am conscious of the very real difficulties which confront you in continuing and enlarging the scope of your good works. But, being so brief, my message to you can touch only lightly, almost perfunctorily, upon one or two of the most important among so many important services you render. I have already mentioned the education of the people in the preservation of good health by the prevention of illness. Correlated with that is, of course, the imperative necessity that the value of all welfare work should be increased by the adequate training of those engaged in social work. For, to be effective, that work more and more demands at least some specialization. You may be sure I have not read your Executive Directors' Report without being keenly aware of the obstacles which temporarily, at all events, bar your progress into fields of larger and less circumscribed usefulness. But I shall be more than satisfied if by public reference to those difficulties I may awaken among some, at least, of the citizens of this Province not only a real consciousness of the splendid work you are doing but a desire to co-operate with you in furthering that work.

It has been said that those who have children have "given hostages to fortune". But in any true scale of values—scales rendered more and more sensitive today, I believe, by a developing social conscience—children are far more than that. They must never again be deemed the playthings of chance, their fate determined by the toss of a coin. A country engrossed with visions of a greater, nobler, better future should never forget that, like any building, that future must be built from the foundations upward. The children of today are the foundations of the future. Poverty must not be permitted to rob them of their strength. Their misfortunes but increase our responsibility to them. May they and their families continue, in time of difficulty, to find in the Canadian Council on Child and Family Welfare, and all such far-visioned and truly humanitarian organizations, that assurance of their well-being on which, ultimately, is founded the well-being of the future of this city, this Province and this great Dominion.

HEALTH AND HOUSES

At the Fifty-fourth Annual Meeting of the
Ontario Medical Association, Royal York
Hotel, May 31, 1934

Mr. President, Ladies and Gentlemen:

Nothing could be more welcome to me than the privilege I enjoy this evening as one of this gathering of the Ontario Medical Association. I am proud that such a privilege is mine by right of my membership both of an honoured profession and of this fine organization.

The public office which I occupy today, and which I am happy to regard as an honour to medical science rather than a purely individual distinction, is one which entails frequent public appearances and numerous public addresses. The diversity of subjects which must be discussed is such as sometimes to demand a considerable amount of research. Occasionally the time available for this research is by no means adequate to the subject. Tonight, however, I am happy in that I can speak to you for a few minutes on a topic to which I have lately given a great deal of time and thought. Furthermore, I have had the collaboration and the stimulation of some very keen and well-informed minds. It is true that I am saturated with this subject as the result of some ten weeks of intensive study and enquiry. I feel justified in speaking of it tonight, first, because of its great importance to our citizenship, and, secondly, because of its relationship to preventive medicine with which we are all so much concerned.

It has been a rule of our profession to understate rather than to overstate cases. No body of scientific men is more insistent than ours upon a full weight of proof for any principles it may wish to establish. That is a matter in which we take pride, for it has saved us from errors that might have resulted in cruel suffering for many people. There is, to my mind, a sufficient burden of proof of the evil effects of bad housing on public health; and there is also, I am satisfied as the result of recent studies, a sufficient weight of proof that bad housing is a present evil in Toronto. But, before I discuss conditions in Toronto, let me adduce some evidence of the effects of bad housing.

Sir John Robertson, medical officer of health of Birmingham, England, published in 1919 a volume entitled *Housing and Health*. Here is a statement from his book: "No single condition in the lives of the masses has such a damaging effect on health or does harm in so many other ways as bad housing."

What evidence does he offer in support of this statement? I think it is sound evidence. He points out that the general death-rate bears a definite relation to the housing conditions. Quoting from the report of Dr. Chalmers, Medical Officer of Health of Glasgow, where sixty per cent. of the population at that time lived in one or two-roomed apartments in tenement buildings, the following data are presented:

In one-roomed houses the death rate was 29.9 per 1,000.
In two-roomed houses the death rate was 16.5 per 1,000.
In three-roomed houses the death rate was 11.5 per 1,000.
In four-roomed houses the death rate was 10.8 per 1,000.

Dr. Chalmers further established that in the City of Glasgow the death rate from measles, whooping-cough and diphtheria was four times greater in one-roomed apartments than in apartments of four rooms or more. "Bad housing," he said, "increases the incidence of all infectious, contagious and verminous conditions, of respiratory diseases and of anaemia, debility and constitutional maladies. The worse the housing, the higher the death rate."

In his annual report for 1926, the chief medical officer of the Ministry of Health in Great Britain, Sir George Newman, said, "There is no subject in the whole range of preventive medicine in which the evidence is so general and incontrovertible as in regard to the bad effects of bad housing upon

the human organism. Commission after commission and
report after report for one hundred years prove the case.

"Forty years ago the housing problem was forcibly presented to public attention, largely through the influence of
King Edward (then Prince of Wales), who held it to be one
of the chief factors in the social condition of the English
people. Since then much has been done, and in the last
fourteen years an immense stride forward has been made.
But the slum remains—what Lord Shaftesbury called 'the
overcrowded and insanitary hovels of the poor'. He named
the two evils with precision: there is insanitation, insufficient
light and air space, often inadequate water supply and sanitary
convenience, no opportunity of battling successfully with
filth and vermin, the home of disrepair, dereliction and discomfort, with their inevitable toll of human misery; and
there is overcrowding of houses per acre, of persons per
house, and all too frequently of the bedstead itself. 'The
one-room system is the one-bed system', was another of Lord
Shaftesbury's terms, and he knew, as we know, what that
means in social and moral degeneration. The slum is,
beyond all question, body-destroying and soul-deadening; it
breeds disease, and it encourages vice; and it is peculiarly
mischievous and dysgenic to child life. The evidence of
the centuries is indisputable."

In connection with the foregoing statement, Sir George
Newman compared Finsbury, one of the poorer districts of
London, with Hampstead, which is, as you know, one of
the better class residential areas. In 1906 the infant mortality
rate in Finsbury was 137 per 1,000 living births, and in
Hampstead only 79. The general death rate in Finsbury was
207 per 1,000. In Hampstead it was 13.5.

Corroborative data of the evil effects of housing on health
were obtained in a survey conducted in Montreal in 1927
under the direction of the Montreal Anti-Tuberculosis League.

Last March I ventured to refer publicly to slum conditions
in Toronto. I believe that the use of the word "slums"
shocked some of our citizens. At the instance of His Worship

the Mayor and the City Council, a committee was formed to enquire into such conditions—to determine if there are slums in Toronto. It is, in my opinion, a well-chosen committee, and the honour done me in appointing me to its chairmanship is one of which I have been increasingly proud as time has passed and all the members of the committee have devoted themselves energetically to their tasks. The amount of work entailed has been perhaps far greater than was anticipated, but it has not been shirked and, in addition to regular daily investigations, we have held weekly meetings to review progress, to consider evidence and to organize and co-ordinate continued activities. It is expected that by the end of June we shall be ready to make a report to the city authorities. We have much evidence yet to examine and assimilate, but I am satisfied that we have already reviewed sufficient evidence to establish, first, that slum conditions do exist in Toronto, and secondly, that there is a serious shortage of physically satisfactory housing. This evidence is in the nature of accurate information which we have taken great pains to procure.

With regard to slum conditions, we have not found them as they exist in older European cities where there are small congested areas where a great number of people are crowded into few houses with inadequate air space. What we have found is a reproduction of slum conditions in numerous scattered dwellings or in small rows of dwellings. Less than one in five of the dwellings which we have investigated so far—and we propose to investigate 2,000 of them before we make our report—less than one in five is structurally satisfactory. Four of the five have defective foundations or no foundations at all. Less than one-third have adequate cellarage. Most have no cellars and are nearly always damp. Walls that crack and sag, ill-fitting windows and doors, fallen plaster, leaking roofs, inadequate heating, deficient sanitation and water supply, heaving floors, sometimes flooded, sometimes dangerously rotten; all these are allied against the good health and ordinary comfort and decency of a number of our citizens. Winter is a season of terror to the unfortunate tenants of these delapidated dwellings. Chills and colds are the daily lot from October to May, and there is no relief from the excessive heat of summer.

It has not yet been possible to make detailed reports on more than 1,000 dwellings, and of these 300 have been carefully tabulated and analysed. One of the most distressing disclosures of these tabulations and analyses relates to sanitation and water supply. At this time I had best pass over the subject of sanitation. It is as bad or worse than the provisions for water supply. Most of the families in the dwellings investigated are dependent upon a single tap. In some cases the water supply is from a pipe outside the house. Occasionally there is a tap and a sink in a hole in the wall between two houses. Less than one house in three has any sort of a bath; very few have hot water. Laundry facilities are such as to tax human ingenuity, and personal cleanliness is achieved only in spite of almost insurmountable obstacles. Food storage is an obvious problem in these houses. Refrigeration is beyond the means of most of their tenants, and the inadequately stored larder is in many cases exposed to whatever insects or germs may be attracted to it. Vermin and rats are common pests. Impure air and foul smells are reported in nearly one-third of the dwellings visited by our investigators.

Overcrowding is frequently encountered. Adolescent boys and girls often occupy the same room. But, although there is overcrowding, there is seldom grave lack of space even in the worse districts, for these can accommodate satisfactorily as many families as now occupy them if better buildings were erected and arranged in a better way. It is the unfitness of the dwelling places and their bad situations that give rise to the slum conditions which we have encountered.

The shortage of physically satisfactory housing is to some extent concealed for the present by economic conditions. As conditions improve it will become more obvious. At present, the city has about 136,000 dwelling units for its

150,000 households. But this apparent shortage of 14,000 dwellings would be greatly increased under improved economic conditions. When work and wages are restored some 4,000 couples who have deferred marriage during the past four years will become family units, and many family units will return to the city as business improves. Probably the shortage at that time will amount to 25,000 or more dwellings.

What is to be done about these slum conditions and this housing shortage? It is not for me to say. Our committee will in due course submit some recommendations. Sir John Robertson, whom I have already quoted, set down what might well be regarded as an axiom of proper housing for those in the lower income brackets. He wrote, "The house must be suited to the minimal requirements of human life rather than to suit the house to the labourer's wage." To do that it seems to me is beyond the ability of the landlord. The slum conditions to which I have referred cannot fairly be blamed either on the landlord or on the tenant because it is beyond the power of either one to rectify them. The property owners have faced many difficulties. Tenants who are destitute cannot pay rent. In many cases properties have reached the limit of their usefulness. To repair or to rebuild them would be futile. To close them up would aggravate the housing shortage. The fault is not, I believe, with the landlord; it lies in the fact that for some years adequate housing has not been provided in those parts of the city in which the more unfortunate families live.

But adequate housing must be provided even though it will in some cases be beyond the means of tenants to pay for it. We shall always have some who are unable to pay, but we cannot condemn them to the misery and sufferings that have been revealed by the reports of some of our investigators. Adequate housing could be provided as a measure of double relief—relief which would provide employment for many who are now idle and which would do away with the almost intolerable conditions under which some of our families are at present living.

In 1919 it was felt that our facilities for technical education were inadequate. To meet this situation the Federal Government appropriated ten million dollars, from which sum it would supply funds to build technical schools, provided that the province and municipality, in which a school was to be built, would jointly make contributions towards the cost. In the course of the long and careful consideration which my associates and I have given to the housing problem in Toronto there has not yet occurred to us any solution other than one along lines similar to the plan adopted to extend our facilities for technical education.

We believe that no problem calls more urgently for solution than the one I have thus briefly presented tonight, both from the point of view of morality and humanitarianism. The thought that some of our fellow-citizens should be compelled to live under such deplorable conditions must be repugnant to our better feelings and must awaken in the hearts of all good citizens an intense feeling of sympathy and an urge to set about immediately to do all in our power to effect a remedy. I am sure that remedial measures will have the whole-hearted support of the members of this Association and of all other citizens who are devoted to the welfare of the community.

THE IMPORTANCE OF THE RIGHT POINT OF VIEW

*Being a Protest or Disclaimer on Being
Toasted at the American Surgical Associ-
ation Dinner Given by the President, Dr.
Daniel Fiske Jones, June 5, 1934*

Mr. President and Gentlemen:

I am very much more appreciative of the undeserved
heights to which you have raised me by your words of
praise than a fellow-countryman of yours who visited Italy—
entering it from the north over the Alps.   He met an Italian
who asked him whether he had just crossed the Alps.   The
American hesitated and cogitated.   "Wal," said he finally,
"Wal, now you call my attention to the fact, I guess I did pass
rising ground."   The height of the Alps evidently didn't make
him feel dizzy—or indeed, have any sensation comparable to
that I feel at this moment.

Since taking office, I have found that even in an official
capacity I do not lack opportunities to undertake quite unusual
operations—operations I would never be called upon to per-
form as a surgeon.   Only the other day, for example, I was
requested to open *up* an Exhibition.   I accepted the invitation, and I have been hoping since then that the little speech
I gave was not regarded as an anaesthetic administered before
the operation.   The patient survived, however, and the
Exhibition is, I believe, still open.

I want to emphasize my desire that whatever honour
accrues to the position I hold in this Province should be
regarded as a tribute to the Medical Profession as a whole
and everywhere, rather than in a narrow sense as a personal
distinction.   That is the point of view which I want to
present to you.   So much, of course, depends on the point of
view.   I am reminded of the man with feet of different

sizes. He ordered his shoes made accordingly. When they arrived he tried without success to put the smaller one on the bigger foot. "Confound the fellow," he burst out, "I ordered him to make one larger than the other; but instead of that he goes and makes one smaller than the other."

Or consider the point of view of the doctor who did a post-mortem on the body of a man who had been murdered. Quite apart from the wound, the body was in very poor physical condition. "This person was so ill," exclaimed our medical friend, "that if he hadn't been murdered he would have died half an hour before." That, if you like, is a triumph of exaggeration, but, at any rate, it illustrates another interesting point of view.

In reply to your very kind words this evening, Mr. President, I cannot insist too strongly that I would be more than pleased were you to take the other point of view and regard all the tributes you have paid to me as tributes which rightly belong, not to an individual, but to the great profession of which we are all members. For there is no greater honour than to belong to that profession, except to be a Fellow of the American Surgical Association, of which I am very proud.

THE COLLEGE GRADUATE

*At the Graduation Exercises of the Ontario
Ladies' College, Whitby, on the Celebration
of the Diamond Jubilee of the College,
June 13, 1934*

Mr. President, Ladies and Gentlemen:

On this, the celebration of your Diamond Jubilee, I have the unique privilege and distinction of returning to you as an ex-pupil of the Ontario Ladies' College. Once upon a time—it was when Dr. J. J. Hare was Principal and Governor of this College—I used regularly to creep with mingled trepidation and bashfulness through the main entrance of this private ladies' seminary. My trepidation was natural—for I always felt that I was entering sacred precincts. My bashfulness, too, was natural and quite excusable—especially since it was always increased by my consciousness that from sundry galleries and doorways startled wide-open eyes were gazing at me—the intruder.

The fact of the matter was that I was being taught to play the pipe organ by Dr. Edward Fisher, a predecessor of Mr. Atkinson. I should add, if only in self-defence, that my education was not then and has not since been limited to ladies' institutions of learning.

In order to enable you to appreciate fully the opportunities you young ladies have had at this splendid College I am going to turn over a few pages of history.

One is not surprised to find that boarding-schools for the upper classes in the eighteenth century supplied only facilities sufficient to enable a young lady who had completed her education to execute a few old airs upon the spinet, dance a minuet, or later on, waltz, and possibly sing one or two of the Italian songs from the foreign operas which were then becoming fashionable in England. At sixteen or even earlier, "Miss" was introduced into the world, and put away all trifling with books for the more serious business of life— routs, masquerades, balls and husband hunting.

In 1740 Lady Mary Wortley Montagu wrote to her daughter, the Countess of Bute: "To say truth, there is no part of the world where our sex is treated with so much contempt as in England. [England was later to lead in women's suffrage!] I do not complain of men for having engrossed the government. In excluding us from all degree of power they preserve us from many fatigues, many dangers and perhaps many crimes. But I think it the highest injustice . . . that the same studies which raise the character of a man should hurt that of a woman. We are educated in the grossest ignorance and no art omitted to stifle our natural reason. If some few get above their nurses' instructions, our knowledge must rest concealed and be as useless to the world as gold in the mine. I am now speaking according to our (English) notions, which may wear out, some ages hence, along with others equally absurd."

The boarding-school (as kept by Miss Pinkerton and her kind) aimed rather at cultivating becoming postures for the ball-room than encouraging bodily health and a natural grace. Open-air games for girls were, of course, undreamed of. Battledore and shuttle-cock, recommended to Dorothy Osborne in the seventeenth century as a cure for melancholy, remained popular; and riding on the rocking-horse was thought good both for old and young.

I do not know if it is still customary for the Principals of Ladies' schools to write to parents about their daughters who have just graduated, but if so, the sample letter written by Miss Pinkerton, the creator of that famous Academy for Young Ladies in Chiswick Mall, may be of service to Dr. Carscallen. Here it is: "Madam: After her six years' residence at the Mall, I have the honour and happiness of presenting Miss Amelia Sedley to her parents as a young lady not unworthy to occupy a fitting position in their polished and refined circle. Those virtues which characterize the young English gentlewoman, those accomplishments which become her birth and station, will not be found wanting in the amiable Miss Sedley, whose industry and obedience have endeared her to her instructors, and whose delightful sweetness of temper has charmed her aged and her youthful companions.

"In music, in dancing, in orthography, in every variety of embroidery and needlework, she will be found to have realized her friends' fondest wishes. In geography there is still much to be desired, and a careful and undeviating use of the backboard for 4 hours daily during the next three years is recommended as necessary to the acquirement of that dignified deportment and carriage so requisite for every young lady of fashion.

"In the principles of religion and morality, Miss Sedley will be found worthy of an establishment which has been honoured by the presence of The Great Lexicographer and the patronage of the admirable Mrs. Chapone. In leaving the Mall, Miss Amelia carries with her the hearts of her companions and the affectionate regards of her mistress, who has the honour to subscribe herself, Madam,

                    "Your most obliged servant,
                        "Barbara Pinkerton."

When people began to laugh at the boarding-schools (as conceived by Miss Pinkerton) their day was over. But the end was not yet. It was left for the nineteenth century to see the dream of Tennyson's *Princess* come true:

                        "Oh, I wish
        That I were some great princess, I would build
        Far off from men a college like a man's,
        And I would teach them all that men are taught;"

And so, in accordance with Tennyson's conception a few public-spirited citizens of Whitby, headed by the Rev. J. E. Sanderson, formed a joint stock company with James Holden as President, and financed the purchase of "Trafalgar Castle" from Sheriff Reynolds, and founded in 1874 this famous residential school for girls—The Ontario Ladies' College.

After you have left this College you may some day be asked the question, "Where were you civilized?" instead of "Where were you educated?" Don't be annoyed at this rude question, which would seem to suggest that you are a reclaimed savage. Only a philosopher, or one who was vividly aware of the true function of education would ask such a question. And what, you may ask, would prompt him to ask that question—especially when it was addressed to such an obviously civilized person as an ex-graduate of the O.L.C.? Well, in the first place, he would know that nobody is born civilized. I am sorry to say it, but there is no such thing as a civilized baby. Every baby has to be trained—civilized as it were—by force of precept and example—in a word, by education.

If I may be allowed to paraphrase some famous words of Shakespeare and use them for my own purpose I would say, not only of babies, but of all people that "None is born civilized; some achieve civilization, and some have civilization thrust upon them"—and very much resent it all the days of their lives.

But I haven't yet told you why I spoke of educating young ladies and of civilizing them, as if the process were one and the same. As a matter of fact, of course, it *is*. For instance, the word "education" comes from a Latin word or words, meaning literally "to lead or bring out of". That explains a great deal about education. When you pass through the process of being educated what is in you is brought out. There is more than a bit of Dr. Jekyll and Mr. Hyde complex in all of us. That is to say, there is both good and bad. Education looks for the best and tries to draw it out and develop it and make it useful and fruitful.

Now, according to your own individuality you will find some kinds of mental food more digestible and more to your liking than other kinds. True education, however, is so comprehensive as to cater to every appetite.

Lord Macaulay once proclaimed that "Men who have been engaged up to one or two and twenty in studies which have no immediate connection with the business of any profession, and the effect of which is really to open, to invigorate and to enrich the mind, will generally be found in the business of every profession superior to men who have (at an early age) devoted themselves to the special studies of their calling."

In the passage I have just quoted you might substitute "women" for "men". In the modern world there has been a good deal of that kind of substitution. But Macaulay was speaking of education, and you will notice how surprisingly apt his words are in any consideration of private schools.

We won't stop to argue about the accuracy of his conclusions, but when he says, for instance, that the effect of studies is to open, to invigorate, and to enrich the mind he defines exactly the whole object of private school education, and, indeed, of education in general.

Now these are not aimless generalizations. They are very pertinent to this matter of private schools. For while every school—public or private—must, as a matter of course, maintain a standard of instruction sufficiently high to satisfy the requirements of public boards of examiners, yet it is the private school which even more successfully perhaps than many others bridges the gap between what I have termed the instruction necessary for examinations on the one hand, and education in a somewhat fuller sense on the other. It should never be forgotten that even the most efficient tutorial instruction may leave a great part of a student's nature, her instincts, her emotions, her secret aspirations—all that we mean by her personality—untouched. A student is, first of all, a person, and only secondarily a candidate for examinations. That is why to fail in an academic examination is not therefore finally and irrevocably to write oneself down a failure. Not at all. And it is because the natural bent of the academic, or scholastic, type of mind turns it further and further away from the practical realities of any given situation that educational authorities are always in danger of regarding examinations as, in themselves, an end, when in truth they are but a means to an end—that end being self-realization in its broadest and its profoundest sense.

So it is that I have but to glance at the curriculum of this College with its great variety of courses to know that here, at all events, the individual student is assured of individual consideration. That shows, among other things, that no student here is ever made to feel that she is a misfit. Never is she allowed to brood and develop a sickening sense of inferiority simply because her personal inclinations, her native desires do not lead her to advance and develop along more generally recognized lines of scholastic tuition. It is not right or seemly that the products of any educational system should be mass-produced. Let a student's natural gifts be what they may, no school or college or university that is not professedly sectarian or vocational in a somewhat limited sense, can be described as efficient which does not encourage the development of that student's gifts and afford an outlet for their expression. Commerce, music and art, public speaking, singing, dramatics, physical culture, swimming, household science, cookery, home nursing and sewing—all these are part and parcel of that unceasing, almost incredible activity which we call life. In one or the other of these the student will find her most congenial subject of study.

I congratulate, therefore, all those responsible for drawing up and making available to students so splendid and comprehensive a curriculum to supplement the more purely academic subjects of study here at the O.L.C. I congratulate all those alumnae present who have been privileged in bygone years to enjoy so liberal and varied a training for that life that has since been theirs beyond these walls and far from the scene of this Jubilee Celebration. And I congratulate, also, all those who are even now studying here, on the opportunity that is theirs of association with their fellow-students during their residence here, of sharing common interests, of learning to respect individual differences.

Nothing that you learn here but is intended primarily to make you a useful citizen. The entrance of women in commerce and trade and the professions—indeed, into all that hurly-burly of life outside the home—is a challenge not so much to the men even, as to women themselves. It means added responsibility for you as the women of the future. I am confident, however, that the all-round training you receive here, the opportunity that is yours to learn how to make all those big and little adjustments necessary before you can live socially, as but one among many others, and the confidence inspired by your own accomplishments as individuals and as students here—these will be excellent equipment for your journey through life.

Even as I say this, however, my eyes tell me that none of you will for long lack a partner in that journey, and I am delighted that household science figures so prominently on your curriculum, and that home-making is a course in itself—as, indeed, it should be. After all, matrimony is itself a career and not by any means the least strenuous of all those open to you.

I feel sure that the comprehensive training to which I have just referred will prevent your partners from expressing such an opinion of their life with you, as did a man about whom I heard the other day. He was a spiritualist, and after some years of married life he died. After an interval he appeared to his wife, who asked him how he was getting on. He answered that he was much happier than he had been on earth. "Oh," she replied, "then you must be in Heaven." To which he answered, "No, I am not."

I welcome the realistic and scientific method of training for a tremendous undertaking, shown by the existence of such courses of preparatory study in your school. Many of you remember the story of the census taker who, in the course of his house to house visits, asked a conscientious married lady for particulars concerning her family. She told him the number and ages of her children and her husband's occupation. "And you, madam," said he, "what do you do?" "Well," said she, "I cook the meals, wash the clothes, nurse my youngest, sweep the floors, polish the furniture, clean the windows, order the groceries —." "That's enough, Madam, thank you," said the man. And with his pencil he wrote on a slip of paper, "Mrs. So-and-So—*No occupation.*"

It is surely a splendid thing that such an attitude toward the duties inseparable from a home has disappeared, to be replaced by an altogether worthier recognition of the realities of home-life. Not the least of the many advantages that are yours as students here is this—that you are able to avail yourselves of the benefits of training that will add to the beauty of your future home-life by increasing, sanely and scientifically, its efficiency.

In mentioning very briefly but a few of the advantages of private school education in general, I wish to pay worthy tribute to the Ontario Ladies' College in particular. I can imagine no more fitting occasion on which to do so than on this, your Diamond Jubilee. Had Sheriff Reynolds but known to what splendid uses his beautiful home would be put in the course of time he would, I am sure, have found in the contemplation of the architect's plans for its erection an additional and deep source of personal satisfaction. I know you will join with me in honouring on this occasion the memory of Dr. J. J. Hare, who, for forty years, guided the destinies of this College with such conspicuous skill and devotion, to be followed by the Rev. F. L. Farewell, who in thirteen years added still further to your achievements as a cultural and educational institution of the highest standing.

I know, too, that I but express the sentiments of all those assembled here today when I pay tribute to your present Principal and Governor, Dr. C. R. Carscallen and Mrs. Carscallen, into whose capable keeping have been entrusted the splendid traditions of all your School's yesterdays and the fulfilment of the hopes you entertain for your *alma mater* for the morrow and the years to come.

In conclusion, I want to read to you the last paragraph of a book entitled *These Hurrying Years*, by Gerald Heard, which was published recently. Whether you have returned today as pupils of the years gone by, whether you are leaving school today, or whether you are still a student here you will, I think, find in these words food for thought, especially as I have been speaking of such things as the cultivation of individuality and self-realization through education in private schools.

"There is a hope, therefore, for our generation", says young Gerald Heard, "in so far as it has a courage intense enough to be quiet, a faith clear, and a kindliness pure enough to be free of any wish to exploit its object; and vision sufficient to realize that its gain is in understanding and in benefiting its fellow-creature; that, in fact, its own individuality is only a phase in its growth and that it is evolving the next stage of its being by co-operation with other individuals." This may be a high fate, but surely one not too stern. Surely everyone who reflects wishes to be possessed of such powers, and with them infinite achievement is possible.

CANNON BALLS AND HISTORY

At the Unveiling of the Tablet to the Pioneers
of Cartwright Township at the Centennial
Celebration, Blackstock, June 16, 1934

Mr. Chairman, Ladies and Gentlemen:

I have often heard the lives of the pioneers, whose memory we honour today, described as lives of grinding toil. That is certainly an appropriate and exact description. But their lives were "grinding" in more senses than one. One of their most important tasks was, for example, the grinding of corn. Man must have bread even though, in scriptural phrase, he shall not live by bread alone. How did these hardy forefathers of ours of Cartwright and of the county of Durham get bread once they had harvested the grain?

Because I know of no better way to illustrate how strenuous and difficult were the lives they led and how grateful we, their descendants, should be for the gigantic labours they undertook so heroically, I want to read you a description of how bread was made or, at least, how grain was ground by the earliest citizens of Durham County. This is how Captain James Dittrick describes the laborious process of grinding grain.

"The mills of rude workmanship", he writes, "were thinly scattered about the country, so that we had to content ourselves with a hollow stump to pound our grain in, which was done with a cannon-ball, fastened to a cord or bark of a tree and affixed to a long pole which served as a lever. The bread or cakes thus made were not particularly white, but were eaten with a good appetite and proved wholesome."

I imagine any man would have a good appetite after grinding toil of that kind and, remembering the biblical injunction to turn the weapons of war into the tools and

281

instruments of peace by beating swords into plough-shares, I really think the pioneers of this township and this county went one better. They actually found a new and most original use for cannon-balls. Instead of dying and being killed by cannon-balls, men and even women and children were kept alive and fed by cannon-balls. Cannon-balls made their bread! And that is not by any means the most remarkable feature of the lives led by the pioneers. I mention it because it will, I hope, give you an even deeper insight into the conditions in which they lived and laboured.

But the story of the making of the bread by which they lived doesn't end with that. No, they weren't content with such rough-and-ready methods. So, far away, near Kingston —they called it Cataraqui then—the Government set up a grist mill. That was away back in 1782—more than 150 years ago. For four years there wasn't another mill available to the inhabitants in this part of Canada, and the pioneers from the County of Durham and, you may be sure, from the very spot on which we are now standing, and where later, exactly a hundred years ago, the Township of Cartwright was founded—from here, from there, from everywhere those old settlers used to travel through forest, over rough roads and by boat to Cataraqui to grind their corn. A man called Roger Bates, for example, used to go regularly from Darlington Township—a little trip that took five or six weeks by boat, and at night he used to pull the boat up on shore and sleep under it. Those were hard days and nights you may be sure. But it's no good having grain unless you can grind it for bread. And there was at least one good thing about such journeys. There was no charge made for grinding grain at the Cataraqui mill; of course, there were no transportation charges, either, since they had to transport themselves as best they could.

If you want to know, by the way, how strong and hard and tireless these old pioneers were, let me tell you the story of the old Scotch settler who once carried on his back one hundred pounds of flour for fourteen miles and, when somebody asked him how he felt after it all, he replied that he wasn't tired "but she'll be a little pit sore apoot the back."

I'm not at all surprised that he was "a little pit sore apoot the back" but I know that when I tell you of such men, this historic occasion will have for us all a new meaning and we shall understand even more clearly what manner of men these pioneers were and, perhaps, recognize with a profounder admiration their splendid qualities of enthusiasm, hardihood and endurance.

I should add, before passing on to another aspect of the lives they led, that by the middle of the last century even when Cartwright was already a township and the conditions of life had improved—even then those who lived in Durham County used to carry their grain eighty miles or more to the mill at Guelph. And eighty miles, over such roads as they had then, was a great deal more than eighty miles would be in this day and age.

It was, after all, the spirit of co-operation and mutual helpfulness that made life in those days bearable. Indeed, it was probably the one great thing that made life possible at all amid such difficulties, surrounded as they were by a country that offered none of the amenities of civilized life such as, thanks to their early labours, we are able to enjoy. Let me give you an example of their generosity to each other, their belief that they should bear one another's burdens. One hundred years ago, in 1831, the home of a certain Mr. Hart was destroyed by fire. It was built of cedar logs. There was, of course, no such thing as insurance in those days. So what happened? Was Mr. Hart to be allowed to bear all the loss and start the battle for life in a comparative wilderness all over again? Never! Here is an item from the little newspaper that reported the fire. "The loss of Mr. Hart, including upwards of $60.00 in cash," the newspaper reported, "must at least amount to $150.00. We cannot express in too strong language the praiseworthy liberality that has been displayed by the inhabitants of our village upon this occasion. A subscription already amounting to upwards of $70 has been raised, and we have no doubt that the entire loss of Mr. Hart will be made up to him."

So life in those days wasn't so terrible, after all. Indeed, life anywhere would be a joyous experience if the same splendid public or community spirit was always being manifested.

Or consider the "Cavan Blazers". Everybody, of course, has heard of the Cavan Blazers—those ardent Orangemen, who, here in Durham County, had many a "run-in" with the Irish Roman Catholics of Peterborough County. And yet, despite all their religious animosity what do we find? Well, when the only Roman Catholic settler in Cavan fell sick at harvest time, it was the Blazers—of all people!—who came secretly and prevented loss by harvesting his crop for him.

So today, standing before this beautiful monument and recalling the lives of the hardy pioneers in whose memory it has been erected and is now unveiled, it is of such men that we think. For a few moments I have lifted the veil that hides the past from us. We have only had time to see a very little of that past but it is sufficient to make us proud of these men—the pioneers, our forefathers; and it fills me with pleasure to be present today when so fitting a tribute is being paid to the lives they led with such fortitude and in such a noble, self-sacrificing spirit of generosity and co-operation one with the other in the building up, not alone of Cartwright, now celebrating its centenary, but of this great Dominion as a part of the Empire. Let me now read to you the names of the men who were residents of the Township of Cartwright from 1837-1845. It is a Roll of Honour and I would like to suggest that all those present stand while I read their names. Adams, Anderson, Archer, Argue, Armstrong, Arnott, Ashton, Axworthy, Bartley, Beacock, Beattie, Bickell, Bolton, Bradburn, Braden, Brandon, Brown, Bruce, Bryans, Burr, Butson, Byers, Caesar, Calwell, Campbell, Chittick, Coulter, Cowan, Crawford, Crawley, Crozier, Darcy, Deacon, Demara, Dever, Devitt, Dinsmore, Earle, Edgerton,

Evans, Fallis, Farewell, Farroll, Ferguson, Fluke, Fowler, Freeburn, Gardner, Gibson, Given, Goggin, Hall, Hambley, Hay, Henry, Hiliar, Holmes, Hooey, Hooper, Howe, Hubbard, Hunt, Hunter, Hyland, Jackson, Jobb, Johnstone, Kissack, Knapp, Lang, Larmer, Lattimer, Lawson, Leddy, Logan, Loucks, Luke, McClenahan, McCracken, McCrae, McCoy, McDougall, McGarrell, McKee, McKinnon, McLaughlin, McNally, McQuaid, Mahood, Mahaffey, Malcolm, Marlow, Martin, Medd, Mills, Montgomery, Moore, Morono, Mugridge, Muirhead, Nesbitt, Parker, Patterson, Petes, Phair, Philp, Potts, Proutt, Prust, Pue, Reynolds, Richardson, Robertson, Sanderson, Saxon, Scott, Seymour, Spinks, Shirks, Smith, Talbot, Taylor, Todd, Torbey, Trick, Vance, Watson, White, Whitfield, Widdes, Willan, Williamson.

When we think of such men as these and of a host of others too numerous to mention, we are conscious that while words will suffice as an expression of our admiration for them, and while, too, such a monument as this is a tangible manifestation of the high esteem in which we hold their memory; yet it remains for us by our deeds further to enrich the heritage they have left us. I am confident that the torch they have handed on will not be permitted to grow dim in the hands of this and succeeding generations. I congratulate the Corporation of the Township of Cartwright on this their Centennial—the celebration of the 100th year since their foundation. I take pride in my family's association with the story of Cartwright and the County of Durham—a story of which we are all justly proud. I welcome the opportunity that has been mine to tell you something—but very little—of this splendid story of the past and I wish you all, and through you, all those communities who fulfill the purpose of their lives within the borders of your Township such prosperity and happiness and success as will be a worthy consummation of the heroic efforts of all those noble men and brave women to whose honour and in whose name we are today gathered together.

YOUTH AND AGE

At the Prize-giving, Ridley College,
St. Catharines, June 21, 1934

Dr. Griffith, Ladies and Gentlemen:

For as long as I can remember, speeches have been an essential part of school prize-giving. I imagine they always will be. Doubtless prizes become even more valuable and gain an indefinable something when they are presented, trimmed and adorned, as it were, with a garland of words. Or it may be that speech-making persists because it is thought that it is never too early for prize-winners to learn that even success has its own inescapable penalties.

More probably, however, like so much else in life, it is all a matter of custom and habit. At one time or another you must all have been conscious of the tremendous and peculiar force of custom—though most of you are too young to know how powerful also is habit, which is, after all, any kind of purely private or personal custom of one's own. Speaking of habits, by the way, I am reminded of a boy's answer to an examination question. The question was this: "Write all you know about Nero." "The less said about Nero the better", wrote the boy.

Some habits are like that; and even the most ancient customs aren't always any more helpful than a certain history book which one schoolboy described as "a veritable millstone on the road to learning". He meant, of course, "milestone", but his description was, perhaps, even then truer than he thought.

I tell you these things because when you leave school and go out into the world you will find it dominated by custom. The habitual thing is always the commonest thing, the thing most frequently done in the world, because it is so very easy a thing to do and to continue doing. But—and

286

this is where you differ so vastly from generations of school-boys in past years and decades—things, conditions, and seemingly the very foundations of life nowadays are changing with a rapidity never equalled in the whole history of the world prior to the era of scientific invention.

"That's a pretty village we're coming to—wasn't it?" said the man who was exceeding the speed limit. That's how quickly the world is changing. You have hardly time to comment on some new production of man's ingenuity before it has been superseded or improved and developed beyond recognition. And what is happening to things, happens also to ideas. They, too, are in a state of flux—unsettled, restless, often formless and rarely, if ever, fixed and definite.

Old habits of thought are changing. In the presence of youth, age is finding it more and more difficult to excuse and impossible to explain away with any degree of plausi-bility the world it will leave to a younger generation. So, in the few words I want to say to you I shall avoid platitudes, and I certainly hope that nothing I say will be as obvious as the answer of a boy who was asked by his teacher to name a liquid that never freezes. "Hot water," said he with pardon-able triumph. That was rather too obvious, but worse still, it was the wrong answer, like so many obvious answers.

I want to say something about youth and opportunity—for opportunity, despite all denials, still exists for the youth of the world, and never so abundantly as in times of unex-ampled difficulty.

Now recently I read a book. Reading, of course, is one of those private, personal customs or habits which I men-tioned just now, and which I cannot recommend to you too highly. Never let your attitude to books—over and above all, books of instruction—become like that of the lady who turned away a man at her door who had asked her if she would like to see the book he had for sale. "A book!" said she, when he offered to show it to her, "No, thank you. I already have a book."

But to return to the particular book I was reading. It concluded with these few lines of verse:

"They do their Maker wrong,
Who, in the pride of age,
Cry down youth's heritage,
And all the eager throng
Of thoughts and plans and schemes
With which the young brain teems."

Those of you who are putting your schooldays behind you; those of you who in all the pride and the uncertainty, the excitement and perhaps, too, the doubt of your young manhood, are trying to imagine what the great adventure of life is going to be like—I know that your brains are teeming with thoughts and plans and schemes. That is why I want this message to be one of encouragement. I want you to recognize that you and all your generation are in truth the world of tomorrow; that whatever drama will yet be unfolded upon the vast stage of the world, you will be the actors in that drama. The destiny of this our civilization will be fulfilled by you who are still at school, or just leaving school. It will be for you to find answers to all the questions which even now are filling the air with clamour. So, you see, you are very much more important than many of your elders would perhaps wish to admit!

I know that young people are thinking of the future with a passionate seriousness, and when I spoke to you just now of customs and habits I wanted to warn you that, as often as not, customs and habits exist to keep you from thinking. In absolute opposition to that, I want you to know that you can never by any manner of means think too much or too intently about the world in which you are about to take your place. The whole purpose of your schooldays is to teach you how to think most fruitfully and effectively. In education—in you, the products of education—the problems of the world await their solution.

Now that, you may say, sounds pretty serious. I can see that some of you are wondering what encouragement there is to be found in such a prospect. But you should first know what you were being encouraged to do, and that thinking is the first of your duties. Have you ever thought that it is only in our minds that the world exists at all—and that what you see, what you touch, is what you think? Apart from our minds, to all intents and purposes, there is no world.

However, that borders on all sorts of terribly deep and involved things like metaphysics and philosophy, and I shall spare you that. Besides, I haven't forgotten the brilliant remark made by a schoolboy who said that in the United States people are put to death by *elocution*. I intend to be brief and not threaten you with such a fate.

When I spoke of custom and habit which are so often used to save people from thinking for themselves or to stop them from thinking about old things in a new way and so eventually to make it impossible for them to think at all, I was actually saying in another way what the Prince of Wales himself said some years ago about youth and young men. "Young men," said he, "should surely have greater opportunities." (I know you will all cheer when you hear that. But now listen to what the Prince said to justify and give point to his demand.) "If anyone says that they lack experience, surely this could be counterbalanced by saying that they lack also bias and prejudice."

Now age, frequently, has plenty of bias and prejudice, because age is often tired and wants to be saved the trouble of thinking all over again about the things to which it has become accustomed and which it accepts unquestioningly. Although travelling by a different route, yet we have arrived at exactly the same point of view as that expressed by the Prince of Wales. The only difference is that what he called "bias and prejudice" in the individual I have termed "custom and habit", since I was referring to people in general. Just as the Prince of Wales was speaking for youth, defending youth, and encouraging youth to assert itself more vigorously, so my message, too, is one of encouragement; and since you should be conscious of your own worth, your own potentialities, your own powers of thinking and the promise that is implicit in all young people, I will read to you a passage about youth in a book by Mr. St. Loe Strachey.

"It is not Age", he says, "but Youth which is the time for hardihood of thought, for the long arduous exploration of the zealous mind, and for the energetic setting up of the great ladders of logic with rung upon rung of syllogisms—ladders by which you mean to reach the skies and storm heaven itself. Why will not Youth understand that it is in possession of the thinking period of life? It imagines that Age is full of wisdom and is always devolving great ideas as well as great schemes and, in a word, making full use of the experience to which it has attained. Nothing could be more untrue. With very few exceptions, Age is resting upon its oars and letting the impulse which it has given to the boat by previous strokes carry it on as far as it will."

Now that sounds very much like one in the eye for age. But while it is perfectly true that youth creates and builds while age is content rather to preserve and guard what has already been built, what has all this to do with those big and little problems which confront a boy as he prepares to leave school?

Well, it is really very pertinent. I want you young people to set out in the world convinced that you have a purpose, a mission, a most important duty to discharge. Don't be too ready to accept as an unalterable truth everything that you are told. You should examine things for yourselves. You should look at this world with the fresh, unprejudiced eyes of youth, and where you find wrong, never be afraid to say that it is wrong. The world needs you. There is always—there always must be—a place for you, and your opportunities are unlimited. Age will always be a little jealous of youth, for youth still possesses what age will never again possess. But age is also your friend.

Prominent men in commercial life say that what is needed in the business world is "new blood in industry" and they speak with all the weight of high industrial positions. Men in every walk of life welcome the energy, the ardour, the enthusiasm and the idealism of youth. If they do not, beware of them for they are the enemies of progress, and the progress of the world depends on you.

I wish you success, and as I do so I wonder what kind of success you are hoping for. Had I time I would speak to you of the true aim of living. As it is, however, I need only say that the very word "success" has been degraded to mean only the acquisition of as great a number of material possessions as possible. And yet it remains true that real success—the real satisfactions of living, are known to many of those who have not "succeeded" in the eyes of the world. If you set out to get as much as you can of things, you may yet learn by experience the wisdom of Benjamin Disraeli's remark that "the feeling of satiety, almost inseparable from great possessions, is a surer cause of misery than ungratified desires."

But I don't want my few words of encouragement and good cheer to develop into a preachment—a kind of sermon. In fact, I don't want it to develop any further. I wish you a full life, a useful life, a life lived with that inward harmony of thought and emotion that is so difficult to achieve, yet when once achieved is the most precious of all possessions.

THE STORY OF ONTARIO

As Told to the Canadian Club, Fort William,
June 25, 1934

Mr. President, Ladies and Gentlemen:

If any one thing more than another can be held responsible for my choice of a subject this afternoon it was a map. When I was thinking of my visit to you today and contemplating my journey I had outstretched on the table before me a map of Ontario. It was a large map—one of those maps that fold up so neatly that you never imagine until you unfold them, how much space they cover. Once I had unfolded it, the map completely hid the large table before me. I found myself glancing at it—north, south, east and west—at the Great Lakes and the innumerable little lakes, the myriad streams, the forests, the towns and cities and hamlets, the great northland, and all the names familiar and not so familiar—until suddenly the thought came to me, "How tremendous a place is this Province of Ontario, what a vast territory it is, how many miles and leagues it covers."

But that wasn't all. For, since nothing, from the human point of view, can be said to have any value except in its relation to the lives of men and women and, since size alone in itself is of but little importance, that map—the very names I read there—evoked thoughts of all that had happened amid the scenes of which it was a diagram.

The fact of the matter is, of course, that history can make even a map—and a road map at that—a living, moving and altogether rather exciting spectacle. Without history it's—well, it's just a road map—a thing to be pored over with keen scrutiny by ardent motorists but not a particularly exhilarating thing in itself unless you're a motorist keen on mileage—that mystic but strenuous cult of as many miles as possible per day.

So it came about that I decided then and there to tell you a story. It is a story of which you members of the Canadian Club, and indeed all the citizens of Fort William and Port Arthur and of the whole of this Province form the sequel. It is the story of Ontario.

One word before we begin. The story won't, of course, be a complete story. We have to travel through time as well as space—and the speed at which we shall travel through this Province will be sure to rouse the hopeless envy of our motoring friends.

A little more than three hundred years ago a young French-man named Nicolas Vignau spent the winter—it was the winter of 1612—on the Ottawa River. Then, like another famous explorer, Baron Munchausen—though he hadn't the peculiarly vivid imagination of the Baron—Nicolas went back and told a pack of lies to Samuel de Champlain. He told Champlain that he had visited a great inland sea—what we now call Hudson Bay. What is more, he described it to Champlain in graphic detail! Now, Champlain didn't know that young Nicolas Vignau was simply telling him a story he had heard from a band of Algonquin Indians, so he set off immediately to Morrison Island in Lac des Allu-mettes. And there, as soon as they found that Champlain had been deceived, the Algonquins wanted to kill young Baron Munchausen or, rather, Nicolas Vignau, so that he wouldn't tell Champlain any more lies. He had never, of course, been within several hundred miles of Hudson Bay—the place he had so clearly and enthusiastically described. Champlain, disappointed by his wild goose chase, went back to Quebec. It wasn't until two years later that he made his second and famous expedition (he left young Nicolas Vignau at home or elsewhere this time, by the way) and the first white man went on to Lake Nipissing, down Georgian Bay to Lake Huron, to Lake Simcoe and so down to Lake Ontario.

But all that was so long ago as to be to all intents and purposes prehistoric.

Now, I think you will agree with me that the ability to make a loud noise never fails to draw a large and curious crowd. People are always attracted by anything or anybody that can roar, even if it's only a lion in a cage or a newspaper headline that screams, or a tub orator who can drown the sound of traffic. So it's not surprising that nearly one hundred years before that first journey of Champlain into Ontario another explorer and a fellow-countryman, Jacques Cartier, had already heard about Niagara from the Indians. Champlain actually referred to the Falls of Niagara in his letters, although he never saw or even heard them, and it wasn't until sixty-three years after Champlain's journey that a certain Father Hennepin wrote the first description of those magnificent Falls—"the noise which they make", he wrote, "is heard for more than 15 leagues." The Indians no doubt referred to them as the "big noise" and it is natural, perhaps, that some of the earliest history of this Province centres around Niagara. Hennepin, by the way, wasn't unlike the imaginative young Vignau. He claimed to have explored the Mississippi Basin before the explorer La Salle; but one writer at least says that Hennepin belongs to "that school of writers who state the truth by accident and a lie by inclination." However, he really did see Niagara and actually drew a sketch of it—the earliest sketch in existence.

He was the first of millions of visitors, and because I have so much to tell you I have time only to quote the words of George Heriot, who saw them in 1801. By that time, incidentally, most of the adders, black snakes and rattlesnakes that infested the district had been cleared away. In Heriot's opinion the sight of the Falls was "the most wonderful and awful which the habitable world presents." Then there was Charles Dickens, forty years later, who found in the Falls "nothing of gloom or terror—but peace and beauty." But, even though Niagara soon became a thriving tourist resort, I doubt if any of all the hosts and hosts of visitors ever got more excitement out of their visit than the coachman, who, in 1850, stopped his coach, as the custom was, on what was known as Table Rock—a large rock jutting far out over the Falls.

Ninety-three years before that a large piece of the rock had broken off; and now suddenly on June 25, this coachman had unhitched his horses on that same Table Rock and was washing his coach when he heard a sudden, strange and terrifying rumbling beneath him.   He jumped for safety in the nick of time; but the coach, the horses and hundreds of tons of rock plunged into the abyss.   Then there was Captain Webb, the first man to swim the English Channel, who was drowned in 1882 trying to swim the rapids there, and Blondin —probably Blondin got just as much excitement out of his visit to the Falls as the coachman—for he walked across the Falls on a tight-rope carrying a man on his back.

But we must leave Niagara, and, because there are so many other places awaiting our attention, we haven't time to watch this town grow into the thriving town of today— a town still visited by hundreds of thousands of sightseers but a town, too, where the tremendous headlong plunge of water is converted into electrical power that is distributed far and wide over this Province.

I would have liked to tell you something of Alexander Henry and that noted company of Scottish merchants who entered the western fur trade—the beginning of the Hudson's Bay Company.   You would have been interested in this heroic old adventurer travelling through a country where, because at every step hostile Hurons were ready to pounce on him, he smeared his face with dirt and grease, took off his English clothes, wrapped a cloth around his middle and made his way past enemy canoes hoping that they wouldn't notice that he didn't use his paddle as deftly as a real Indian should.   But that is too long a story, although when I tell you that at least once he and his party saved their lives by eating the bones of an elk which the wolves had left only partially devoured (fortunately for them!), you'll see that it's a great pity that we must leave such an exciting tale of adventure untold.

The true story of Ontario, however, is the story of its settlement. When people began to come in the wake of the explorers to what became known as Upper Canada and later Ontario, and decided to live here and settle down— then the real story of this Province, as we know it, begins. Unfortunately, so many of them settled in so many different places all at once that it's not easy to decide which particular group of settlers I shall mention first.

However, there's nothing like beginning as the day begins— in the east; and when a group of Glengarry Highlanders emigrated to New York from Scotland after the Jacobite Rebellion because their own country was rather more than they could endure with reasonable comfort—they were, though they didn't suspect it, already on their way to Canada to found Glengarry County in the eastern corner of this Province. What with the Revolutionary War in the States and the ill-treatment they received because they remained loyal, however, their troubles weren't by any means over even in that country. So, once again, they emigrated, this time to Canada. Here they sought and found refuge under the British flag. That was in 1776 or thereabouts and they numbered about 300.

There was nothing in those days that corresponded to a civic reception so, I'm afraid, they were left pretty much to themselves when they arrived here and had to work out their own salvation. But ten years later—they'd probably been writing home to bonny Scotland in the meantime— a large number of Scottish Highlanders left the land of the leal and came out to join them. They were about 500 in number and they were nearly all called Macdonnell because— believe it or not—they were all relations of their priest who had charge of them—the Rev. Alexander Macdonnell. True, they were followed by other settlers of other and lesser tribes like the McLeods, Camerons, McPhersons, and Macmillans— but to all intents and purposes it was a rip-roaring Macdonnell invasion of what became known as Glengarry County.

So far—so good.

The clan Macdonnell, nevertheless, were not by any means

the only newcomers to Canada.   While they had been settling in Glengarry County and, no doubt, congratulating themselves that they'd escaped from Scotland or the States or wherever they happened to come from—companies and battalions and whole regiments of disbanded troops were making their way over the border of the States, where, because they were Loyalists, life wasn't worth living—at least for *them*! For example, at about that time, no less than 1,462 officers and men of the King's Royal Regiment of New York (the Royal Yorkers, as they were called) settled in the first five townships west of the Quebec boundary.   Now, that was pretty near the Glengarry Highlanders.   But, these Loyalists were also Highlanders.   So there was no declaration of war and they all settled down to make the best of the wilderness in which they found themselves.

As you would expect, however, the Macdonnells ruled the roost for quite a long time.   No less than eighty men of that name received grants of land and it was the Macdonnells who, for many years, held the most important civil and military positions.   Indeed, two of them, the brothers John and Hugh, were members of General Simcoe's first Parliament, 1792-96.

Did you notice, by the way, that I spoke of grants of land? That shows that the Government was already taking upon itself the responsibility of settling these ex-soldiers or, as we call them now, Loyalists, and their families.   They didn't do at all badly considering the rough-and-ready administration of those days.   A private soldier (grants of land were based upon army rank) received one hundred acres on the river front and two hundred in addition; 50 acres were allowed to his wife and each child; and each son or daughter on coming of age received 200 acres.   Land was plentiful in those days.   As for the officers—well, if one had attained field rank a grant of 5,000 acres was regarded as a slight compensation for a return to the more humdrum civilian life of a settler.   So you see that a commission in the army was even more than now, perhaps, a matter for congratulation.

While, to make prospects for the settlers even brighter they were supplied for the first three years—officers and men alike—with most of the necessities of life—food, clothes, seed, cattle, horses and implements and so on—not to mention coarse cloth for trousers (what the Victorians of that day called the "unmentionables"); Indian blankets for coats, boots made out of skins or heavy cloth and last but not least, a "firelock" or musket which was used, no doubt, to keep Indian peddlers away. For all these excellent arrangements Governor Sir Frederick Haldimand was largely responsible—indeed, in his desire to help these settlers he didn't hesitate on one occasion to disobey the instructions of the Imperial Government, and continued supplying the settlers with these things despite orders to stop doing so.

As for the settlers in Glengarry, they farmed and built up a lumbering industry, but the Scot, as you know, is not easily changed even by a new country. So in 1819 we find John Goldie writing in his diary that he entered Glengarry, "of which", he says, "the Highlanders boast so much", and found that they retained all the habits and customs of the Highlands of Scotland—pure and undefiled. In 1852, the middle of the last century, Colonel Alexander Chisholm found 3,228 Macdonnells or McDonalds in Glengarry, and thirty other clans numbering from 50 to 545 in each clan. Those clans doubtless, and in Kipling's words, were regarded as "lesser breeds without the law" to be tolerated but not encouraged by the Macdonnells! I should add, however, that during the Rebellion of 1837-38—less than a hundred years ago—the regiments of militia from the shores of the St. Lawrence were conspicuous for their gallantry.

So much, then, for Eastern Ontario where we have spent so long, that we shall have to redouble our speed if we are to get a glimpse of what was happening at this time in the rest of the Province. But we shall stay long enough to glance at Carleton County and Bytown which are also in the East, and where events had been moving so rapidly that in 1829 the settlers held their first fair—and a very large agricultural fair it was. However, as a minor poet of that region said:

> "Twas not to buy or sell 'they came;
> They all assembled, wild and free
> To have a ranting, roaring spree."

and the result of that first fair was that after the horse race at the end of the fair the lumbermen and the Irish labourers had a glorious dust-up. They didn't dare have another fair for years. Those were wild days in more senses than one. For instance, in Richmond—named after the Duke of Richmond, who was then Governor-General and who died after being bitten by a pet fox that had rabies—in Richmond the inhabitants excelled Bytown by having two fairs every year; and whenever the lumbermen and the ex-soldiers began fighting (and they never failed to fight) a gigantic Irish priest called Father Peter Smith used to lay about them with a long whip and restore law and order. The Irish "shiners" as they were called, used to shine brilliantly and with a rare, wild, unrestrained effulgence in any and every one of these brawls; but for all that, the population grew and progress was being made in the intervals between fights and fairs—real progress in every part of the East of Ontario. Then came the day in 1857 when Queen Victoria chose Ottawa as the site of the future capital. Of course, the whole country of Carleton took on much greater importance. The citizens walked, you may be sure, with heads erect and a lighter step because of the presence within the borders of their county, of Ottawa—which was described by one man (Goldwin Smith) as "a sub-arctic lumber-village converted by royal mandate into a political cock-pit."

Meanwhile, what was happening in other parts of Ontario? To be quite frank very much the same sort of development was taking place wherever immigrants had settled; land was being farmed, mills were being built, lumber was being hauled and little communities were being formed, growing gradually into towns and some of them much later into cities. I don't wish to give the impression, however, that fights and brawls were an inseparable part of life in every community, and that all fairs ended with a skirmish between rival contenders who doubtless regarded fisticuffs as not the least of the day's pleasures. Election days at all events rarely passed anywhere without their free-for-alls. Politics and pugnacity went together. Voters vowed vengeance on everybody who didn't think as they did. That was the rule! Now, it's going to be impossible, in so short a time, to tell you the story of Ontario in detail, taking in turn county by county as I have done thus far. A short time ago I had the pleasure of delivering an address to the Empire Club in Toronto. It concerned, appropriately enough, the history of Toronto. As you may have heard, Toronto is celebrating its centennial this year and it occurred to me even then that the life led by the pioneers in every part of this Province differed in different localities only in minor aspects. The conditions of living were pretty much the same in the scattered communities of those days. Bill Jones in Toronto and Elisha Smith in Niagara—and there must have been some people of that name then—must have lived lives that were very much alike.

What I propose to do, therefore, is to tell you something about the lives of the Jones and the Smiths, the Browns and the Robinsons and all those hardy forerunners of ours who came to, and saw and conquered a wilderness and made of it the Province of Ontario as we know it.

Let us begin, then, with the first English-speaking settlers in Upper Canada. There were about 5,000 of them and they were the United Empire Loyalists. Now, irrespective of where they went in the Dominion they had to have a house, a shelter, a home—even if it was only a shanty ten feet long, eight feet wide and six feet high, and that was the beginning for almost all of them without exception. They had a tent— an army tent usually. The tent would be pitched on the land granted to them and then they would begin felling trees, making a clearing in which their little house would be built. Later the shanty would be enlarged. If they prospered they would build a larger, more commodious log house—or even a frame house on the popular colonial pattern with, perhaps, a huge fireplace eight feet or more wide.

Fires, by the way, were a problem. For one thing there weren't any matches. It was not until less than one hundred years ago that the ubiquitous lucifer was invented. So that if the fire went out, they would have to carry live embers or burning wood from the nearest neighbours—to start the fire again. I don't imagine that happened often, however, because they made sure of slow-burning fires by having huge logs pulled right into the house, and placed near the fireplace, by oxen. They burned a great deal of wood, of course. Mrs. Ann Macaulay in Kingston wrote to her son John in Toronto in 1837 describing the previous winter: "If I may judge by the quantity of ashes", she wrote, "I burnt an immensity of wood, for in February I was obliged to take out 12 bushels as the ash house was quite full." It must have taken them all their time, I imagine, to keep even moderately warm, and thinking of those days, we cannot but be amazed at the progress that has been made since.

It is, after all, unnecessary for me to tell you how the houses became more and more comfortable as the years passed and as the hard-working pioneers achieved the comparative prosperity they worked so hard to realize within their own life-time. Stone houses, brick houses, began to be built in every community, and gradually through the years the towns of the Province assumed the appearance with which we are familiar today.

By a natural association of ideas, however, this brief reference to fires reminds me that fires cook—and cooking (the ladies present will agree with me)—cooking, good and bad, has played a much more important part in shaping world events and, of course, events in this Province than most historians would seem to believe. What did they live on—these pioneers?

Well, the soldiers—and they were the first inhabitants of Upper Canada excluding, of course, the Indians—the soldiers had bully beef, pea soup and hard tack. By way of a luxury, they consumed a considerable amount, too, of salt pork. But that is not all—not by any manner of means. In the lakes and the rivers were whitefish, salmon, sturgeon, and in the air, or on the ground, or in the trees were ducks, turkeys, pigeons, deer, raccoons and, of course, rabbits. So even the soldiers' fare wasn't to be sniffed at—or at least not merely to be sniffed at.

Nevertheless, Governor Simcoe, whom I have already mentioned, once told a traveller that they often had to depend on getting their flour all the way from London, England. Think of it!—and their salt meat was shipped across the Atlantic from Ireland.

But I'm afraid that the cooking was bad—unendurably bad. In 1835 Patrick Sherriff, travelling through the Province, stopped at Richmond Hill for dinner. Listen to his description. He had "roast beef alone, so tough", he says, "that my friend remarked that the animal must have died in the yoke from distress. Human teeth could make little impression upon it, and I satisfied hunger with bad bread and water." When poor Patrick asked for breakfast at a little inn between Amherstburg and Sandwich he was served with "poor green tea, rancid butter and worse bread."

Now before I leave this all important matter of food and cooking I would like to read for the edification of the ladies present a recipe devised, concocted, invented or simply made up by a certain "Tiger" Dunlop who strenuously objected to food being "deluged with grease and butter" as was the custom in taverns and inns in those days. Here is his recipe. "To dress beefsteak: Cut the steak about ¼ inch thick, wash it well in a tub of water, wringing it from time to time after the manner of a dish cloth; put a pound of fresh butter in a frying pan (hog's lard will do, but butter is more esteemed), and when it boils put in the steak, turning and peppering it for about a quarter of an hour; then put it into a deep dish and pour the oil over it until it floats, and so serve it."

I wish I could tell you more about food and cooking in

the days of yore, but, please, don't imagine from what I have already said, that there weren't sumptuous meals in those days. Here at Fort William, for example, the North West Company had great feasts in an immense wooden building—"venison from the woods and fish from the lakes—buffaloes' tongues and beavers' tails and various luxuries from Montreal served by cooks brought for the purpose."

Even the rather unappetizing fare with which, for many reasons, other pioneers usually had to be content was better, at all events, than the food people had to eat in that terrible year—the hungry year, 1788, when a drought killed everything. In that year people ate dogs in St. Catharines. At Niagara they ate whatever roots they knew the pigs ate, because that was the only way they could be sure that they wouldn't themselves be poisoned. Bull-frogs were delicacies in other communities, and starving children stood on the shores of the St. Lawrence begging for biscuits from passing boatmen and traders. Fortunately, that was a very exceptional—indeed a unique year—and it was long, long ago.

As I tell you of these things I would like you to fill in with your own imagination all that one must omit in so brief a story of the past. I have told you of how people came to Ontario. I have given you some idea of their little homes, the fires with which they kept themselves warm and the food with which they strove to build up strength and endurance to meet the rigours of early life in Canada. There they were, these valiant people, clearing the forests, building log roads and log houses, log schoolrooms and little log churches; fishing and hunting for their food; farming and lumbering. What a great industry, by the way, was that of lumbering and what wild, devil-may-care and immensely powerful men were those shantymen with their red or tri-coloured red, white and blue sashes, their cow-hide boots with heavy spikes, their blanket coats and their red caps, risking their lives rolling the logs down the rivers.

Here's an old song about the shantyman. It describes the wooing of a bonny lassie by a shantyman come to the little

town on holiday from the woods.   This is the last verse.
The girl's Mother is speaking:

"O daughter, dearest daughter, you grieve my heart full sore,
    To fall in love with a shantyman, you never saw before!"
"Well, Mother, I don't care for that, so do the best you can,
    For I'm bound to go to Ottawa with my roving
        shantyman."

Nothing in the world, you see—not even a Mother's solici-
tude—could prevail against the fascination of this wild
young man from the woods, this lumberman, this shantyman.
Many, many a young farmer left the quiet routine of his
farm to become "a roving shantyman" in the great forests
of Ontario, there to live a life of adventure.

Little by little this great Province was being settled by
farmers and lumbermen, by builders and merchants and by
the labours of men and women engaged in subduing nature
so that it might supply their needs.   The years passed and
roads were being built.   Villages sprang up; and as their
population increased and the activities of their citizens multiplied they became towns with duly appointed officials whose
responsibility it was to serve the inhabitants.

I have no time to tell you of historic events such as are
to be found in all history books.   The occupation of York
by the Americans in 1813, the battle of Montgomery's farm
in 1837, the battle of Windmill Point in the following year
in Prescott when the Hunters, republican immigrants from
the United States were defeated.   Nor is it my intention to
speak of Government administration during those years, of
the steady growth that continued despite such events as the
Fenian Raids, and the Riel Rebellion of 1870.

Once development had begun nothing could halt Ontario's
persistent march forward and upward—just as nothing will
ever be able to check the continued progress of this great
enterprising Province.   What I have told you, however, is
something that is so often overlooked—the lives led by men
and women, as it were, behind the scenes.   For it is they with
their carts and their canoes, their little sailing ships and later

their bigger steamers, their stage coaches and their roads labori-
ously cut through the wilds of that primitive country—it is
they who made Ontario what it is today.   That is why their
lives are so interesting and inspiring.   That is why the men and
women of today owe these strong, simple, courageous men and
women of the past such a tremendous debt of gratitude.   Even
though their own toil was never ending yet they found time to
help each other.   They had their logging bees and the women
their sewing bees.   In co-operation, in mutual helpfulness
there was something that compensated them for the hardships of their lives.   In all this life of the past, Fort William—
situated almost at the heart of this vast Dominion, 1,700
miles from Halifax and 1,900 miles from Vancouver, with
its thriving population of more than 26,000—Fort William,
your own city, has played a most worthy part.   How far
you have travelled since those early days when Indians and
French and Scottish voyageurs of the North-West and Hudson's Bay Companies used to set out from here on expeditions
into the Far West, taking with them bears' grease and coarse
cornmeal on which to live.   Fort William was then the
Grand Portage; everybody going West would pass by the
fort that stood here on the banks of the Kaministiquia River;
for two centuries this was the most famous, perhaps, of all
meeting-places for the old fur-traders.

What developments there have been since then!   How
important a position you occupy today as the terminus of all
westward traffic on the lakes and with the greatest in-turn of
freight in any city in Canada.

For you are still the Grand Portage, even as you were
during all those years—and long before those years—of which
I have attempted to tell you as much as I could in this necessarily brief story of the past.

How nearly, by the way, both Fort William and Port
Arthur came to being placed within the boundaries of Manitoba and out of Ontario altogether!   It was only forty-five
years ago that the Federal Government, under Sir John A.
Macdonald claimed that the Manitoba line should be a line

drawn due north from the confluence of the Ohio and Mississippi Rivers, 300 miles east of its present position. You would have been lost to this Province—but our loss would have been Manitoba's gain.

I, too, would very probably never have had this opportunity of coming to you. Certainly I couldn't have chosen as my subject the one I have presented to you today.

Yet, in a very real sense your railways and the great Trans-Canada Highway that will one day span this great Dominion —these link you with not one Province but with every part of Canada, making of you a point of concentration, ideally situated, a centre that will flourish, whose importance—great though it is today and for three centuries past—will increase as the years pass.

I trust that in the story I have told you, you have been given a glimpse of the past—a past of which every citizen of Ontario may well be proud.

It is a past that tells of the emerging of this vast, progressive Province from virginal forest and wild lonely stretches of country known only to the wandering Indian.

Such a story of superb hardihood and the courage of generations of pioneers is at once an encouragement and a promise. For nothing can impede the forward surge of progress, and here in Fort William I hope I have once again reminded you not only of your own magnificent part in that story but also of the tremendous sweep of history, the dangers and the toils, the courage and the self-sacrifice, of all those actors for whom this Province was a vast stage on which they enacted the drama and sometimes, too, the comedy of their lives.

THE BRITISH EMPIRE—A SYMBOL AND A PHENOMENON

Before the Canadian Club, Port Arthur,
June 25, 1934

Mr. President, Ladies and Gentlemen:

I am indeed privileged in being able to address so large and distinguished an assembly as I see before me this evening, and I want to express my very sincere thanks to those who have given me the opportunity to meet this representative gathering of the citizens of Port Arthur. I need not say how deeply I appreciate the courtesies that have been extended to us, and, searching my mind for words that would express something at least of what I feel at this moment, I am reminded, curiously enough, of the text of a sermon I once heard—"Lord, it is good for us to be here."

However, that is not the text or subject of the few words I want to say to you tonight. Nor have I any intention of preaching a sermon. When I was considering what I could say to you, and when, as you may well imagine, different subjects were suggesting themselves to me, I found one of these subjects returning again and again to my mind, demanding, as it were, very special attention. The thought came to me, "How many things there are that we take for granted, when in reality they are very special privileges which have been made possible for us to enjoy by years and even centuries of the devotion, sacrifice and toil of others." I wasn't thinking, by the way, of such things as the radio, the cinematograph, the motor car and all those gifts of Western civilization to men and women everywhere. But suddenly I found myself thinking of the British Empire as a reality, as a promise, and also as a fulfilment of much that for centuries was little more than a vision or an idea that spurred men to high endeavour.

I once heard the story of a speaker in the Oxford Union who traced drunkenness to three causes: "The first," he said, "was the adulteration of liquor; the second was the desire for drink; and the third, and above all, Sir, was the desire for more."

Now I find these words are apt to this occasion in two respects. They are an illustration of what must at all costs be avoided in a speech of this kind. For I am convinced that he who sets out to explain something, however many the thoughts and ideas that crop up in any consideration of so vast a subject as this British Empire, must use no "firstlys" and "secondlys" and "thirdlys"—you all know that wearisome method of enumerating the points of a speech.

It has very much the same effect as counting sheep going through a gate—a process recommended, I believe, for bringing sleep to the sleepless. But I want you to notice four words, "the desire for more"—those words that came so trippingly off the tongue of our Oxford Union friend.

Now, I am not so dyed-in-the-wool a romantic as not to recognize in these four words the primal impulse, or first cause which in the course of time led by manifold paths to the creation of the British Empire. You may be sure that long before the Empire existed even as a wild fancy in the mind of a poet—far, far back when the world was a very tiny world surrounded by the unknown world, a place of terror and darkness inhabited by fabulous monsters—you may be sure that even then the call of the sea awakened dreams of adventure. To be "cribbed, cabined and confined" as it were, on an island where the sea was always knocking at your door, made the Viking blood that flowed even then in the veins of the inhabitants of that little island stir restlessly and thrill to thoughts of conquest. Let us be frank then and make no bones about it. It was the desire for more, the desire for growth, the desire for something bigger, freer, richer and fuller than could ever be found sitting by the family fireside—it was this desire that first drove the youth of England and Scotland to seek a fairer fortune over the seas.

John Morley once referred to the newspaper press of a certain country as "that huge machine for keeping discussion on a low level." I have no means of knowing precisely how just that description was. But I do know that I must hasten to correct any possible misapprehension that may already exist in your minds. This brief discussion would have reached a low level, indeed, if it is being assumed that the heritage of Empire—that heritage which we take so much for granted—is nothing more than an expression of whatever philosophical or ethical content is to be found in "the desire for more" regarded as an expression of rank materialism. Let me say at once and with all the emphasis of which I am capable, that the expansion of the Empire by conquest and exploration would be of no more than passing significance— indeed, the fate of the Empire itself would have been far different if not actually involved in utter disaster—if those who built it had no higher promptings than personal, material or pecuniary gain.

How can I explain what it is that lifts the whole history of Empire far above the humdrum, commonplace level of practical, uninspired self-aggrandisement to the higher and intrinsically nobler realm in which the ideals of generations of men and women have sought their surest realization? If such other motives—such ideals—are to be found they must be sought for in history.

There is an amusing parody of some well-known lines of poetry which runs thus:

"Lives of great men all remind us
    As the pages all we turn
That we're apt to leave behind us
    Letters that we ought to burn."

Now one of the men who left letters, or at all events, a diary that very fortunately was never burnt, was Samuel Pepys. On the 30th of January in the year 1649 he saw with his own eyes the execution of King Charles I. Pepys was at school then, and years later—after the Restoration—when a king was again on the throne, he was terribly afraid lest it should ever be recalled that when Charles was executed at Whitehall, he (Samuel Pepys) had declared that he would like to preach a sermon, taking as his text, "The memory of the wicked shall rot."

Charles I was doubtless a man of charming personality in private intercourse with his friends. What then was his great, his unforgivable crime—the crime that could only be expiated by his death? What was it that made young Samuel Pepys so highly incensed that he, a schoolboy, could think of a text so full of unconcealed, youthful bitterness for a funeral oration over the headless body of his King?

Before I answer that question I want you to notice that we are now dealing with something far greater in its magnitude than colonial expansion, something that touches men and women more closely, more intimately than even fresh conquests over the seas. Centuries before this, yet another king—a king less pleasing in his person than Charles I—had sat sullen and resentful, surrounded by his watchful barons, and with pen in hand had affixed his name to a Charter that deprived him, for all time, of what he considered to be his God-given rights. To what purpose was he taken to the field in Runnymede? He saved his life, no doubt, by signing the Magna Charta, but what had he done to make the people turn so fiercely upon him as they were later to turn, so fatally, upon Charles I?

The answer is, like most tremendous things, a simple one. King John was made to renounce his tyrannic privileges and King Charles I paid with his life for the unforgivable crime of seeking to rule without justice and of despoiling his people—the nation over which he ruled—of that liberty which is the inalienable and rightful possession of every man.

I have heard it said—and that very recently—that the trouble with public opinion is that so many people only express it privately. But throughout the history of the Empire never has public opinion been so vigorous and so vociferously public as when the freedom of the individual subject is endangered or his personal integrity is being tampered with—even tentatively—by those who wish to arrogate to themselves the autocratic power which can never, by any windy plausibility of argument, be rightfully theirs.

Now, the point I wish to make is this. Such historical acts as I have just mentioned have sent repercussions down the long corridors of time and,—to change our metaphor—like the widening circles made by a stone in a pool, have extended gradually to embrace all those countries, all that world-wide commonwealth of nations which we habitually refer to as the British Empire.

Samuel Butler once wrote that "all the animals, excepting man, know that the principal business of life is to enjoy it." But he didn't add (no doubt because it was not a part of his purpose at the time) that whatever be the particular kind of enjoyment we seek in our lives one thing above all is needful—to be free to pursue it. All the titanic struggles of the past, the wars, the revolutions, the executions of kings and the crowning of emperors, persecutions and massacres, triumphs and mistakes, shame and glory, what lies behind it all but the struggle of a world of conflicting desires to find unity and harmony, peace and enjoyment of life for the individual man and woman? And in the whole history of the world what more powerful agency than the British Empire has been seeking by trial and experiment, such as is possible only under a true democracy, to find the fulfilment of every man's legitimate aspirations?

Once upon a time a city wanted a new hospital and funds were low. So the City Council promptly voted and passed a set of resolutions:

1. Resolved, by this Council, that we build a new hospital.
2. Resolved, that the new hospital be built out of the materials of the old hospital.
3. Resolved, that the old hospital be used until the new hospital is finished.

Do you detect a flaw, somewhere, in those resolutions? Now, he who regards the story of the Empire as a blunt, bald narrative of territorial expansion is making just as obvious a blunder. For, side by side with the story of Clive in India, of Cook in Australia, of Wolfe in Canada, of Wellington at Waterloo and Marlborough at Malplaquet, there is a story that deals with events of deeper import and profounder significance. It is the story of a magnificent determination to achieve a full life by affording the individual every opportunity for self-development with due regard, I need not say, for the rights of his fellow-men. I know full well that long ago Machiavelli stated that it is impossible to define what democracy is. But had he lived to watch the struggles by which and through which the democratic institutions of the Empire have been evolved and brought into being, I know he would have found in its Parliaments, its press, its freedom of speech, its broad tolerance of religious and political differences and in all those other tangible and intangible benefits of which we are the heirs, more than a hint of that rich, free, ennobling life toward which democracy at times painfully and, at times, triumphantly makes its way. For it can never be said of the Empire as Emerson said of his generation that "Things are in the saddle and ride mankind." I don't propose to attempt in so brief a discourse, a definition of democracy. But I am convinced that we who live in a democratic country, we who are citizens of the Empire to which I am paying all too inadequate a personal tribute, will agree that, although a true democracy may be difficult to achieve, it is not, as some would have us believe, impossible of achievement. No, the very difficulties make it all the more desirable as an objective, all the more worthy of attainment and all the more magnificent an aim for our individual and collective striving.

Of course, democracy, and with it the Empire which remains a bulwark of democracy, is being almost savagely decried in this our modern world. There's too much freedom about it! It's altogether too easy going! As Shakespeare says, "Ambition must be made of sterner stuff." Many people, as you know, find their life purpose—their principal enjoyment (and in a democratic country they will not be denied this enjoyment)—in a wholesale condemnation of everything that savours of liberty—which they quite mistakenly confound with licence.

Matthew Arnold, a delightful man in many ways, a writer of distinguished prose and some poetry, had a perpetual grouch against people and things in general because they weren't perfect. If progress springs from a "divine dissatisfaction" with things as they are, then in Matthew Arnold that dissatisfaction had found a congenial habitation. Then came the day—as it comes for all of us—when Matthew Arnold died.

"Poor Matthew," wrote Robert Louis Stevenson, another celebrated author, "Poor Matthew, he's gone to heaven no doubt—but he won't like God." Some people are like that!

Now, when I began I intended to speak rather more specifically of the history of the Empire. But in a world that is filled with the clamour of contending ideas it was, perhaps, natural that I should be led to rediscover and to insist that the real strength of any institution—even of such an institution as the Empire—is its rightness as an idea. Ideas are, of course, abstract things but, none the less, they are the most powerful things in the world. They build and they destroy. They can create and they can strangle and put an end to all growth. I chose the British Empire as my subject this evening simply because it seemed to me that we are inclined to take for granted the hard-won privileges which we enjoy as citizens of Empire. That is why I thought it would be both interesting and instructive to say something of the Empire and what it stands for, which meant, of course, that I had to direct your attention to some of the ideas underlying all that we mean by the Empire.

I think it has been the experience of all of us that in conversation or at public meetings references to the British Empire are always liable to be exclusively concerned with its size, its power as an economic unit and what I may call, in general, its external aspects. But the stability of this great commonwealth of nations can't be explained by reference to such obvious but superficial features. Indeed, the actual story of how the Empire came into existence isn't by any means the epic story of impossibly perfect men. It is the story of human beings with all the good and bad which we find in human nature, expressing themselves in the actions history has recorded. It is above all a story of the gradual emergence of certain definite principles of Government and of the formation of a certain attitude toward life which, if not a fully formulated philosophy, is at least noticeably and distinctively British. And the records of Empire history— and not least the history of this Dominion within the Empire —are all the more moving, all the more an inspiration and contain an even deeper and more heartening promise for the future because they are records of progress made as true progress is always made—that is, by trial and error, by some- times devious routes, by backslidings checked and mistakes corrected, and rarely, if ever, by any sudden ebullition of a superhuman intelligence or a godlike wisdom. The men who built the Empire were first of all men, and as men, with all their faults, they succeeded in raising the structure of that Empire of which we are citizens.

Tyranny was never permitted for long to make bold experiment impossible. Above all else they wanted liberty— liberty to undertake for themselves that most difficult of all tasks, the building of an Empire in such a way that its foundations would rest upon the free consent of all its citizens.

That is why the story of the Empire is, like human nature itself, so full of seeming contradictions. The country that was at one time so deeply involved in the slave traffic that Lecky, the historian, described slavery as "a central object of the British policy"—it was that country which led in the work of emancipating slaves and making due reparation, once public opinion had been aroused by men like Wilber- force. The country whose prisons at one time were described with such painful accuracy by its leading novelists, was also the country that produced such ardent and successful prison reformers as Elizabeth Fry. Today England is second to none in the variety of the Social services it renders. The freedom that is possible in such a developing democracy not only implies the freedom to make a mistake but also, and above all, to correct it and never to make it again. And that is true, sound progress.

One day a farmer presented himself before a very famous European Marshal who, in his day, had enjoyed almost unlimited power. Owing to political change and revolution, however, he was now virtually impotent, a prisoner in fact if not in name.

"Excellency," said the farmer, "I found your handkerchief in the park, but it would mean great happiness to me if I were allowed to keep it as a souvenir."

"No," said the Marshal, "please give it back to me. It is the only thing into which I may still poke my nose."

He had, you see, lost his freedom, that democratic freedom which consists in being able to investigate or, if you will, to "poke one's nose" into anything that seems to threaten the well-being of a democratic community or nation or people.

Now, I should say something about that much-maligned, because misunderstood, word—freedom. Never for a moment does freedom mean that there shall be no restrictions. Freedom simply means that you are free to choose and have the power to decide under what restrictions you wish to live. It also implies that you shall be free of force, of coercion and of interference in bringing about that condition of things in which you and your fellow-citizens wish to live your own lives in your own way. Beyond that, freedom, in its personal or private sense, is whatever you like to think it is.

Confronted with the spectacle of freedom lost and liberty despised in the world of today, how splendid a thing it is that through the years the ties of loyalty and sentiment, of sympathy and of a common heritage which bind this great country to the Empire over the seas, remain firm and enduring.

The necessary restrictions which exist in a well-ordered state are embodied, of course, in laws. In a democracy such as the Empire, "law and order" are in reality cause and effect. It is the law—an even-handed justice acceptable to the people

—that establishes and maintains that order which is the guarantee of freedom. But it does not follow—though this is a common mistake—that the more laws there are the better order there will be in the State. Far from it. I haven't time to do more than make a passing reference to a subject whose ramifications are infinite, being the very heart and foundation of democracy. A recent and noteworthy remark made by a visitor to this country will be sufficient, I believe, to illustrate the point I wish to emphasize. The President of the Kiwanis International, in the course of a Convention held in Toronto a few days ago, spoke with great enthusiasm not only of the police, who are the visible, active symbols of the law, but, in general, of the administration of justice in this Dominion. It was a well-turned compliment; and I know you will not miss the significance of the remark that followed his word of praise: "The United States of America," said this visitor, "has no less than 1,900,000 laws."

May it not be, gentlemen, that even the justice of law courts must itself be justified? May it not be that laws themselves, even though they are backed by the full authority of the State can, in effect, annul themselves if they arouse the resentment of liberty-loving citizens on whose behalf they are, ostensibly, enacted? May it not be that there is a lesson that law itself must learn if it is to be worthy of of respect—the lesson King John learned—the lesson King Charles never lived to benefit by, and the lesson King George III learned only when the great democracy to our South had been lost forever to the British Empire?

In the whole history of the world the liberty of the private, individual citizen has never yet been violated with impunity. At the heart of every man there is a shrine. It is his holy of holies. Over that shrine is inscribed the one word Freedom. Woe betide the legislator, the autocrat, the dictator who desecrates that shrine. Woe betide the man who, unheeding and ruthless, tramples down those barriers which protect every man's dearest possession—his freedom, his personal integrity—the shrine at which he worships—though it be in secret.

A man thirsting for personal power at the cost of the people's liberty may and does, as we know, sow the wind of specious arguments, wild promise, and fervid propaganda. But he will certainly and inevitably reap the whirlwind of revenge, of hate, and it may be, too, of bloody revolution. For the people know that a desire for power is the love of self but that a desire for liberty is the love of others. Vaulting ambition always, in fact, o'erleaps itself and the people are the instruments by which a dead freedom is avenged. Some of you will recall Voltaire's famous words in defence of Freedom of Speech when he wrote to Jean Jacques Rosseau, whose books had just been burned—much as books have been burned in our own time—"I don't agree with a word that you say," wrote Voltaire, "but I will defend to the death your right to say it."

So much then for the freedom which like a precious jewel is preserved in the heart of the Empire—its world-wide democratic setting.

Now, it happens that I have spoken of three kings, and by a coincidence, it has been my good fortune and that of many of you present today to live under the beneficent rule of three British Monarchs—Queen Victoria, King Edward VII, and now King George V, our beloved sovereign, in this year of Grace 1934—to whom be happiness and length of days.

Of all the bonds of Empire, our King and our Royal Family are one of the strongest. Indeed, all that I have said may be regarded as but a preamble to what I shall now say. You will recall what I said of freedom, of law, which is a concomitant of freedom, and of democracy, which seeks by law to preserve freedom and to create those conditions of life best suited to the fulfilment of the whole purpose of living which, in a word, is self-realization for the individual in the fullest and profoundest sense. Now it so happens that all these lines of thought converge upon, and the whole structure of the Empire and consequently the very spirit of democracy is symbolized by, the Crown.

The implications of Royalty and all that it stands for

are therefore tremendous.   The King of England and the present Royal Family are not only dear to the hearts of the citizens of this great Empire but they are pledged to govern according to their own laws and customs and usages.   The King pledges himself so to rule.   How many of you know that at a coronation the King is, to this day, presented to his people as their choice?   The people are told to look upon their King; the people recognize their King; they accept him as their King.

I know that you share with me a warm, whole-hearted admiration and affection for our King and his gracious Con-sort, Queen Mary, and I have shown what it is of which they are the emblem.   I know of no better tribute that I can pay them than to read to you Lord Asquith's words when seconding the address of congratulation in 1918, shortly after the Armistice:

"I had the privilege", he said, "to be Prime Minister when His Majesty ascended the Throne, and I continued to hold that office until more than two years had passed of the progress of the war.   There is no one who can bear testimony—first-hand testimony—more authentic or more heartfelt then I do to the splendid example which His Majesty has set in time of peace, as well as in time of war, in the discharge of every one of the responsible duties which fall to the Sovereign of this Empire.   In the crash of thrones, built, some of them, on unrighteousness, propped up in other cases by a brittle framework of convention, the Throne of this country stands unshaken, broad-based on the people's will.   It has been reinforced to a degree which it is impossible to measure, by the living example of our Sovereign and his gracious Consort, who have always felt and shown by their life and conduct that they are not there to be ministered unto, but to minister."

In the year 1919 the Prince of Wales, returning from a tour of the Empire, stood in the Mansion House in London to deliver an address.

"I should like to tell you," he said, "what I feel I have

learned. I have come back with a much clearer idea of what is meant by the British Empire, or, as it is often more appropriately called, the British Commonwealth. The old idea of Empire handed down from Greece and Rome was that of a mother-country surrounded by daughter-states which owed allegiance to her. Now, we left that obsolete idea behind a long time ago. Our Empire implies a partnership of free nations, nations living under the same system of law, pursuing the same democratic aims and actuated by the same human ideals. The British Empire is thus something far grander than an Empire in the old sense of the term." Perhaps, at this point, and because I am, after all, addressing a Canadian Club, it would be very appropriate to emphasize that such words are sterling evidence of that quality, that spirit within the Empire which is at once its magnificent characteristic and, also, I suspect, the cause of considerable confusion to many of those who overlook the fact that the British Empire has become in itself the embodiment of an ideal—or to be more explicit—a democratic ideal. You may be sure, too, that that ideal—and we as citizens of the Empire are all conscious of its many manifestations—that ideal must have a very considerable power, it must possess a truly tremendous cohesive force, when it is able to preserve in linked harmony a whole commonwealth of nations which are yet so loosely knit together from a purely constitutional point of view.

Heirs, as we are, to a heritage that comprises liberty, representative government, political equality and tolerance of race and creed; determined, as all British subjects are, to retain their personal political liberty; and desirous, as the great majority of us are, for a more equitable distribution of the fruits of production in a world where our environment has been altogether changed by new scientific invention, new economic demands and new industrial organization, we can—because we are free to do so—we can retain the essentials of our heritage while ridding ourselves of the inessentials. We can adapt some things rather than lose everything. We can curb our impatience and avoid violent change whereby both good and bad alike may be lost; for our democracy is such that we can preserve what we cherish most and can reform all that is an anachronism and a hindrance to progress.

Thus shall we avoid the fate that has overtaken those who sought by violence to substitute for the old, something new and incompatible with freedom. Thus shall the Parliamentary system be preserved as the ultimate guardian of liberty, equal justice and free government.

The guardianship of these rights of every citizen is implicit in a limited monarchy. Because the King gives the due and necessary authority to the sanctions and desires of the people he is, therefore, both the ruler and the servant of the people. The very motto of the heir to the throne, the Prince of Wales whom I have quoted, is "Ich Dien"—"I serve". The principle behind it all is that there is a body of rights belonging to British citizens which any and every government is bound to regard.

Unless such a principle were formally acknowledged the multitudinous voice of a democracy's free citizens would soon be involved in Bedlam—unless, of course, that voice were silenced outright by force. That has been done; and under the heel of a dictatorship men and women have lost not only the power of giving weight and authority and even majesty to their freely spoken desires as expressed through elected representatives in Parliament, but they have lost freedom itself—that political and constitutional freedom of which I have already spoken in some detail.

What does all this mean to us as Canadians? Without appeal to emotion and sentiment, and regarded frankly and realistically, it means that Canada is aligned with all that gives stability and security. It means that liberty is still regarded as the prerogative of every man. It means that self-determination in all matters affecting the future of our citizens will never be denied the duly elected administrators of government, and it means a conception of the intrinsic value of human life, the reverence that should be accorded the potentialities of every man and woman which will never be thwarted and made mock of by harsh tyranny or a brutalizing autocracy.

It means, too, that with such traditions of freedom as are cherished within the Empire it is possible for that Empire to cultivate and strengthen in the great democracy to our South such a sentiment of goodwill as will make of the English-speaking peoples of the world an abiding guarantee that war shall never again despoil the beauty of this world and destroy, beyond all hope of recovery and restitution, all that humanity deems most precious.

OUR INHERITANCE

*At the Dominion Day Luncheon Given by
the Mayor of Toronto and Members of the
Council to Commemorate the Centennial of
Toronto, July 2, 1934*

Your Worship and Gentlemen:

In the presence of this great representative gathering of the citizens of Ontario it is a great pleasure and a quite unique privilege to respond to the toast so eloquently proposed by His Worship the Mayor of Toronto.

Rather more than one hundred years ago the employees of what was known as the Canada Company near Goderich held an impromptu celebration. News had arrived of the coronation of King William IV. The news was a mere two months overdue, but that didn't matter. And to show you the contagious quality of the enthusiasm manifested on that occasion, even the American millwright was infected. He joined in the celebrations with great gusto. "I do declare," he exclaimed, "I do declare, if this don't almost put me in mind of the 4th of July. Well, I vow if I don't feel quite *loyal*. Come let us drink the old gentleman's health again. I guess I feel as dry as a sand bank after so much hollerin'."

Today, gentlemen, we celebrate not merely the 150 years that have passed since the foundation of this great Province— we celebrate also Ontario's unwearying, persistent, youthful vigour and its undiminished vitality. We recall not merely the number of years that have passed since municipalities, villages and towns came into existence within our borders, but we call to mind also the superb buoyancy of spirit by which those years have been animated—and during which so many great things have been accomplished.

To return for a moment to Goderich and our friendly American millwright. You probably noticed that he, too, became imbued with something of the spirit of that day. It pervaded the very atmosphere he breathed. It placed in the forefront the men who were making history as pioneers, as legislators, as farmers, as lumbermen, as soldiers or simply as men—the United Empire Loyalists.

I don't know why it is, but if at any time any of you gentlemen should open at random a history book dealing with that period, you will in all probability find yourself reading some such statement as this: "The Government intended to give a cow to each two families, but there weren't enough cows." As soon as you read that you may be sure that you have opened the book at the very page on which the story is being told of the splendid work done by Governor Sir Frederick Haldimand. How magnificently he strove to help those disbanded soldiers and their families settle in Upper Canada, as it was then called. How generously he sought to do all he could for the United Empire Loyalists who came over the borders to a Northern wilderness to found and develop the Province in which we live today. One hundred acres on the St. Lawrence River front were given to each private soldier and two hundred acres behind that; fifty acres to his wife and to each child an additional two hundred acres when each son and daughter came of age. Food and clothes and seed and farm implements—hoes, spades, mattocks, sometimes ploughs and farm animals were supplied to them for the first three years. Not much of anything, of course, but enough to keep every Loyalist going—every Loyalist, that is, but the Glengarry Highlanders. They kept going, nevertheless! And I know of nothing which illustrates the indomitable spirit of these hardy old pioneers so vividly as the fact that although they didn't receive the supplies given to other and later Loyalist arrivals, yet they went straight ahead and, unaided, built up flourishing communities in the east of this Province. That was a magnificent achievement.

Perhaps I should state at this point, gentlemen, that it isn't my intention to undertake anything in the nature of a historical survey of Loyalist history. I mention these historical facts because it is in this manner that we became heirs to a rich heritage. Indian blankets for coats, boots made out of rough skins, trousers of extremely coarse cloth, and all those other necessities with which most of the Loyalists were supplied—what significance have these things? The answer is obvious. All too inadequately equipped as they were, those ex-soldiers, those settlers, those United Empire Loyalists quite literally pitched their tents in that corner of a wild country which had been allotted to them and which had never been cultivated since the dawn of civilization, and forced it, by dint of their incredible labours, to yield to them and their families those things by which all men must live.

May I, for a moment, raise the curtain on the past so that we may look at life in the developing municipalities of Ontario? With so many of them represented here today I can imagine nothing more appropriate. We have time only for a few brief glimpses of the past. However, they will be typical of the years we are celebrating—and because this is a happy occasion they will be in the lighter vein.

The early settlers—the citizens of Old Ontario—were always ready to celebrate and they did so in a very whole-hearted manner. Of course, they were born far too soon to have such an occasion for celebration as has brought us together today. Nevertheless, they could always invent occasions and find reasons. Consider, for example, the case of a builder named Bradbeer. You know that these early pioneers sought and found compensation for their loneliness and the hardships of their lives by co-operation and by helping each other at what they called "Bees". In return for all helping, for example, to build the barn of one member of their community, they would expect that member to supply them with, shall we say, refreshment—a little celebration! One year the ignoble Bradbeer refused the refreshment which would reward them for their labours. The next year, when he tried to build another barn he had to send to the Methodist Indian Mission on the Credit River before he could get anybody to help him. That happened in Wentworth County.

Or consider a parade day at Springfield (or Erindale) on the 4th of June, 1837, in the County of Peel. The Militia is on parade and this is how Miss Jameson describes it: "A few had coats, others jackets; a great number had neither coats nor jackets, but appeared in their shirtsleeves—in edifying variety. Some wore hats, others caps, others their own shaggy heads of hair. Some had firelocks, some had old swords, suspended in belts, or stuck in their waistbands; but the greater number shouldered sticks or umbrellas. Mrs. M. told us that on a former parade-day she had heard the word of command given them—'Gentlemen with the um-brellas, take ground to the right! Gentlemen with the walking-sticks, take ground to the left!'"

That was less than one hundred years ago. In all serious-ness it appears little less than miraculous that the intervening years have witnessed such great changes. Living as these men and women were, in a country beautiful but uncultivated, picturesque but with none of those amenities to which we of a later day are accustomed, how tremendous was their task, how hard they must have laboured and how fantastic it would be to imagine that these parades and celebrations, these family gatherings and merry-makings were anything more than the briefest interludes in lives of toil.

In such a setting the families of early settlers formed little village communities that became the towns and cities of today. Logging, lumbering, farming, opening little stores, hunting, fishing, building houses, making roads—in a multi-tude of such ways they subdued a wilderness. Ottawa, to take a single example—and what better example than the capital of this Province—Ottawa began when, about 1817, two brothers named Burrows built a house on the site of the present capital. Then one of the brothers, John, sold his land to Nicholas Sparks, who built a log shanty. Others joined him. They called it Bytown in 1826. It prospered until 1857, when Queen Victoria chose Ottawa—it had changed its name again—as the site of the future capital.

But I must resist the temptation to speak more of all those past events which bewilder by their number and their variety. Like little tributary streams they all flow into and contribute to that broad flowing river of life in this Province, which has carried us forward to where we are today. Thinking of the past of this Province, how many pleasant scenes come to mind. The young lady, for example, on the occasion of the Public Examination of the Upper Canada Academy in 1840 who read for the edification of the audience an original composition on "The Pernicious Effect of Novel Reading", only to find that as a result the booksellers were sold out of novels a few days later. Or the holiday celebration in the same year, of Queen Victoria's marriage when, according to the Toronto *Mirror*, "one ox, roasted whole, was brought into the centre of the Market Square, and every person, man, woman and child was requested to come cleanly attired, each with knife, fork and plate." How fortunate we are that our invitations to this celebration contained no instructions or even suggestions of that kind. The benefits of the progress made since then are indeed manifold.

A hundred years ago when York became Toronto, Brockville and Brantford, London and St. Thomas and Bytown (or Ottawa) were all thriving towns, and Chatham, Sandwich, Amherstburg and Richmond (or Windsor) were villages ready before many years had passed to assume the status of towns.

With seventy or so municipalities represented here, I cannot hope to pay adequate and individual tribute to the part everyone of your communities has played in the development of the Province of Ontario. I have attempted to do so, as it were, collectively by telling you some of those happier incidents which occurred in every community—incidents characteristic of lighter moments in the lives of our forefathers whom we honour to-day.

I am confident that when we think of these men and women of old in their little and big settlements scattered over this vast Province, we are aware not only of their essential and invincible humanity, but also that we share with them a common heritage. Some weeks ago, addressing a meeting of the United Empire Loyalists, I attempted to express what it was that motivated the lives of these men, why it was that, with the milder, more temperate climes of the South beckoning to them, they yet chose to return to that wild northern wilderness which was to be known as Upper Canada, there to lay the foundations of Ontario.

Still more recently I addressed the Canadian Club at Port Arthur. My subject was the British Empire as an embodiment of an ideal—or to be more explicit, a democratic ideal—an ideal of such power that it has preserved in linked harmony a great commonwealth of nations which are yet so loosely knit together from a purely constitutional point of view. I would conclude with the words I then used: Heirs, as we are, to a heritage that comprises liberty, representative government, political equality and tolerance of race and creed; determined, as all British subjects are, to retain their personal and political liberty; and desirous as the great majority of us are for a more equitable distribution of the fruits of production in a world where our environment has been altogether changed by new scientific invention, new economic demands and new industrial organization, we can—because we are free to do so—we can retain the essentials of our heritage while ridding ourselves of the inessentials. We can adapt some things rather than lose everything. We can curb our impatience and avoid violent changes whereby both good and bad alike may be lost; for our democracy is such that we can preserve what we cherish most and can reform all that is an anachronism and a hindrance to progress.

Thus shall we avoid the fate that has overtaken those who sought by violence to substitute for the old something new and incompatible with freedom. Thus shall the Parliamentary system be preserved as the ultimate guardian of liberty, equal justice and free government.

The guardianship of these rights of every citizen is implicit in a limited monarchy. Because the King gives the due and necessary authority to the sanctions and desires of the people he is, therefore, both the ruler and the servant of the people. The very motto of the heir to the throne, the Prince of Wales, is "Ich Dien"—"I serve". The principle behind it all is that there is a body of rights belonging to British citizens which any and every government is bound to regard.

Unless such a principle were formally acknowledged the multitudinous voice of a democracy's free citizens would soon be involved in Bedlam—unless of course, that voice were silenced outright by force. That has been done; and under the heel of a dictatorship men and women have lost not only the power of giving weight and authority and even majesty to their freely spoken desires as expressed through elected representatives in Parliament, but they have lost freedom itself—that political and constitutional freedom which is the very air breathed by the citizens of a democracy.

What does all this mean to us as Canadians? Without appeal to emotion and sentiment and regarded frankly and realistically, it means that Canada is aligned with all that gives stability and security. It means that liberty is still regarded as the prerogative of every man. It means that self-determination in all matters affecting the future of our citizens will never be denied the duly elected administrators of government, and it means a conception of the intrinsic value of human life, the reverence that should be accorded the potentialities of every man and woman which will never be thwarted and made mock of by harsh tyranny or a brutalizing autocracy.

It means, too, that with such traditions of freedom as are cherished within the Empire it is possible for that Empire to cultivate and strengthen in the great democracy to our South such a sentiment of goodwill as will make of the English-speaking peoples of the world an abiding guarantee that war shall never again despoil the beauty of this world and destroy, beyond all hope of recovery and restitution, all that humanity deems most precious.

THE RETURN OF THE MACE

*At Fort York, on Receiving the Mace Taken
by the United States Army in 1813 and Returned by the Honourable W. D. Robbins
Representing President Roosevelt, July 4, 1934*

Your Worship, Ladies and Gentlemen:

As the representative of His Majesty the King in the
Province of Ontario and at the request of the Government
of Canada it is with the greatest pleasure that I accept this
Mace from you, Mr. Robbins, as the personal representative of
the President of the United States of America.

It is my duty and my privilege, Sir, on behalf of all Canadian citizens, to request you to convey to President Roosevelt,
at whose suggestion and with whose congressional sanction
this Mace has been returned to Canada, our sincerest admiration for his magnanimity and our most cordial appreciation
of the enduring spirit of friendship by which so noble an
action has been prompted.

In the British Empire the Mace has been for many centuries
an emblem of sovereignty and authority borne by the Ser-
geant-at-Arms as his warrant for demanding obedience to
the commands of the people's representatives assembled in
Parliament. It is likewise a symbol of those democratic
ideals of free constitutional government by which the splendid
history, also, of your own great nation has been illuminated
and ennobled in the sight of all men.

The friendly association of our neighbouring democracies
during the past twelve decades has been, we believe, a shining
example to the world and a magnificent vindication of the
principles by which our citizens are inspired.

We believe those principles of freedom permeate individual and community life on both sides of the geographical

boundaries which separate us.   They are our common heritage as English-speaking peoples.

We thank you, Sir, and through you, the citizens of your great nation for this token of their amity.   Through the courtesy of your President we receive this Mace as a tangible expression of goodwill.   Its value is therefore inestimable. For a time it will be placed on view in the Royal Ontario Museum as a visible symbol of our enduring friendship. Seeing it, the citizens of Canada will recall this historic occasion with the liveliest sentiments of affection and gratitude.

A CENTURY OF PEACE

*At the Unveiling of a Tablet Erected by
the United States Daughters of 1812 in
Memory of General Zebulon Pike and
United States Troops Who Fell in the Cap-
ture of York, 1813, July 4, 1934*

Your Worship, Ladies and Gentlemen:

The death of brave men is commemorated by this tablet.
The names of General Pike and those soldiers of the United
States Army whom he led, brings to mind historic events which
shaped the whole course of development on this great North
American continent, and determined its destiny.

Never, I am convinced, has any tribute to the memory
of the valiant men of the past been paid with a greater
sincerity than that which we feel and manifest on this historic
occasion. Long before the memory of living men, there
was war between the nations represented here. In the name
of duty, true to their individual loyalties, men laid down
their lives that those who followed might gain by their
self-sacrifice.

How triumphantly does the unbroken, tranquil record of
peace between the two great democracies represented here
vindicate the part played by General Pike whose name we
honour as one who died gallantly on the field of battle!
He and his army left behind them no heritage but that of a
peace which has endured throughout the intervening years.
May this memorial tablet be not alone an emblem of the
respect we accord to valiant foeman of the days of yore;
not alone an acknowledgment of our gratitude for the
abiding peace which has followed those far-off days of strife
between the contending armies of two great nations; but
also it is our earnest prayer and our heartfelt hope that it

331

will forever symbolize the perpetuation of that peace with which the English-speaking peoples can enrich the world beyond all human computation.

As representative of His Majesty the King in this Province of Ontario, and on behalf of the citizens of Canada, it is my unique privilege and my great pleasure to unveil this tablet erected by the Daughters of the United States of 1812 to honour the memory of their brave fellow-countrymen who, with General Zebulon Pike, fell in battle at Fort York in the year 1813.

COMRADESHIP AND THE TRAGEDY OF PEACE

On Opening the Eighth Annual Convention
of the Ontario Provincial Command of the
Canadian Legion, British Empire Service
League, at the Royal York Hotel, Toronto,
August 1, 1934

Mr. President and Gentlemen:

The name of the Canadian Legion brings memories. Those memories lose nothing of their poignancy with the passing of the years. I know that to you, as ex-service men, the Great War itself must at times seem as unreal as a dream. It couldn't be otherwise. It was another life on a lower, more elemental plane of being. It was more barbarous than the jungle, more merciless than disease. It was all so different from anything you had ever known or imagined.

Gentlemen, you are survivors of the greatest disaster in the history of the world. It must all seem incredible to you at times—those training camps and route marches—screaming shells and creeping poison gas—stretchers and hospitals—night glares and the roar of guns—crowded boats and trains—mud and blood—the trenches and the sickening, unforgettable stench of decay. You must often ask yourselves, was it only a nightmare? Yet the fact that you can recall these and a thousand other things so vividly, is proof enough that it was all very real.

Ypres and the Somme, Passchendaele and Vimy Ridge—how far away they seem now, today.

Yet, despite all your memories of mass murder there come times also, I believe, when you find yourselves thinking, perhaps a little wistfully, of the comradeship, the camaraderie, the loyalty of friend to friend, the good fellowship that existed in platoons and companies, batteries and battalions when you were marching to meet possible death or waiting for it to come.

You wonder why that spirit of comradeship seems to disappear in times of peace when death is no longer a collective menace. You wonder why the cheerful friendliness that existed between soldiers on all fronts and on all sides has vanished. Why? I cannot answer the question.

I sometimes feel that the tragedy of peace is this; when, like a great wall that had protected nations, the army was scattered, it fell apart into hundreds of thousands of small pieces, individuals, each going about his own business. That wonderful *esprit de corps* that had bound them together was lost. If only that one thing had been saved from the ruins; if only the spirit which animated the men who actually did the fighting, who themselves endured the torment of wound and disease; if only that comradeship, which, like a single ray of sunshine struggled through the clouds of war and touched with its brightness some of the most sordid and bestial scenes ever enacted on this planet—if only that spirit had been brought back by soldiers to their separate countries and given full scope and authority in the counsels of men and nations, then, I am sure, the world wouldn't be in the mess it is today; the newspapers would have other topics than the imminence of new wars—wars that will, of course, settle nothing.

But in the Canadian Legion and the British Empire Service League a valiant and most successful attempt has been made to perpetuate that spirit. Who can read of the Douglas Haig Memorial Homes in England without being touched by the so evident desire to make the phrase, "A land fit for heroes to live in", something more than a catchpenny piece of war propaganda? Who can learn of the work being done here in Canada by the Canadian Legion without feeling more hopeful for humanity in general because of this evidence that the spirit of comradeship is still alive among you. It has been preserved as a potent force in your mighty organization. Its fruits are to be found in all that you have done to help the widows and children of dead comrades and those of your wounded comrades who will never again be the men they were. In the Statute Books of Canada such legislation as the Pension Act and the War Veterans' Allowance Act prove the part you have played and the service you have rendered to those victims of war—who might otherwise have been forgotten; for such is the way of the world. That is why to describe any members of the Canadian Legion as Ex-Service men, is in one sense at least, a misnomer. You still serve. You are still on active service—very active service.

On behalf of the citizens of this Province—who will never forget your sacrificial services—I wish you every success. May your deliberations be fruitful. May this Convention be the most completely satisfactory Convention you have ever had. May the decisions you make and the plans you draft here enable you in the days to come to add still further to the magnificent contribution you have already made to life in the Dominion of Canada.

It is with the greatest pleasure that I declare the Eighth Annual Convention of the Canadian Legion of the British Empire Service League now open.

BRAINS AND HANDS

In Which a Theory is Stated but not Discussed When Presenting Scholarship Awards to Boys of Ontario on Behalf of the Fisher Body Craftsman's Guild, at the Royal York Hotel, Toronto, August 3, 1934

Mr. President, Ladies and Gentlemen:

I want to pay you boys a well-deserved compliment. If I tell you something about a theory—a scientific theory—you will, I feel sure, recognize that by winning these prizes you have done very much more than you imagine. And you won't miss the compliment.

But, first of all, about this theory; it isn't more than a theory and it is thought by many scientists to account for man's mental superiority over all other orders of creation.

You know, of course, that scientists are always asking themselves questions just for the fun of finding answers to them. Sometimes they are questions about chickens and eggs and which came first. But they ask themselves other and more important questions too and do their best to answer them, not always satisfactorily.

So you can imagine a scientist saying to himself one day, "How is it I can do all the things I do—how is it that men can write books and make clothes, paint pictures and build cities, fly in the air, sail boats on the sea, invent radios and manufacture motor cars, and even—if they are quite exceptionally brilliant—win valuable prizes as craftsmen—how is it that they can do these and a thousand, thousand other things, when a horse, a sheep, a cow, a camel and even an elephant, big as it is, literally cannot add two and two together."

And then not one scientist alone but scores of them decided that there was only one answer—a man has hands. Because

336

he has hands he is the highest of all living creatures. By using his hands his brain developed. He was always thinking of new ways of using them. And now he is thinking of new ways of *not* using them. He has invented the machine—with his hands and his brain. And he's wondering now where all his cleverness is going to lead him.

Now, that seems to me a pretty sound theory. It certainly explains a great many things about men and women and why they are so very different from other living, breathing things on this planet. It seems to show you how they have been able to build a world all their own—which we call civilization—within the world of nature. If they had had hooves and paws, or no legs and arms at all—like a snake—they obviously wouldn't have got very far away from those holes in the ground, those caves that they once lived in just like other animals.

But—and this is the point I wish to make—all this means that you, as craftsmen, as workers with hands, and brains that direct your hands, belong to those men who have done more for humanity's progress than any others. You have already proved yourselves to be the very type of young men that the world most needs—builders and not destroyers. We have too many skilled destroyers in the world as it is. They get prizes too—for leaving in ruins everything they touch.

Men's hands are subtly and perfectly connected with their brains. Because you have shown yourselves so skilful as builders and creators it is right and proper that you should be given this splendid opportunity to develop yourselves to the full bent of your physical and mental powers. The world owes everything to its craftsmen.

On behalf of the citizens of the Province of Ontario I most cordially congratulate you. I know that you are very happy at the thought of your prizes and all that they mean to you. I know, too, that you would like me to thank all those who have made it possible for you to win these scholarships by initiating and holding the Fisher Body Craftsman's Guild competition. So I will take this opportunity in your name to express your thanks and that of all other competitors who were able—equally and without distinction—to enter the competition. Then, secondly, and solely on behalf of you, the winners, I want to express your unbounded pleasure—for I know there are no limits to it—and your gratitude that your ability as craftsmen has been recognized by the granting of these prizes which it is my pleasant privilege to present to you.

THE ALLEGED IMPOTENCE OF DEMOCRACY

Before the Fiftieth Annual Meeting of the
Trades and Labour Congress at the Royal
York Hotel, Toronto, September 10, 1934

Mr. President, Ladies and Gentlemen:

It would be no exaggeration to say that there have been more changes—more radical, fundamental changes in life and thought in the past one hundred years than in all the preceding centuries of history. That fact alone is sufficient to give to this Trades and Labour Congress a significance that will not escape the notice of intelligent men and women. I am sure that all the delegates here assembled are conscious that this year marks the completion of a chapter in human history, telling of developments in industry, in science and in invention more startling, more profound and more truly revolutionary than have ever been told or even dreamed of by preceding generations of men.

For this your fiftieth annual congress is also the centennial of the formation of the first Trade Unions, which actually put into effect the legislation that already existed for such Unions. I am correct, I believe, in saying that before the date the Tolpuddle martyrs were banished to Australia, Trade Unions were such only in name.

However, I do not propose to say anything of Trade Unions as an essential and most important part of the story of human progress in the past one hundred years. That would be the story of trade and labour grappling with the tremendous problems and difficulties and dislocations that came in the wake of the machine. It is a story all too well known to you. But I do want on this historic occasion and on behalf of all men and women who champion the cause of humanity to congratulate you. Throughout the past century you and

339

your organizations have consistently upheld the rights of man against the threatened depredations of the machine. And, although the machine came in the guise of an enemy to man it will yet prove to be—as it *must* be—and as it was intended to be—mankind's greatest friend. Of that I am convinced. It is at once your duty and your privilege at such congresses as this, to find a way whereby the machine may be transformed into a docile and no longer a tyrannical partner in this our great democracy. May the difficulties that confront you never daunt you. The solution of the problem may not be easy, but, gentlemen, there is a solution. And it is a problem which democracy can solve—a problem which democracy is peculiarly fitted to solve.

Now, whenever I think of conferences, congresses and conventions I visualize groups of men surrounded by problems —groups of men sitting, let us say, in the rather ponderous attitude of thought that characterizes Rodin's celebrated piece of sculpture entitled, "The Thinker". I have been invited to add to your problems by bringing to your attention yet another problem, and one of the greatest. I do so the more readily because, with the problem, recommendations for its solution will be presented. It is a problem that challenges thought, it is the problem of every man in a democracy. It demands your most earnest consideration. I am speaking, of course, of the problem of slums—those centres of social corruption which exist in every city—which infect every city—which, if disregarded, grow and grow—so that the older a city is, the greater is the slum area.

Some time ago, in the course of a function which celebrated the centennial of this city, I seized the opportunity to direct attention to a state of affairs which seemed to detract somewhat from the greatness of a great city. The response was immediate. I venture to say that there has never been in the one hundred years of Toronto's history a more gratifying and heart-warming manifestation of true civic pride than the speed and enthusiasm with which citizens undertook to examine every aspect of the housing problem in Toronto.

So long as the pride of our citizens is so quickly touched, so long as they remain so sensitive to all that concerns the health and the beauty, the decency and the dignity of this city, so long as they regard the welfare and happiness of the men, the women and the children within the borders of their city as their own greatest responsibility, a responsibility not to be relegated to others—so long as humanity always comes *first* in all their considerations—just so long will that city be great in the real sense of the word and its progress assured.

After all, progress—*all* progress—will cease only when there are no more problems for mankind to solve. Hope itself will die when the ultimate goal of mankind has been won, the last difficulty overcome; for in such a far distant Utopia hope will be unnecessary, out of place, impossible. There will be nothing more to hope for. That is why, encountering the difficulties that face democracy, those difficulties of adjustment that have multiplied with inventions, we should be inspired by a spirit of bold challenge. For they are by no means insuperable difficulties. There is no need for pessimism, but there is every reason for optimism.

That is why the message of the President of the Trades and Labour Council of Canada reflects an attitude of mind and an energy of spirit which will receive universal commendation. May I quote it to you. It is taken from an editorial which appeared a few days ago, and with the housing problem in mind, as one of many problems that await solution, it forms a convenient starting point for my brief message to you.

"Labour Day, 1934", says Mr. Tom Moore, "finds organized Labour once more on the *forward march*, determined to abolish the prevailing system of destruction and waste, and to use every constitutional means at command to secure the right to participate in the enjoyment of those things which, by their labour and with the aid of modern machinery, are today produced in such abundance."

Now may I add some footnotes to this frank statement of the aims of organized labour? The housing problem, to which I shall return in a moment, is but one of the many problems crying aloud for solution. I am not an economist and I must leave any political implications of such a message—if there are any—to be dealt with by those best qualified to do so. But in my representative capacity I can at least direct attention to one phrase. It is the phrase "to use every constitutional means at command."

The man who wrote that message and the men whose views were therein expressed recognize what is so often forgotten. The constitution was made for democracy and not democracy for the constitution. Democracy is an ideal that necessarily embraces economics and must, more and more, find its most concrete expression in economic action. Brought face to face with economic facts, democracy cannot, will not, and, I am confident, has no wish to ignore such facts. The constitution does not give authority to any citizen of a democracy nor secure to any body of citizens the power or right so to conduct themselves or their affairs as to harm their fellow-citizens. No mandate, no charter, no law, no verbal or written order, for example, has ever gone forth over this city or over Canada, commanding, "There shall be slums in every city of this fair Dominion."

The very phrase "to use every constitutional means at command" is proof that these are truths recognized by the men who use that phrase. Constitutional means can be used because they are free to be used. What is more, they are at the command of a free citizenry. They are there to facilitate and not to check what, in the words of your President, has been described as the "forward march"—a much more graphic phrase, by the way, than the word "progress". There is something more active and purposeful about it.

Now this may appear to be a digression from my main subject—which, by invitation, is the housing problem in Toronto. But slums are but a part of the great problem confronting us all as members of a democracy—the problem of enforced unemployment and the machine, of inequitable distribution of wealth, of faulty economic functioning, of plausible economic theories and distressing every-day realities, and of all those things of which it would be idle for me to tell you. And it occurs to me that there are certain questions which every man must ask himself concerning the manner in which these and allied problems should be solved, the spirit in which the solution must be sought for. Let me make my meaning clear.

When any speaker uses such words as "freedom" and "democracy", particularly in moments of impassioned oratory, he is usually suspected of one of two things. Either he is popularly supposed—especially nowadays—to be speaking of vague abstractions which he knows and his listeners know have no existence in reality; or he is floating these words like large airy balloons to see which way the political wind blows.

Let us bring these words down to earth and briefly examine them. Does democracy, in fact, protect freedom? And if it does, what is this thing called freedom? Wherein does it exist? Would the loss of this freedom be too high a price to pay for guaranteed economic security, even supposing it were possible to guarantee such bovine security under an autocracy, a dictatorship, a form of undemocratic tyrannous government under which you could not have and would not have any freedom of thought, of speech and of action? Before the problems which you will attempt to solve in such congresses as this—before the problem of such evils as slums— will the difficulties of economics lead us to clamour for a world without liberty—a world in which any attempt to be yourself would be high treason? A world in which, if I may parody Kipling for a moment:

"—— only the State shall inspire you and only the State
        shall maintain,
And no one shall vaunt his visions and no one shall use
        his brain;
But each shall wait for his orders and each with obedient
        hands
Shall do the things he is told to, as the Lord High Boss
        commands!"

What a pleasant prospect that would be—even if it meant three meals a day—which it doesn't!

Now, democratic freedom is of many kinds. Each kind has been consciously striven for and even fought for. Democracy is no accident. It is a form of government, a way of life which was deliberately chosen by the British people as promising most good collectively and individually. The ideas of this generation are not *new* ideas. Tyranny, with plausible but false pretences of omniscience has reared its ugly head many times ere this. Briefly then, and for the purposes of what I wish to say, there are four principal kinds of democratic freedom.

First, there is national freedom—that is freedom from foreign domination. Second, there is constitutional or political freedom. That is the liberty to rule yourself through a representative government elected by the people and responsible to the people. Only by a long struggle was this priceless freedom secured by the British people. Democratic government is a peculiarly British institution and has never been successfully transferred to other countries—countries that have abandoned it without ever really trying it, because it was foreign to them in more ways than one. Democracy is a gradual growth; it is evolution in politics; it is therefore perfectable and progressive above all other forms of government. It can and does change to suit the hour. From the day the barons met King John at Runnymede—from the day King Charles I was executed, through the centuries the government of the people by the people has met ten thousand hazards and triumphed.

Thirdly, there is what one might call personal liberty. The liberty to think, say, write, read and do, eat and drink pretty much what we like with due regard—as every intelligent man realizes—for the rights of others. If, however, any man doesn't realize that liberty doesn't mean licence, then there is always the law to aid his understanding.

And fourthly—and this is where democracy has not yet completely triumphed—there is *economic liberty*. The chains of poverty, the manacles of want—until these have been struck from the wrists of citizens of a democracy, true perfect freedom has not yet been attained. No man who is unemployed, no citizen, no family of citizens forced by circumstance to eke out a precarious sordid existence in slums, can be said to possess liberty. But are we, therefore, to despair? Must democracy with all its hard-won, precious victories be therefore abandoned?

The liberties we cherish are not thus lightly to be foregone. The political persecutions we see in the world today are prompted by the same motive—by the same hatred of liberty —as the religious persecutions of the past. Freedom—free thought and a free way of living—may be taken by force from a large part of the world. Their citizens may for a time be transported back to the middle ages. Mediaeval intolerance will find its victims today as it did in the past. But not under a democracy. Not where British institutions exist. There is no reason why the essential form of liberty— the fourth I mentioned, economic liberty—shall not be assured every citizen of our democracy.

All the materialistic philosophies in the world today seek to deny the fact that a man is bigger than his job and that life is too varied to be contained within any ready-made system. It is individual, independent thought that has enriched the world. Liberty demands law and discipline if it is to be preserved.

But the solution of that economic problem lays upon every citizen of a democracy the moral obligation to be intelligent. It was Carl Sandburg, the poet, who, thinking perhaps of the crimes that have been committed in the name of brotherhood and equality, remarked that the brotherhood of man "is sometimes not so much a beautiful dream as a humiliating reality." But he was not thinking of the free brotherhood such as can and will yet, even economically, exist in countries where democratic ideals beckon to greater heights yet to be attained.

The interests of the people as a whole must be considered

as beyond and above the private interests of social class or political party. And here, gentlemen, let me sound a note of deepest import. Has it ever occurred to you that only very recently has poverty been regarded as a curable thing and not as an inevitable condition imposed by some divine dispensation? Every century that has rolled over this planet has found the poor taken for granted, their abject condition of helplessness looked upon as incurable, not amenable to human treatment. Today, every intelligent citizen of our great democracy knows that poverty is democracy's final problem—the crucial test, if you will. But, just as democracy has secured for its citizens and has maintained for them those liberties I have mentioned, so it will secure for them this liberty also and maintain it in the face of every tyranny that threatens it.

So it is that when we turn our attention directly to the problem of slums we can do so in the knowledge that we are free to get rid of them by wisely conceived, well-disciplined action—just as we are free to tackle and find solutions for any and all the multitudinous problems that confront democracy. If what I have called the "tyranny of the machine" does, in fact, exist, then we shall be too wise to believe that it can be banished by substituting for one kind of tyranny another kind—the tyranny of man.

And now in considering the housing problem as it exists in Toronto, I should like to explain that when I promised to speak to you on this subject, I had hoped that our Report would be completed.

However, in the course of the next few weeks the complete text of our findings and recommendations will be in the hands of the Mayor and Corporation of the City of Toronto, for whom we have undertaken this work and from whom I have received permission to present to you our conclusions and recommendations so far completed.*

* As this was an interim report and anticipating the final report of the Housing Committee, since published, it is omitted here.

ODD FELLOWS ARE ODD PEOPLE

*A Welcome Extended to the Officers and
Members of the Sovereign Grand Lodge of
the Independent Order of Odd Fellows at
Their Annual Meeting in Toronto,
September 17, 1934*

Grand Sire and Gentlemen:

As the representative of His Majesty the King in the Province of Ontario it is my pleasant privilege to extend cordial greetings to the officers and members of the Sovereign Grand Lodge of the Independent Order of Odd Fellows here assembled in session.

My pleasure is not in the least diminished by a certain uncertainty as to the correct name by which I should address you. There would be no doubt whatever in my mind and I would have addressed you as Odd Fellows if I didn't know that your Order includes Rebekeh Lodges and Encampments and Cantons and even subordinate Cantons—not to mention Patriarchs Militant. It would seem that even the old men in your Order are getting on the warpath. But they are engaged in a kindly, beneficent war—not a war that causes distress and pain and suffering, but one that is far more glorious—a war directed against these very things. A war to overcome them wherever they may exist.

That is excellent. We cannot have too many people engaged in that kind of warfare. The more the merrier. The more warriors we can enlist in the cause of Humanity the merrier will be this world of ours.

So that I am assured that to address you all as Odd Fellows, irrespective of the titles you bear within the Order, is, after all, the finest compliment I can pay you.

I don't know whether it has occurred to any of the Members of the Independent Order of Odd Fellows here assembled that the greatest contributions made to progress have come from men who were regarded, in their day, as odd fellows—fellows who were odd because they were out of the ordinary, above the average.   Odd men and odd women.   Women like Elizabeth Fry, who clamoured so loudly for the reform of prisons that she disturbed the sleepy officials of her day and awakened them to the fact that there was something wrong—*everything* wrong with prisons.   Or odd women like the lady of the lamp—Florence Nightingale—pottering about at night among the tents in which lay wounded men.   An unheard-of thing!   Certainly not a very nice thing for a lady. How odd she must have seemed to her generation!

And then all those scores and scores of odd men—odd fellows, they were, in their day and age.   The thing that was odd yesterday is a commonplace today.   You can yourselves recall the names of these odd fellows—odd fellows like Stephenson and Watt who were so hare-brained, so odd, as to imagine that the power of steam might be used to do things.   Odd fellows who thought they would be able to fly if they tried hard enough.   With what a superior smile people must have watched the quaint antics of those earliest aviators—those very odd fellows who thought they could conquer the air by making wings.   Men like Alexander Bell—a queer Canadian, a very odd fellow who actually imagined that the sound of a man speaking could be carried thousands—tens of thousands of miles—along wires.   An incredible, foolish, preposterous, impossible thing.   And as if there were not enough odd fellows in the world, along came Marconi with an even wilder fancy, a fancy so odd that people must have tapped their foreheads significantly whenever they heard of what he was trying to do—whenever he suggested that wires were unnecessary and that the sound of one man speaking in ordinary tones could be made audible all over the world—*at the same instant* and without any wires at all. These were all odd fellows—decidedly odd—but the oddest thing about them was that they actually did do what they set out to do.

Gentlemen, you can call to mind other odd fellows—men who were different, men with vision, men who would not keep to the broad, straight highway trodden by their ancestors, but went off alone along queer-seeming by-paths and returned with great treasure wherewith to enrich those more ordinary folk who had not been lured by new adventure and fresh discovery.

I like to think that the Odd Fellows of this gathering are akin to the odd fellows I have mentioned. I verily believe that there is here a crystallization, as it were, of a spirit in mankind which becomes more manifest as the years pass. It is a spirit which, more and more, finds its way into the hearts of men and women. It is a spirit of responsibility. It is a brotherly spirit. It is a spirit of community—a spirit strengthened by the adversity through which the world has been passing.

The pleasure with which I welcome you to this Province and greet you in the name of His Majesty the King is a pleasure that has its roots in the knowledge I have of the great humanitarian work being done by the Independent Order of Odd Fellows. May you always be *Odd* Fellows, inspired by that spirit of brotherhood which is so manifest in your activities. Thus shall you be set apart, thus shall you lead in the progress of the world toward a better life for all and, thus too, in the words of one of your own booklets you will keep the pledge your members make, the pledge "to mutual assistance, goodwill and the amelioration of those ills that are inseparable from human life."

THE PIONEERS OF CANADA ARE NOT DEAD

*A Radio Address on Behalf of the Canadian
Red Cross Society, September 26, 1934*

We are all apt to forget that there are still pioneers. Men and women and children in Northern Ontario are still living lives of hardship and difficulty—the same hardships and the same difficulties as those met with by the pioneers of old who have been so often praised in speech and song during this historic year.

It is the easiest thing in the world to read of the pioneers of old and forget the pioneers of today; to be moved to deep and almost tearful sympathy by stories of the sufferings of those pioneers long dead and do nothing for pioneers still living. It is pleasant to pay lip service to those who founded the cities of today, and to render no service whatever to those who, even now, are founding the cities of the future—great cities that will yet spring up in the vast hinterlands of Northern Ontario.

To the everlasting honour of the Canadian Red Cross let it be said as forcefully as possible that they have never forgotten these fellow-citizens of ours—the pioneers of the future. The Red Cross has removed from the hearts of innumerable little communities of people—lonely people, people isolated in the wilderness—that haunting fear, that ultimate horror of sickness or accident, with no one within a hundred miles to render prompt, efficient aid.

After all, the poetic beauties of the scenery in the wild northland does nothing to overcome the prosaic realities of life lived there—far, far from the great hospitals of the cities. But the Red Cross, year after year, valiantly carries to them the message of the practical good wishes and the efficient medical aid which their more comfortably situated fellow-citizens wish to extend to them. May it never be said of us that we refused to help them. There are still communities which must face the perils of the future with no hope of medical assistance. It is here that the Red Cross is most helpful.

I feel confident that the play which is to be presented to you this evening will conjure up in your minds and imaginations ten thousand similar moving scenes and incidents illustrating the splendid work being done by the Red Cross of Ontario—it will bring home to you vividly the epic grandeur of the part played by the Red Cross in this great Province.

The full scope and significance of this great international organization is not, however, fully appreciated until we realize that its ramifications extend far beyond the boundaries of this Province to the uttermost parts of the world. Sixteen years after the War, the Red Cross is one of the world's great agencies for peace and goodwill among all nations.

The Ontario Branch of the Red Cross has special reason for gratification in that one of its former Presidents, a lady who has been identified with educational, charitable and humanitarian work in this city—Mrs. H. P. Plumptre—has been selected to represent Canada at the International Red Cross meeting in Japan next month.

May the Red Cross be enabled always to express in action the high ideals of service for which it stands, and may those ideals one day reign in the counsels of nations as even now they reign in the hearts and minds of these devoted men and women.

ON SIR PEREGRINE MAITLAND AND A PET FOX
—AND WHAT THEY DID

At the Unveiling of a Monument Erected
in Memory of Lieutenant-Governor Sir
Peregrine Maitland by the Lundy's Lane
Historical Society and the Stamford Town-
ship Council at Stamford, Ontario,
October 5, 1934

Mr. President, Ladies and Gentlemen:

I greatly appreciate the opportunity to unveil this Cairn erected by the Lundy's Lane Historical Society to the memory of Lieutenant-Governor Sir Peregrine Maitland—one of my predecessors in office, who lived here at "Stamford Cottage" rather more than a hundred years ago.

I very much suspect that Sir Peregrine made "Stamford Cottage" his permanent residence because he was fond of a quiet life. Until his arrival in Canada he had had the adventurous career of a soldier in the Napoleonic Wars. Old Dr. Scadding, who often saw him going to church on Sundays, described him as "a tall, grave man, his countenance ever wearing a mingled expression of sadness and benevolence." Evidently Sir Peregrine was just the type of man who would appreciate to the full the quiet rural beauty of this countryside so near the great Falls of Niagara.

Now, I do not intend, of course, to trace Sir Peregrine Maitland's history in any detail. In dealing with history in the open air, in October, brevity will be the soul of consideration for others. But Sir Peregrine didn't have the quiet life to which, perhaps, he looked forward. Perhaps, too, that's why Dr. Scadding noticed that the Lieutenant-Governor wore such a sad expression. These are, of course, only suppositions. They must not be regarded too seriously.

At all events, Sir Peregrine Maitland had been a soldier

ever since the age of fifteen.   Three years before he came to
Upper Canada he had fought at Waterloo.   At the Ball at
Brussels on the eve of the Battle, Major Maitland (as he then
was) met his bride-to-be.   It was a most romantic setting
for such a tender scene.   You remember Byron's description
of that ball in *Childe Harold* in the lines beginning, "There
was a sound of revelry by night."   Well, it was in the course
of the revelry that night that Major Maitland's eyes met
those of the daughter of the hostess, who was the Duchess
of Richmond.   Major Maitland went into battle the next
day a marked man, his fate already sealed, his life forfeited
—to Lady Sarah—the daughter.

   The Duke and Duchess of Richmond objected strenuously
to any hint of marriage.   Who was this man, this Major
Maitland?   But even in those days young women had wills
of their own.   So Lady Sarah ran away and married the
soldier who had survived Waterloo only to capitulate to her.
And it all turned out for the best.   She was forgiven.   They
were both forgiven.   And when in 1818 the Duke of Richmond was appointed Governor-General of the Canadas what
could be more timely and appropriate than that Sir Peregrine
Maitland, his son-in-law, should be made Lieutenant-Governor of Upper Canada?   They came to Canada together.
It was, you see, quite a family affair.   And it sounds very
much like the happy ending of a popular work of fiction.

   However, this is history—a very different thing—and I'm
afraid that it wasn't long after their arrival in Canada that
trouble started.   There was, for one thing, a pet fox.

   The Duke of Richmond had a pet fox.   On the return
journey from a visit to his daughter and son-in-law at York
the pet fox bit the Duke.   Nobody knows why it bit him,
nor indeed, why he had a pet fox.   But the bite was fatal.
The Duke died shortly after at Richmond from hydro-
phobia.   He had only been in Canada a year or so.   And
then, as if determined that the Duke's son-in-law, Sir Peregrine, should not be left in peace here at Stamford Cottage, two gentlemen from Scotland, one named Robert

Fleming Gourlay and the other William Lyon Mackenzie, began to make their presence felt. It would seem that the old governmental doctrine of *laissez-faire* already had its opponents. I needn't remind you, of course, that this was the beginning of one of the most exciting episodes in Canadian history. But I do not propose to tell you of those events— events which years later, and when Sir Peregrine had already left Canada, led, among other things, to the Battle of Montgomery's Inn. As members of the Lundy's Lane Historical Society you are all familiar with the devious course which events took in this Province at that time. I shall leave the story of them untold. Even if it were necessary to do so it would take too long to tell you of them. It is enough to say that the first bubblings and eddies of that tempestuous stream of political ideals and opinions which was later to be churned into the fury of rebellion and conspiracy, battles, skirmishes, victories and defeats, were already discernible in political happenings during Sir Peregrine Maitland's administration. I will content myself with but two incidents connected with the men in whose memory this memorial has been erected. They both illustrate—each from different angles—life in Canada a century ago.

First of all, there was Jacob Bromwell. Jacob Bromwell— long-forgotten Jacob—lived in Smith Township in the back-woods. One day he came all the way from his home to Sir Peregrine to make a complaint. He said that he had been forced to make a miniature mill of himself. It was a fact. There simply were no mills—or at any rate, insufficient mills for the grinding of corn. And poor Jacob had been forced to chew corn until it was soft enough to bake into bread for his children. To the credit of Sir Peregrine, let it be said that it wasn't long before the Government had erected a good mill to replace those very uncertain, very temperamental and very delapidated mills called Scott's Mills— where Peterborough now stands.

Such an incident shows that for all the apparent seclusion of Stamford Cottage, Lieutenant-Governor Sir Peregrine

Maitland was not out of touch with the needs of the people. It affords us also a vivid glimpse of the difficulties which faced men and women and children making their livelihood in a land still wild and stern, a strange land, a land yet unconquered by the labour and skill of man.

One more story and I have done. One hundred and ten years ago Sir Peregrine Maitland took part in a ceremony not unlike this. Those were the days when Generals still led their men into battle—the first in the fray. Major-General Sir Isaac Brock had died twelve years before, heroically leading his men—not, you will notice, telephoning instructions to his men—at Queenston Heights. A memorial was to be erected in General Brock's memory. In 1824 Sir Peregrine Maitland laid the foundation stone of the memorial—a huge block which in one part had been hollowed out. Into this hollowed portion of the block several documents were placed. Later, in the absence of Sir Peregrine and unknown to him, Mr. William Lyon Mackenzie, for good measure, inserted a copy of his paper, *The Colonial Advocate*, into this same hollow. Let Mr Mackenzie tell the rest of the story. "Many days afterwards," he writes, "when the column was 48 feet high, Sir Peregrine Maitland, who was terribly annoyed by the first *Advocate*, ordered his courtier, Thomas Clark, to go and dig it out again. Clark obeyed, and after three days' excavation, they exhumed the record with the otter's skin in which it was wrapped".

That happened in 1824. It was on Christmas Eve that same year, by the way, that the new Parliament House in York (Toronto), erected to replace the one the Americans burnt, was itself accidentally destroyed by fire. So that Sir Peregrine opened the first session of the Ninth Parliament in 1825 in the General Hospital. Those were eventful days! There can't have been many opportunities for a quiet life even here at Stamford Cottage.

And yet, stranger though he was in a strange country, with habits of thought moulded by other and older traditions, and with, perhaps, rather too much of a soldier's belief in the efficacy of unquestioning obedience, Sir Peregrine Maitland has left behind him an honourable record.

His limitations were, in part, those of his time and in part, also, those of his upbringing.   If there was at times something dictatorial in his attitude toward popular questions, it was because traditional beliefs, firmly rooted in the mind of this soldier, unconsciously usurped the function of free, frank criticism.   There is always a tendency in such a mind to find answers to questions and solutions to problems without ever really considering the questions as new questions, and approaching the problems as new problems raised by new circumstances in a new land.

No man is entirely free from the limitations of his nature, and to say of the man we honour that he was not perfect, is but to say that he had the failings of our common humanity. Much more significant is the fact that when the term of his office expired addresses poured in upon him from different parts of the Province, all expressing sentiments of personal regard and respect for his administration of the Government.

More than one hundred years later we add our tribute to those of another day and age.   Sir Peregrine Maitland surmounted the difficulties of his time with soldierly courage. At no time did he by speech or act betray the trust which he felt was reposed in him by those for whom he held office. To know the difficulties by which he was surrounded is but to esteem the more highly those fine qualities which he possessed.

It is with the greatest pleasure that I now unveil this memorial erected by the Lundy's Lane Historical Society in honour of Lieutenant-Governor Sir Peregrine Maitland.

CONCERNING EDUCATION IN ONTARIO

*Before a Combined Meeting of the Annual
Teachers' Institute of Welland East and
the Hamilton Branch of the Women's Press
Club in Falls View Consolidated School,
Niagara Falls, October 5, 1934*

Mr. President, Madam President, Ladies and Gentlemen:

I have it on high authority that no state schools in any English-speaking country have instructors and teachers superior to those we have here in Ontario. That is high praise—the highest praise. You will recognize, therefore, with what pleasure I come to you today. Not only do you belong to a most distinguished profession—but you are actually the cream of that profession in the English-speaking countries of the world.

There is, of course, no profession—unless it be that pursued so ardently and arduously by the ladies and gentlemen of the Press—in which so much power for good and evil is ultimately reposed. The school and Press are as one in this power. They are the most potent instruments humanity possesses—far more powerful than all those armament firms of whose nightmarish activities we continue to hear so much. Indeed, if any of you should try to trace all the channels through which the power of your respective professions is directed, you would find that you had set yourselves an impossible task. There are literally no limits to that power. I need not add that the responsibilities of those in whom that power is vested is correspondingly great.

Here in Ontario there are more than 20,000 certificated teachers. University graduates in our High Schools and even, not infrequently, in our primary schools, are men and women possessing high qualifications for their work. To give a single instance of the manner in which education in this

Province has steadily and purposefully pushed its way forward to a position second to none in the world, a significant change for the better was recently brought to my attention. Teachers with third-class certificates are now practically non-existent in this Province. They have been supplanted by men and women with second-class certificates who, by dint of private study and additional courses of instruction, are continually swelling the ranks of those who possess first-class certificates. This is perhaps the most significant educational development of recent years. I am delighted and I am sure that every citizen of the Province would be gratified to know that the standards of education—which, after all, intimately concerns every home and family in this Province—are so consistently being raised.

So that I am not disposed to regard with any great apprehension the case of a girl who, on the occasion of her 21st birthday, received a birthday gift from a lady of my acquaintance. The girl had been at school until the age of sixteen and yet admitted that it was quite beyond her powers to spell sufficiently well to write a few words of thanks. She tried—for days she tried. Then she abandoned the attempt and begged the whole question by sending a printed card of formally phrased appreciation.

It was a revelation to me, but it only shows that however carefully the educational net is spread in any place or province, there are always those who contrive, somehow, to elude it or to slip through its beneficent meshes and to emerge from their schooling without any obvious advantages. I would very much like to know how it is done. But, after all, education doesn't confer brains; it only helps to develop them.

Once upon a time Mark Twain, who was then editing a paper called *Galaxy*, received an enquiry from a young man who signed himself "Young Author". This was Mark Twain's reply.

"Yes", he wrote, "yes, Agassiz *does* recommend authors to eat fish, because the phosphorous in it makes brains. So far you are correct. But I cannot help you to a decision about the amount you need eat—at least, not with certainty. If the specimen composition you send is about your fair, usual average, I should judge that perhaps a couple of whales would be all you would want for the present. Not the *largest* kind, but simply good, middling-sized whales."

It may be that the pardonable omission of fish in the diet of the young 21-year-old girl I mentioned had something to do with the curious predicament in which she found herself. I very much doubt it, however, and it must not be thought that I am championing the cause of fish as brain builders, nor that I am suggesting that whales be enlisted to forward the march of education in this Province.

But, at least, in Mark Twain's reply you all meet on common ground, for you all recognize the peculiar potency of the written word as a revelation of the thought behind it. As teachers you know how unerringly a student's written work reveals the progress a student is making. It reveals, too, what progress you yourself are making with your students. And as members of the Press, I need not remind you that it is you who reveal yourselves on every page of the newspaper for which you write. The well-worn adage that "the teacher is the school" is paralleled by one just as true, namely, that "the journalist is the newspaper".

The Press and the School are, of course, our greatest educational forces, but, for a moment, I would like to speak rather more specifically of certain phases of school education in this Province. They become more and more apparent as the years pass. Teaching shares with other professions the unfortunate distinction of being overcrowded. For many reasons which I need not enter into here, it is an attractive profession. It appears even more attractive during a time when so many useful channels of commercial and other activities are closed. For young men and women it then becomes not so much a matter of choosing the profession of teaching; they are driven toward it rather by the economic urgency of making a living. Let this be granted. Let it also be admitted that when industrial and commercial activity revives, this overcrowding will thereby be lessened—appreciably lessened. Overcrowding will, nevertheless, continue to be a problem in the teaching profession—a profession affecting the destinies of thousands of young men and women. And because it affects them so deeply it would be manifestly unfair not to seek some solution—even if that solution proposes some sort of planning that would more efficiently and more justly balance supply and demand. Now, as I have shown, there is already in force a type of planning whereby teachers with first-class certificates are taking the place of those with lesser qualifications. Might not there be some sort of scheme put into effect whereby those not yet in the profession, but who propose entering it, might be selected according to the promise they have already shown as potential teachers and assured of a position on the completion of their training? This is necessarily only a rough-cast suggestion, but it might well be moulded into more definite, concrete form, I imagine, by those qualified by their knowledge and experience of the teaching profession. Such a proposal demands, of course, a careful, statistical tabulation of population areas, and of schools in their relation to these areas; the number of teachers necessary for a given number of pupils if their teaching is to be most effective, and a consideration of all those other facts without which no plan of any kind can hope to be anything more than makeshift. Year by year, the existing and probable vacancies would then be known and planned for. In this way it should be possible for young men and women to be saved the disappointment, the humiliation, of studying for a teaching career and being actually, even though tacitly, encouraged to do so—only at last to be denied a teaching position. It is a difficult problem, a problem requiring intricate re-adjustments of the present system—but surely it can be solved at least to the extent that students will be warned, before entering their courses of study, that they do so at their own risk of eventual disappointment. For it must not be forgotten that while, doubtless—and especially during times of economic difficulty—many try to become teachers who are much better fitted for other callings, yet it is just as true that there are many also who, given the opportunity, would have become ornaments to their profession.

Of course, overcrowding is a problem that has come to the fore comparatively recently. I am convinced that in urging that steps be taken to find a solution, I am but voicing the desire of all those who wish to remove from the minds of student teachers any fear of undeserved failure to obtain a position. And that fear will continue to hang over their heads like a veritable sword of Damocles until the statistical relation which should exist between the supply of teachers and the demand for teachers has been determined rather more scientifically.

Now, I am very far from any desire that this should be construed as adverse criticism. I am speaking of difficulties which exist, problems that await solution. And I do so the more readily because I know of no educational organization in the world better able to remedy defects, and with fewer defects to remedy, than that of the Province of Ontario.

May I, therefore, bring forward one or two other proposals in the spirit of one who wishes, above all, to add his mead of praise to that of all citizens who admire the splendid work done by the teachers of this Province. Please do not imagine for a moment that I am forgetting the members of the Press who are present and who have also earned the gratitude of their fellow-citizens by the type of newspaper which they have created for our delectation and information. For them I hope to have a word or two later.

I have always found it very difficult to reconcile my reason to the belief that great age always implies great merit of some kind and that the two are, to all intents and purposes, synonymous terms. I know, for example, that it does not follow at all logically that the longer you have resided in a certain town the greater is the service you have rendered that town. So it seems to me that it is not quite logical to make the length of a teacher's employment the only qualification for promotion in our schools. Ready recognition of any service rendered to schools and to students makes for better and greater service. The brilliant teacher—the successful teacher—the energetic teacher who transmits to his pupils something of his own enthusiasm for learning—such a teacher deserves to be promoted—such a teacher should have special consideration even though, in years and length of service, he may be junior to many others. To emphasize the element of time in appraising a teacher's work and the promotion due to him, is to encourage the kind of uninspired teacher who is content to amble more or less methodically through his duties, confident that as long as his work is not glaringly bad, promotion will come with clock-like regularity. Promotion by merit should be just as certain as promotion by seniority. Such promotion would be an incentive to the best that is in our teachers. Its benefits would be reflected, of course, in the work of the students themselves.

It may be that even these suggestions would not be as important as they undoubtedly are were it not that the twentieth century has witnessed a remarkable change. Sociologists have noted it again and again. Those interested in what may be called the general trend of development and change in our times have indulged in a good deal of speculation as to whither it will lead us eventually. Schools, as you know, were originally church foundations. It is many years now since the expansion of education made it impossible for the church any longer to assume sole responsibility for the instruction of youth. At first, private individuals, and then the State became interested in education. And now education is firmly established as a State responsibility and a governmental duty.

Meanwhile, parents have inclined more and more to relegate to schools the responsibility for the proper upbringing of their children. The function of schools consequently is no longer, even principally, an academic function. Schools are no longer merely educational institutions. They are the very foundation of the society of tomorrow. The teaching of the "three R's" has now been extended to embrace the specialized training of boys and girls for every sphere of commercial, industrial and professional activity.   It is the school also that largely determines their character.   The school has thus become one of the greatest of all social forces. And in that capacity its importance is all the greater because, whether we choose to admit it or not, we are now living in a time of social reorganization.

It was nothing less than an inescapable sense of the tremendous importance of education that made it impossible for me today to choose—as, for a time, I thought of choosing —a historical subject for my few words to you.   This is a countryside rich in history.   It would have been pleasant to wander along the highways and bypaths of the past.   But the future is far more important.   Life goes on.   The dead may well be left to bury their dead.   For the living, life beckons to fresh endeavours and new conquests.   Liquid, malleable youth in the crucibles of the schools of today will tomorrow be poured into new moulds, assuming new forms. Their thoughts, their ideals will undergo new orientations. Progress does not proceed in a straight line.   Knowledge of the past will help us only to get our bearings before we set out on our journey to the unknown destinations of the future. For youth, at all events, thoughts of the future are far more exciting than remembrances of the past.   Indeed, the examples of history are sometimes a handicap, since the motives of today are not those of yesterday.   The future—the future is youth's province.   It is also the territory of education—to be mapped and planned by all the powers of intelligence and farsightedness possessed individually and collectively by our educational institutions.

To return, however, to a rather more practical consideration of education.   I am sure that many welcome the announcement recently made by the Minister of Education, Dr. Simpson, changing the time at which examinations are to be held at the end of the school year.   To hold these examinations in June instead of a month or so later, when the heat of summer is already upon us, is a threefold boon—to students,

to teachers and, not least, to parents.   For reasons which
I need not enumerate, I am convinced that the boys and girls
in our schools will welcome the change.   To them, examinations are at best a necessary evil.   And an evil is not the more
easily endured when it is allowed to encroach upon the golden
and sometimes uncomfortably hot days of their summer
vacation.   Studies then become tyrannical.   To be forced to
remain at their books when the whole world of nature is at
its most alluring and beautiful can only accentuate the sus-
pense and nervousness with which our boys and girls approach
and undergo the ordeal of examinations.   That is not, needless
to say, conducive to the best work.   It is unnecessary to remind
you, too, that the end of the examinations is but the beginning
of the teachers' work marking the examination papers.   And,
thirdly, parents are in many instances forced to continue in
residence conveniently near schools and examination centres
much longer than they wish, and much longer than is actually
necessary.

It is quite impossible, therefore, to imagine that any
objection to such a very desirable and altogether beneficent
change will come from any quarter.   To have examinations
earlier than July has been for many years a not altogether
secret desire of many students, teachers and parents.

And now, in conclusion, may I draw your attention to a
comparatively recent and important addition to the subjects
taught in our schools.   You will recall that a short time ago
I spoke of schools as social units of tremendous power and
significance.   They can no longer be regarded as purely
academic institutions, set aside from the main stream of
practical life in a workaday world.   In Canada, in the United
States and in England much more attention is being paid
to what is termed "civics"—a rather bleak name for all that
we mean when we speak of the rights and the duties of men
and women as citizens—in a word—citizenship.   The very
fact, of course, that this subject is now being taught is gratifying proof that educationists recognize the futility of any
education which is not a complete preparation for life *as it is*

lived, politically, socially, intellectually, physically and even commercially. It is proof, also—but only incidentally—that when I spoke a little earlier of schools as the very foundation of the society of tomorrow, I was not indulging in mere rhetoric. Mankind is discovering, after many hard and painful lessons, that co-operation is not merely desirable but absolutely imperative. When I learn, therefore, that "civics" is being taught in connection with such subjects as history and geography, and that it is being expounded also to give the student a grasp of the whole system of representative government—municipal, provincial and federal—I hope it means, too, that the history now taught has a rather more cosmopolitan flavour than formerly, and that the geography teacher tells his pupils not only about rivers, lakes and towns in distant lands, but also about the people who live there. I hope, too, that he will not only name the products of foreign fields and factories, but describe, too, under what conditions they are produced. This type of knowledge should not be denied students.

That is true civics, practical civics. It definitely removes civics from the realm of pure theory devoted to the expounding of doctrines and gives to it a practical application. And, if I am told that civics is only a form of sermonizing and does not include such practical considerations, then I can only reply that it ought to.

When the study of history is made to embrace an examination and explanation of the whole structure and development of this our civilization, that, it seems to me, is true civics. It is, perhaps, too complex a structure to be studied in any detail by school students, but the men and women of the future should be given an opportunity *now* to learn something of it. In the days to come it is they, and not we, who will be called upon to pass judgment upon it and, if necessary, to build a new structure on new foundations.

In a little-read novel by the American author Howell, one of the characters exclaims to another, "Both our education and our civilization ought to bring us in closer relations with our fellow-creatures, and they both only put us *wide* apart! Every one of us dwells in an impenetrable solitude! We understand each other a little if our circumstances are similar, but if they are different all our words leave us dumb and unintelligible."

May it not be that it is by education that the world of the future will be brought into a closer harmony? May it not be that the "impenetrable solitude" of which Howell spoke will yet be pierced by the warm rays of a truly social friendliness and mutual understanding? Such understanding can only be born of greater knowledge—knowledge unwarped by fear and prejudice—knowledge such as it is the exalted privilege of every teacher to impart to youth.

May it not be, too, that the public Press, by emphasizing more and more those things we all have in common, the needs and desires of our common humanity, will gradually destroy and reduce to nothingness all those things which continue to hold us apart—as men and as nations—and so help to usher in those longed-for days of peace and plenty which can never be realized individually and while we are still divided one against the other, but only by whole-hearted, ungrudging co-operation?

"This being of mine", said Carlyle, "this being of mine, whatever it really is, consists of a little flesh, a little breath and the part which governs—be it mind or spirit."

Every man and woman comes at last face to face with that truth. When, no longer as individuals, but collectively as communities and as nations this, the basic fact of our existence, is recognized and acknowledged, then the regeneration of the world will have begun and a truer, finer civilization will have been born.

May you long be spared to aid by your spoken and written counsel and guidance the boys and girls of today in their march toward such a world—a world that I know you would wish them to inherit and enter into possession of in the days to come.

SLUMS

A Presentation of Some of the Findings and Recommendations of the Housing Committee Anticipating the Final Report yet to be Published, and Made at the Opening Meeting of the Women's Canadian Club of Toronto, October 12, 1934

Madam President and Ladies:

During many years I have enjoyed and benefited by the privilege of membership in a Canadian Club, although not, because of constitutional disabilities, in this particular club I am honoured to address today. I have even gone so far, on occasion, as to speak before some Canadian Clubs, and no ill effects having followed, as far as I was concerned, I did not hesitate to accept the kind invitation for this afternoon. Toleration and patience characterized the reception of my previous efforts, and Mrs. Bruce assured me that I could expect at least as much from you ladies. Anyhow, I have chosen as a subject something that I am confident will appeal to that public spirit, that devotion to the progress and sound development of our city and country which is the *raison d'etre* of this Women's Canadian Club, and I think that if my ability to state my message were equal to the importance of the message, I should leave you spellbound indeed.

Lately, some acquaintances of mine engaged a new maid whose blood was purely African. Shortly after this dark servant had taken up her position the telephone rang and the mistress heard the following part of the conversation: "Hello! Yes! Yes, this is Mrs. Jones' residence. Yes, yes, it is, isn't it?", whereupon the receiver was restored to its hook and the servant resumed her work. Only a minute or so elapsed before the telephone again rang and again the maid answered and again the conversation was "Hello!

Yes! Yes, this is Mrs. Jones' residence. Yes, Ah said so. It is, isn't it?'', and again the receiver was hung up. When this happened a third time the mistress summoned the maid and said: "Mandy, is that some friend of yours who is telephoning you?" "No, Ma'am," answered the darky, "Ah don' know jes zackly who tis." "Well," asked the mistress, "what do they say?" "Well, Ma'am," answered the darky, "Ah says 'Hello!' and they says 'Is that Mrs. Jones' residence', and Ah says 'Yes, this is Mrs. Jones' residence,' and they says 'Long Distance, Montreal,' and Ah says, 'Yes, it is, isn't it?' and that's all."

Now, not all of us are as literal-minded as poor Mandy, and few of us are less ready to perceive such obvious facts as that Montreal is a long distance away. I want to take you with me today to visit a certain city not nearly so far removed as Montreal and one from which I think we must all draw certain obvious conclusions. It is a visit that will, I think, be interesting and instructive and suggestive to anyone, but more particularly to women. This is an age of emancipated womanhood. In government, in the professions and the arts, in commerce and industry, woman stands on an equal footing with man. But there is a sphere in which she stands even higher and in which she acquires added prestige and glory. It is the sphere of the home. As guardian of the home she enjoys a privilege that is not entrusted to mere man—more than man she makes and moulds national character because she presides over the home.

You all come from comfortable, healthful homes. You all enjoy at least the ordinary amenities necessary for health and comfort. You probably consider, and should consider, that such is no more than your right. And it is your right. But it is also, I believe, and I think you will agree, the right of every man and every woman and every child in this city and country. I shall go further and say that it is *your* right that all our people should be decently housed because, although you may not suffer the actual discomfort of bad housing, you must nonetheless pay the price of any bad housing that exists. You pay it in a greater incidence of disease and crime, both of which are reflected in heavier charges upon the State. You may not shiver when chill winds blow through cracked walls and ill-fitting casements. You may not feel the goose-flesh rise as verminous hordes set out on their nightly forays. Your stomachs may not be revolted by evil odours. Your aesthetic senses may not be subjected to unceasing bombardment by unsightly dilapidation, but nevertheless you and all of us suffer and pay, and the price we pay—altogether apart from the shame we must feel— is the price of a lower mental, moral and physical status of citizenship.

Let us now set out on our little journey to this city I want you to see. We shall not go far, nor shall we stay very long, for I cannot promise a pleasant visit. I am sorry I cannot expect that you will enjoy the trip, for we are going to a city of misery and shame and degradation. Yet it is well that we should see and study it. It is well that we should know of its existence, for if after our visit we are agreed that it should with all possible speed be razed to the ground, we shall have accomplished something.

It is a city of at least two thousand dwellings, and because its homes are crowded far more than ordinarily, its population is in excess of ten thousand. You know where it is. It is right here about you. It is Toronto's slums.

Now, the word "slum" is one of the ugliest words in the English language. It is an offensive, odorous, deformed, slovenly and anguishing word. It should be used with discretion, because it is an irritating, challenging word, and when one says that there are slums in Toronto one arouses that spirit which has made Toronto so beautiful and splendid, though not perfect, a city of homes. Many will be reluctant to accept any statement to the effect that there are slum conditions in Toronto, but on our visit today we shall accumulate evidence that will, I am sure, prove convincing. Toronto has no slums in the sense that slums exist in some of the old European cities. There are no large areas in which all or nearly all the houses are decayed and dirty, in which the decencies of life are non-existent and in which families live in crowded squalor. But there are small and scattered groups of dwellings that have no place outside a slum district. Here and there, throughout Toronto, conditions of slum life are in full evidence, and this city which I ask you to visit with me today is a concentration of those small and scattered groups of miserable homes, their number as I have said, is at least two thousand, and their sorry tenants are at least ten thousand.

During the past seven months much time has been devoted to the study of slum conditions in Toronto, but I do not intend today, nor would it be possible in the course of an address not so long as to exhaust your patience, to cover fully the voluminous report which we have prepared, which is now in the hands of the printer and which will shortly be transmitted to His Worship the Mayor. This report is the work of an expert committee whose members have been more than generous in their contributions of time and talent. But we are not competent, although we have been unsparing of effort, to say just how great is this slum problem in Toronto. That is to say, we cannot state the problem in terms of exact figures. But we know that there are far too many homes that do not measure up to the standard of "fitness" which we have adopted. It is not an over-exacting standard and it is based upon the verdict of experts in many countries. I shall state it briefly:

A fit dwelling is one which is free from serious dampness and which gives adequate protection from rain, snow and wind. It is adequately lighted and ventilated and heated. It is properly drained, is furnished with sanitary conveniences, including at least an inside sink with water tap and escape pipe and has separate water closet accommodation, to which there is an entrance from within the dwelling. It is equipped with accommodation for preparation and cooking of food, and for storage of food in a reasonably cold place and protected from dust and flies. It is capable of being kept free

from rats and other vermin. I think you will agree that
that is not an unreasonably elaborate specification of a dwelling for any Toronto family. I think you will also agree that
Toronto wants no homes that do not measure up to this
standard at least.

In the course of our work as members of the Committee
on Housing we conducted two surveys. One was an "intensive survey" and called for a careful study of selected districts
in which there was a great concentration of unfit dwellings.
The second survey was an "extensive survey", and was concerned with detailed investigation of dwellings in all parts
of the city. I shall give you some figures from the extensive
survey in which 1,332 dwellings and 1,421 households were
investigated.

Of the dwellings 75 per cent. fell below the minimum
health standard, and a further 21 per cent. below the standard
of amenities necessary for reasonable comfort and decency;

57 per cent. were damp and 20 per cent. flooded;

43 per cent. had no cellars;

59 per cent. had no bath, 57 per cent. were verminous, and
40 per cent. were malodorous;

39 per cent. had unsatisfactory toilet accommodation;

88 dwellings (not rooming houses) contained one or two
extra families;

57 per cent. averaged more than one occupant per room,
and 43 of the households averaged three or more persons
per room;

82 per cent. had no method of central heating, 9 per cent.
had no electricity.

These, I think, are shocking figures. Can we find even a
shred of consolation in the thought that foreigners are repro-
ducing here slum conditions with which they have long been
familiar in Europe? No, we cannot, for only 25 per cent. of
the households were foreign; 75 per cent. were Canadian and
other British households.

Figures are cold. They appeal to reason. Reason tells us
that these conditions should not exist in Toronto or in any

other city.   But reason will not impel us to action so readily as will our emotions if we will stop a few times in our journey through this sorrowful city of slums to enter and inspect some of its houses.   What is that great stain on the wall?   It is where the rain blew in a few nights ago.   Why is the floor uneven?   Because the house sits on bare ground and dampness has warped the wood.   What are those smaller spots on the walls?   They are the remains of things that crawl and have been crushed to death while their more nimble fellows escaped back to the cracks in the wainscotting.   Why the cloud of flies in that corner?   Because the food is stored there and because the food is not in good condition through lack of refrigeration.   Why the rag tucked into a hole in the corner?   To exclude an over-bold rat that bit the baby's cheek last night.   What is in that pail?   The drinking water, carried in from a tap that stands between this house and the next and thus serves both dwellings.   Perhaps you will be glad now to step outside and inhale the fresh air, as fresh as it can be in a dilapidated, dirty, squalid district.

We shall pass by one house in which a family of seven, with five children between the ages of six and fifteen, live in one room.   We had better pass, too, a four-room cottage in which a family of eleven live.   There would be scarcely room for us to enter.   We shall also pass many houses in which families live in two rooms, father and sons occupying one bed; mother and daughters the other.

These things mean misery, sickness, disease, death.   These things reflect not upon the people who endure them—for who would willingly endure them?—they reflect upon us all. In homes occupied by such as we who are here today, the presence of vermin would suggest a culpable uncleanliness. But how shall we achieve cleanliness when we have no bath, perhaps not even running water in the house; or how shall we carry on when in winter the water in the sink freezes to a block of ice?   What measures will avail to exclude bugs, roaches and rats from one dwelling if they overrun an entire area?

I have on another occasion quoted Sir George Newman, Great Britain's Chief Medical Officer, who said: "There is no subject in the whole range of preventive medicine in which the evidence is so general and so incontrovertible as in regard to the ill effects of bad housing upon the human organism."

After the reconstruction of slum areas in Edinburgh, the death rate of those areas fell from 45.5 per thousand in 1892 to 15 per thousand in 1910.

But bad housing does not prejudice physical health alone. The influence of physical environment on crime and in cases of mental breakdown is an important one.

I should like to speak to you for a few minutes of the evil effects of bad housing on health. No single condition in the lives of the masses has such a damaging effect or does harm in so many other ways as bad housing. The evil effects of bad housing on health are demonstrated by the relation between slum conditions and tuberculosis. For Toronto's seven ward divisions of poor housing, the tuberculosis rate last June was 37 per ten thousand of population. The highest rate, 64 per ten thousand, was in Subdivision 3 of Ward 4, which has the highest population density of any subdivision in the city. For four districts of good housing, the incidence of tuberculosis is 25 per ten thousand. The correlation between dark, poorly ventilated houses and the presence of tuberculosis has been clearly shown.

Infant mortality is influenced to an important degree by bad housing. In 1933 the infant mortality rate for Toronto as a whole was 63.4. For the seven areas of bad housing it was 72.6. For the four areas of good housing it was 58.3. In Moss Park it was 121.2 and in "the Ward" 83.3.

For our report on housing conditions in Toronto our Committee has had prepared a spot map of unfit dwellings. For several years the Big Brother Movement in Toronto has charted the court cases of juvenile delinquency by residence, and it is instructive to note that these charts almost completely parallel the spot map of unfit dwellings. In 1933 delinquency cases in the Toronto Juvenile Court showed a rate of 7.9 for districts of good housing, and a rate of 24.9, 27.6, and 36.6 for three areas of poor housing. But these figures do not reveal the full measure of the influence poor housing exerts on juvenile delinquency, because in the area chosen to represent good housing most of the court cases concerned youngsters from the "bad spots" in that area. It is only logical that areas of poor housing should furnish most of our cases of juvenile delinquency. The areas of poor housing are near the centre of the business and industrial and commercial life. In these districts it is most difficult to organize the leisure time of the children. Overcrowding in the home leads the children to use the streets for playgrounds. They form play groups or gangs, and it is natural, because there is no proper guidance either from the home or the community, that these gangs breed crime.

The problem of juvenile delinquency grows into the larger subject of adult crime.

Toronto enjoys a reputation as a law-abiding city, and I am happy to say that the situation in respect to crime in our areas of poor housing is not as yet a serious one. Nonetheless it is true that a slum area is a potential breeding-place for crime, and that is just one more reason why we should not tolerate slum conditions in our city. Shattered nerves and frayed tempers are the inevitable accompaniments of constant friction and quarrelling which are inherent in poor housing conditions. An increasing number of broken and desolate homes because of desertion by husband or wife is directly traceable in many cases to intolerable housing conditions, and is part of the price we must pay for the toleration of such conditions. The plane of sex morality is likely to be lower in areas of poor housing. Self-respect is broken down by lack of privacy, and indiscriminate intermingling of the sexes increases the tendency to delinquency.

A low standard of housing is one of the important factors in the problem of child neglect. Most of the wards of social agencies come from areas of bad housing. When it is realized that the estimated potential liability of wardship is from

$5,000 to $7,000 per child, it is apparent that in this connection alone, slum conditions impose an enormous financial burden upon the city. We cannot estimate the cost of the misery and suffering of those who spend their lives in blighted districts, but some slight measure of the heavy expense to the community is revealed by the cost of certain civic services, such as public welfare, public health, police and police court services, etc. Moreover, areas of poor housing do not meet their full share of the tax burden. The rate is already low because of exemptions to dwellings assessed at less than $2,000, and collections are not as good as in the areas of better housing.

My statements today are all based upon observations and studies which we have made as a committee investigating housing conditions in Toronto. Housing problems and slum conditions are not, I am sure, peculiar to Toronto alone among Canadian cities. These things exist, I should say, in every Canadian city and even in the smaller centres. A few days ago, a friend, for whose judgment I have great respect, told me that in his home town of less than 15,000 people a housing problem exists, and in relation to the size of his town it is just as pressing and difficult as Toronto's. So housing and slum conditions are not local problems. They are national problems. I stress this fact because it has a bearing upon the solution of which I shall speak later.

The inescapable conclusion based upon our investigations is that there exists in Toronto a physical shortage of suitable dwellings for the existing population. Economic conditions have partly hidden this fact because there has been much doubling up and over-crowding. If wage earners were able to procure reasonably full employment it is probable that a shortage of 25,000 dwellings would soon be apparent. This is a striking figure. If we allow four persons to a dwelling, which is not excessive, it means that we are short of suitable housing for 100,000 people.

First of the major reasons for our housing problem is the inability of many tenants to pay rents high enough to procure good houses. Even many regularly employed heads of families do not earn enough to obtain good housing. At least twenty-five to thirty dollars is asked for satisfactory dwellings for families of average size, but many employed heads of families cannot afford to pay more than fifteen or twenty dollars. There are numerous families whose wage earners are only partially employed. Certainly they can pay no more than ten dollars.

Then we have the unemployed, most of them quite without means to pay for proper housing. Toronto's relief system has made only partial provision for payment of rents. Consequently, the unemployed and their families have been driven into the poorest, most unsanitary dwellings, dwellings that could not easily be rented to anyone with the capacity to pay.

Home ownership is not to be considered as a solution of our housing problem. We speak of Toronto as a city of homes, but not more than half of the family units in the city own the dwellings in which they live. For the poorer wage earners home ownership is completely out of the question, and there are many objections in a world of unemployment and of economic insecurity to the acquisition of homes even by the better paid workers. In a great urban industrial community home ownership is really a luxury available only to the more prosperous minority.

A second reason for the existence of the housing problem is that it is not financially practicable to supply new housing in place of the old. This is so because in certain districts where there are bad housing conditions, notably in the downtown sections, land is held in the expectation that it will be in demand for business purposes, and consequently prices are very high. Housing cannot yield sufficient revenue for adequate returns on such prices. The old dwellings are rented for what they will bring, and often landlords do not find it worth while to keep them in repair. Furthermore, the use of land in Toronto is very uneconomical. This is so in part because Toronto, like Topsy, "just grew" and did not have the guidance of far-sighted planning. Consequently, even in the down-town sections there is a relatively low density of population and a large proportion of land is devoted to streets, with a resultant heavy mileage of sewers, lighting systems, paved roadways, sidewalks, etc. But even were land cheap and taxes low, it would be difficult or impossible with existing methods of building and financing to provide good houses at rentals that poor tenants could pay. Existing building and finance methods are wasteful and expensive. Construction of a single home on a single lot is uneconomical. But, altogether apart from considerations of cost, the system which prevails of building one house at a time on a single lot or a row of houses on a row of lots is unsatisfactory and out of date, at least as a means of providing good dwellings for wage earners. It involves waste of land. It does not provide open spaces for child play and for adult recreation. It creates drab environment.

Certain of the older districts in the down-town section of Toronto have been deteriorating for years and have now reached the status of the slum. Other districts are deteriorating and will deteriorate to slum conditions as the years go by. There is no prospect of clearing up existing slums or of preventing the development of more slums without a planned community attack on the problems of bad housing and of bad environment. Municipal regulations based upon provincial legislation are insufficient to protect us against the slum menace. The present health and building regulations do not give sufficient powers to the city to demolish unhealthy homes. Zoning in Toronto is but slightly developed. Town planning has not gone nearly far enough to bring about the destruction of old slums and to prevent the emergence of new ones. The slum menace can be met only by demolishing unfit houses and by building new houses to provide poorer people with good sanitary low-cost dwellings. There is need for a three-fold programme; town planning, demolition of unfit houses and construction of new ones. Private enterprise cannot initiate such a programme. It must be done by the municipality, assisted by the Provincial and

Federal Governments, because the problem is a national problem.

As a Committee, we are of the opinion that Toronto should set up a modern, efficient system of town planning. This planning should be extended beyond the problems of street and traffic adjustment to take account of all geographical, industrial, economic and social factors which affect urban life. Concrete plans should be formulated whereby the future development of the city would be directed and controlled in the interest of the whole community. A permanent town-planning commission would be required. It should be guaranteed complete independence and its duties would be to initiate schemes of development. It would be essentially an advisory body with executive functions vested in the elected representatives of the people. It would be the duty of the commission to arrange for a master plan to guide the development of the city for a long period of years.

Our second recommendation is that the city should have repaired or demolished all houses which are manifestly unfit for habitation. This should be done as soon as possible. To effect this proposal the health department of the city should be reinforced by provincial legislation to increase the powers of the medical officer of health, and from that officer, capable and vigorous administration with respect to housing should be demanded.

Thirdly, it is recommended that the city with the assistance of the Dominion and Provincial Governments should institute a comprehensive programme of slum clearance and rebuilding designed to meet the need for low-cost housing. There should be social management of any housing scheme, and this would go far to prevent people making slums out of their new quarters. Managerial methods of this type were developed many years ago in England by Octavia Hill, and have been very successful.

We must have some one supervisory authority to regulate housing development and housing conditions. At present there is no such authority, but there are several departments of government who concern themselves with one aspect or another of the problem. Responsibility for maintaining healthy conditions in houses rests with one department, responsibility for structural soundness rests with another. It is difficult, if not impossible, to achieve anything without a centralized and all-embracing authority. Those preventive checks of bad housing which are applied in Toronto are so unco-ordinated, so complex and so difficult to enforce that a unified city planning authority is an obvious need.

We believe that action to produce new housing should be undertaken at once. It would require considerable time to carry through a complete programme for solving Toronto's housing problem, but early action in the actual clearing of certain blighted areas is demanded. There is in Moss Park an ideal opportunity to take such action, which I will now illustrate by some lantern slides.

The evils associated with bad areas may best be illustrated in detail by reference to a single area, and more specifically to a single block within the area. For this purpose we have chosen for analysis the block situated in Moss Park bounded by Oak, Dundas, Sackville and Sumach Streets.

The block has been selected for illustration because it offers a relatively simple field for the work of reconstruction, while at the same time presenting one of the most pressing problems in the city. Land cost in the area is relatively low as compared with other bad areas; the buildings are mainly of frame construction, are over fifty years old and are worn out. Moreover, the buildings are of low value and many of them fall below our minimum health standards. The land in this district is not required for business purposes so far as one can judge from the fact that the growth of the city has largely been north-west from the City Hall, and from the fact of relatively low assessment. Further, industrial areas where wage earners may expect to find employment are very close to the Moss Park district, so many should be able to walk to work without having to pay transportation charges.

While the block under consideration has been replanned

separately, it could only function properly as one unit of a large area.

In the block selected for illustration fifty-nine houses are under six owners, with one owning twenty-eight, and most of this group ownership occurs in interior streets. The condition is admirably illustrated in the accompanying ground plan. These small dwelling house families often number seven, eight or even nine, and crowding seems to be more prevalent than on boundary streets.

Suggested Plans for Rebuilding the Bad Areas.

In order to illustrate the possibility of rehousing in an area such as this, three alternative schemes have been drawn up by architects as an example of block rebuilding. The suggested plans are illustrated. All three are designed to show that with more careful planning of streets and greater economy in the use of land, the existing population, or an even greater population, may be suitably housed with full consideration for the needs of health and comfort, and with reasonably good environment.

The Third Scheme.

This scheme differs from the others in several important characteristics. These differences are clearly seen in the block model of which a picture has been shown. This scheme combines, with one and two-family dwellings, two large and four small apartment houses, each of three and a half stories. By this arrangement a larger number of families may be housed on the area—196 in all, or 46 more than are provided for in either of the other plans. Further, this arrangement has the advantage of leaving a much larger space available for rest and recreation; the central square would be large enough for soft-ball games. In addition, it is to be noticed that the living-rooms of most of the dwellings face the open square, while those of the other dwellings face relatively large open spaces. It is at once apparent that very remarkable advantages in light, air and play space are gained by adding two extra stories to the majority of the buildings.

The roomy balconies provided, together with the flat roofs, are practically the equivalent of the yard spaces in the single dwelling groups; though you may not dig in them, you may cultivate plants and enjoy a broad view. The trees and smaller spaces provide resting places for the parents and older tenants.

There is, of course, the question of preference for one type of dwelling rather than another. It is usually assumed, not without some reason, that the great majority of the people for whom the dwellings must be provided have a strong antipathy to large apartment blocks, and a very decided preference for single family houses. It is certainly true that the large block buildings which are common in the heart of many big cities, especially in Europe, would not be popular in Toronto at present. But it must be remembered that the three-and-a-half-storey dwellings contemplated in the plan now suggested are vastly different from the great block tenement houses to which reference has just been made; and, further, that few, if any, of the occupants have ever had the opportunity of living in such spacious surroundings as those now contemplated, with a building coverage of only 16.1 per cent. If this ratio were adhered to, the usual objections to the additional storeys, namely, that they bring more noise, additional traffic and deliveries, and that the demand is limited, could not justifiably be raised. A certain amount of this kind of dwelling will be required in any new housing development, and the indications are that the normal demand will increase.

Although our committee has compiled figures relating to costs of solving the housing problem, it is not my intention to go into the matter of costs today apart from emphasizing the fact that the problem cannot be solved unless financial support is lent by the provincial and federal governments. The provincial government would also lend important assistance in the way of enabling legislation.

It is usual, particularly in these hard times, to sigh and shake our heads when we come to the question of funds. We

all know how heavy are the demands upon our public trea-
suries, but it seems to our committee that the Federal Government can enormously assist housing reform if it will provide
relief funds for housing projects.   As an item of permanent
policy I think that the Dominion Government should go
beyond this, providing advice and assistance in various ways,
and generally giving leadership to a movement that is of
infinite importance to the national welfare.   Over a period
of years such a programme would do even more than merely
solve our housing problem.   It would stimulate employment
and reduce the need for relief.   Every technician knows that
housing makes heavier demands for labour than the more
rationalized industries.   About forty per cent. of the total
costs go to labour on the job, and labour represents approximately another twenty per cent. of the costs of materials.
As the land costs and the financial costs of private buildings
are diminished, in a non-profit government-aided project, the
amount that goes to labour increases.   So housing has great
possibilities as a palliative of unemployment.

The slum is the front line of nearly all anti-social forces.
Behind its parapets lurk misery, unrest, disease, depravity and
crime.   These are relentless enemies.   Their defences must be
levelled and they must be destroyed.   Frankly, I am here today
as a recruiting officer.   I want to enlist your opinion and your
support in this just and righteous cause, and I can think of no
body of our people to provide better recruits than your organization of public-spirited women with their high ideals of
citizenship.

The work necessary for an adequate survey and comprehensive report on housing has been heavy.   I welcome this
opportunity to pay tribute to the devotion of all the members
of the Committee to the tasks imposed upon them.   They
gave unselfishly of their time, their energy and specialized
knowledge.   They were painstaking in carrying out their
various and numerous assignments.   If, however, as a result
of this work, there is launched a movement to rid our social
organism of radiating centres of depravity and disease, if this

urgent economic and social problem is vigorously attacked, if our people accept, as they should accept, the principle that provision of proper housing at a rate within the means of every family is a public responsibility, and if, consequently, the shame and degradation of slum conditions are banished, then, I am sure, every member of the committee will feel that his efforts have been fully justified and generously rewarded.

MR. FRANK O'CONNOR

At a Complimentary Dinner given by the
Newman Club, at the King Edward Hotel,
October 24, 1934

Mr. Chairman and Gentlemen:

I know Mr. O'Connor best as a farmer. I am not referring now to his relationship with that wealthy lady in the United States, Miss *Fanny Farmer*, but rather to his occupation as an agriculturalist. I should think he is about the smartest farmer in Ontario, and I, who am also a farmer, should be competent to judge him. He has about 600 acres of good land in the County of York. Recently, and as is usual when Fall comes around, quite a lot of it needed to be ploughed. Mr. O'Connor didn't follow the ordinary course of getting out and doing it himself. No! He started an argument up and down the side lines as to who was the best ploughman in the Province, and when he had worked up a lot of rivalry, invited one and all to demonstrate their ability on his property. Consequently the argument is more or less settled for the time being and all the ploughing at Maryvale is finished. The furrows are straight, too.

Mr. O'Connor is an amazingly complex person. He is, as I have said, a farmer, but he is also an industrialist, a salesman, a stock-breeder, a horseman, a sportsman, a philanthropist, and an all-round good fellow. In short, he is a white-haired boy. In business he is courageous, enterprising and keen but, withal, he has a very *sweet* way. He is one of the few farmers I have ever heard of who has a summer cottage. I myself am of the more conventional type of farmer who has—temporarily—a city home.

A few days ago in one of the financial papers I saw Mr. O'Connor referred to as a "Candy Head". That's wrong! There is more in it than that.

As a charming companion, a splendid citizen, as a staunch churchman and firm friend of education, as an inspiration to youth and encouragement to enterprise, Mr. O'Connor has a very definite and important position in our society, and I am more than glad to have been able to come here tonight and join in this public testimonial to so fine a man and so good a friend.

A LAYMAN'S THOUGHTS ON ART

*At the Fifty-fifth Annual Exhibition of
the Royal Canadian Academy of Arts,
November 2, 1934*

Mr. President, Ladies and Gentlemen:

I have often thought that the secret of perpetual motion is no secret to those who discuss art. And although in the act of formally opening this Exhibition I am in duty bound to say something concerning Art, I am well aware that everything worth saying has, in all probability, already been said.

However, that will not prevent me expressing with what extreme gratification I read the foreword of your President, Mr. Wyly Grier, contained in the Art Gallery bulletin for the month of November. You should all read it. It is brief but very much to the point, and I was particularly pleased by the last paragraph. Here it is. "The forthcoming Annual Exhibition of the Academy", says Mr. Wyly Grier, "will appeal to the lay public—*from which it makes no boast of being estranged*—and it hopes to share with that public the enjoyment of beauty, the appreciation of which is not the exclusive gift of the artist."

I very much doubt whether any wiser words have ever been written or spoken about Art. Art is the enjoyment of beauty and the function of the artist is to share that enjoyment with everybody, by making it accessible to, and realizable by everybody. I congratulate you, Mr. Grier, upon stating so clearly a basic truth—a truth which people in general are so prone to forget.

For it seems to me that the pleasure every true artist finds in doing his work should be transmitted to those who see his work. I know that in the minds of many, an Art Gallery is a place of sepulchral silence—except on opening night—a place where people with very serious faces creep about on

tiptoe and look at pictures, with their heads all on one side.
But that is simply the result of surrounding art with a cloak
of mystery, making of it a mystic cult.   And that is wrong.
It is not fair to art, nor to the artist, and least of all to the
general public.

May I add but a few personal thoughts on art and artists.
They are, of course, the observations of a layman.   They are
contained in no book or books for the very simple reason that
they summarize a few of my own thoughts on seeing certain
works of art.   I shall state them as briefly as possible.   And
if any apology is necessary for the temerity of a layman in
presuming to speak on matters artistic, then I am afraid that
your President must shoulder a great deal of the blame.   Has
he not said that "the enjoyment of beauty is not the exclusive
gift of the artist"?

Firstly then—the pleasures of art, of which Mr. Grier has
written, are primarily *emotional*, and only secondarily *intellectual*.   The emotional pleasures are those of recognition, of
memory and of recaptured vision.

Something grey and melancholy creeps over all art that
attempts to be too intellectual and abstract.

Great art is often unfathomable.   But that does not mean
that what is unfathomable is always great art.

No matter how seemingly profound the thoughts that come
to him, the real measure of an artist is his ability to express
those thoughts clearly. Obscurity is not profundity. It
reflects the artist and not his subject.

The chief virtue of modernity is that it is still with us.
To that extent we all share in whatever distinction it possesses.

All art must be, in part, derivative.   There is nothing so
original as to have no relation with any other thing.   If any
man insist that, although what he produces is unintelligible,
yet he is painting things, or saying things in his own way,
then he should be reminded that many others say things in

their own way—a way that has no meaning for any but themselves. Originality is not enough and has never been the sole prerogative of genius. In order to be quite original it is not necessary to be quite mad.

Colour and line and form—these are the hurdles every artist must take if he is to find himself as an artist. They lie between him and every artistic goal—not excluding his own. If he ignores them or seeks to evade them, then he cheats and will deceive no one for long.

The difference between imitation and interpretation is not great enough to cover every artistic sin against the canons of common sense.

Art should make people see more clearly, not confound their vision. Artists may make rules and adopt certain arbitrary conventions, but Nature also has its laws. And Nature is the greater artist.

There is such a thing as artistic honesty, which is a kind of morality. But that has everything to do with art and nothing to do with morals.

A picture in an Art Gallery may not lead a gay life, but it should be very much alive. It should speak, though it need not tell a story. If it says nothing, it is dead—even before it is hung.

If the pictures of an artist express something that nobody but the artist has ever felt, then the public cannot be expected to take any interest in it—except as a curio.

No picture dies of old age. It must have been still-born. It is possible and frequently happens that what are called "moving pictures" have less life in them than a study of still life.

Great art has no affectations. It has too much to say to study its tone of voice.

If a man standing before a picture says, "I'm afraid I don't understand", may it not be just possible that it is the painter of the picture who lacks understanding?

And finally, let me add that if you recognize something of yourself in an artist's work, then, to that extent, you recognize him as an artist.

Nothing so clarifies one's mind about such perennial topics as art and its purposes, as to express one's own opinions concerning them as succinctly as possible. I do not, for a moment, expect all those who hear me to agree with all that I have said. Perhaps, this being the Fifty-fifth Annual Exhibition, there should have been fifty-five thoughts on art for the day. But, happily for all concerned, I have not attempted anything so exhaustive and exhausting.

And now in conclusion may I say with what interest I have learned of the educational activities of the Art Gallery. I congratulate all those responsible for planning so comprehensive a programme for the study of art, the practice of art, and the appreciation of art. Children and grown-ups, those who paint pictures and those who look at the pictures they have painted—there have been placed at their convenience such advantages as, I feel sure, few cities enjoy.

May the interest in the work being done here grow greater as it becomes more widely known. Interest in art must precede its development and is essential to the progress of art here in Canada. Life is short but art is long, and it is the artist who confers upon the greatness of a nation its immortality.

It is with the greatest pleasure that I declare this Fifty-fifth Annual Exhibition of the Royal Canadian Academy of Arts now open.

ENVOI

At St. Andrew's College Prize Day,
Aurora, Ontario, 1934

Dr. Macdonald, Ladies and Gentlemen:

When science first began making great strides forward during the reign of Queen Victoria everybody who wasn't hopelessly dull became conscious of new disturbing forces let loose in the safe world of conventional ideas. Men like Darwin and Huxley began propounding new scientific theories. Some people were shocked, others became terribly angry and a very few welcomed what they hoped was the millenium presided over by a very young and somewhat immature goddess called Science—with a capital S.

A poet summed it all up by saying that in those days people were living in a half-world, full of shadows, a world in which nothing was definite, precise, conclusive, a sort of no man's land between the entrenched forces of Past and Present, over which clouds drifted, making it impossible for anyone to see anything clearly. Some called them clouds of poison gas— these pernicious new scientific doctrines. To others, however, they were very pleasant and welcome clouds bringing refreshing rain after centuries of the drought of old, dried-up, fixed, immutable theories concerning such things as Nature and Man's Place in the Scheme of Things.

But you mustn't think that the poet described this condition of things in such a prosaic way. No, what he said was that people were living—at least, to be more precise, that *he* was living—between two worlds: "One dead—the other powerless to be born."

And that, you boys will agree, is, to say the least, a most unfortunate state of affairs.

However, all that the poet meant was that he was living in a period of transition, a time when everything seemed to

390

be and was changing—rapidly changing, taking new forms, opening up new vistas of progress. Old things were disappearing and new things taking their place almost overnight.

And that is exactly what is happening today in the world you boys will enter when you leave school. The whole world in these days has set sail on a voyage of discovery. Like Columbus, people of every nation are looking for a new world, a better world, a happier world—because it will be a juster world and a very much better regulated world.

It is an exciting thought but it demands that everyone should play his part heroically, manfully. You remember that Columbus had to contend with mutinies and was beset by storms, just as the world—as you will read in any newspaper—has its storms, its mutinies, but, I hope, never again its wars.

All that we, who are older, can ask of you who will follow us is this. We want you to regard the knowledge you will acquire through education and through your own private study and thinking, as the finest, in fact, the *only* ammunition with which you can ever hope to overcome all the forces of darkness and ignorance and folly, forces that will try to stop your search for a better world and bring to naught your voyage of discovery.

And remember this. You will read, you will hear, perhaps, that youth is not wanted. The surly, embittered, tired old world may seem to say to you, "What do I want with you youngsters? Leave me alone. I can look after my own affairs without your interference. I'm old enough to know better than you, am I not?"

Well, boys, with all due respect to a very old world, that is a lie. The world needs the help of youth, the energy of youth. It needs youth's generosity and freedom from ancient prejudices. It needs all that you have to give it, now more than at any time in all its history.

So as you go out into the world I bring you this word of encouragement. Learn to think for yourselves. Be brave enough to think new thoughts, cherish new ideals and embrace splendid new doctrines of the brotherhood of man. They are really old, old doctrines, old as the hills, but they seem to be new because for the first time the modern world is recognizing the wisdom of ideals for so many centuries thought to be hopelessly impracticable. Nevertheless, economically, socially, internationally, in many, many ways, these old-new doctrines still wait to be put into practice.

May your voyage of discovery lead you to the new world in which such doctrines will be universal laws. And may you live to bring honour to your school, as you will to yourselves by the courage, the devotion and the hardihood with which you help to bring the tempest-tossed ships of your own lives safe into the pleasant harbours of a brave new world.